The Official Record

Manchester University Press

The Official Record

Oversight, national security and democracy

Edited by

Peter Finn and Robert Ledger

MANCHESTER UNIVERSITY PRESS

Published by Manchester University Press
Oxford Road, Manchester, M13 9PL

www.manchesteruniversitypress.co.uk

British Library Cataloguing-in-Publication Data
A catalogue record for this book is available from the
British Library

ISBN   978 1 5261 7432 1   hardback

First published 2024

Typeset
by New Best-set Typesetters Ltd

Contents

Figures and tables

Figures

Tables

Notes on contributors

Rubrick Biegon is a Lecturer in the School of Politics and International Relations at the University of Kent. His research focuses mainly on US foreign policy and international security. He currently serves as the editor-in-chief of *Global Society*, an interdisciplinary journal of international studies. His recent work has been published in *Geopolitics*, *International Relations* and *International Politics*, among other outlets.

Peter Finn is an award-winning Senior Lecturer in Politics at Kingston University, London. He has published on a broad range of topics related to democracy, with a particular interest in national security oversight and US elections. His work has gained significant domestic and international press coverage, and he is Web Team Lead for the American Politics Group of the Politics Studies Association.

Louise Kettle is an Assistant Professor of International Relations at the University of Nottingham. Her research focuses on British foreign policy in relation to the Middle East and she has published widely on this topic including her latest book entitled *Learning from the History of British Interventions in the Middle East*. She is an Associate Fellow of RUSI and a Fellow of the Royal Historical Society and is currently working on her new project focusing on British–Iranian relations.

Robert Ledger (Goethe University Frankfurt) has a PhD in political science from Queen Mary University of London. He currently lives and works in Frankfurt am Main, Germany. He is the author of two books on contemporary British history and political economy.

Christine Sixta Rinehart is a Professor of Political Science at the University of South Carolina (Palmetto College) in Columbia, South Carolina. In addition to other scholarship, she has published three books: *Volatile Social Movements and the Origins of Terrorism: The Radicalization of Change* (2014), *Drones and Targeted Killing in the Middle East and Africa: An Appraisal of American*

Counterterrorism Policies (2018) and Sexual Jihad: The Role of Islam in Female Terrorism (2019).

Luca Trenta is an Associate Professor in International Relations in the Department of Politics, Philosophy and International Relations, Swansea University. He is the author of the upcoming book *The President's Kill List: Assassination in US Foreign Policy since the Cold War* (Edinburgh University Press). He has published extensively on assassination and US foreign policy. Dr Trenta has participated in several national and international events, and in History Channel documentaries. He is a contributor to The Conversation, BBC Radio Wales and *History Today*.

Preface: Defining and 'reading' the Official Record

Peter Finn and Robert Ledger

This volume primarily focuses on the intersection between national security, oversight and the Official Record. It does so in the context of the United Kingdom (UK) and the United States (US) and, to a lesser extent, Canada. Added to this intersection is the democracy that (to some degree at least) exists in all three countries. The volume consists of an Introduction, which explores literature that grapples with the volume's conceptual and empirical territory, seven empirical case study chapters and an Afterword. The bulk of the Preface introduces the rubric that will be central to the discussions of case studies, themes and material (whether official or not) with which the volume engages. As shown in the rubric visualised in Figure 0.1, this volume conceptualises the Official Record in terms of two related concepts: the Public Record and the Historical Record. These concepts are conceptualised as three overlapping and interconnected rectangles. Following the introduction of this rubric, the importance of the Official Record is illuminated. Finally, this Preface discusses how to 'read' the Official Record.

Defining the Official Record, the Public Record and the Historical Record

Defining the Official Record is an important task, especially in the context of a volume dealing directly with state action that engages with events as varied as the Pergau Dam scandal, the Mueller investigation and drone strikes, and deals with concepts as diverse as citizenship, extradition and assassination. Useful guides can be found in state definitions. In this vein the US federal government, for instance, defines an – rather than the – official 'record' as

> all recorded information, regardless of form or characteristics, made or received by a Federal agency under Federal law or in connection with the transaction of public business and preserved or appropriate for preservation by that agency

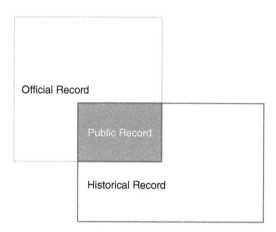

Figure 0.1 Visualisation of the Official Record, the Public Record, and the Historical Record

or its legitimate successor as evidence of the organization, functions, policies, decisions, procedures, operations, or other activities of the United States Government or because of the informational value of data in them.[1]

Similarly, in the UK, a record 'includes not only written records but records conveying information by any other means whatsoever'.[2]

In reality these definitions are subject to numerous caveats and exclusions (the CIA, for instance, is able to define some documents as 'nonrecords').[3] Yet they are both relatively expansive and allow a myriad of material to be subsumed within them, especially if one extends them to include records generated by legal processes that occur within a state's judicial system. Building on these definitions, this volume defines the 'Official Record' as visualised in Figure 0.1 as the sum total of records or information made or received by a state in connection with the transaction of public business, regardless of whether such records or information are in written form. For clarity, this volume subsumes the judiciary within the state, and thus information collated, and documents created, as a result of legal cases, within this definition.

The Public Record, as visualised above, will be defined as the sum total of records or information from the Official Record which is in the public domain, regardless of whether this information was deliberately placed into the public domain by a state or another entity such as a whistle-blower or entered the public domain by mistake.[4] Finally, the Historical Record, as visualised above, will be defined as the sum total of records or information about the activities of a state, or the effects of state activities, in the public domain. This encompasses the entire Public Record, but also encompasses records or information not included in the Public Record such as statistics developed by non-state organisations and oral testimonies collated by bodies or individuals operating outside of a state. It also includes material that is not currently in the public domain, such as diaries, which could one day inform an understanding of state activities. This rubric is visualised in Figure 0.1.

As is highlighted in the Introduction, and demonstrated by numerous chapters, the relationship between the Official Record, the Public Record and the Historical Record is dynamic rather than static. The same principle is true for those responsible for generating the Official Record and the Historical Record, along with the Public Record that sits between the two. As we shall see in the case of Robert Mueller and material related to the investigation into Russian interference in the 2016 US presidential election in the Introduction and Chapter 7, for instance, individuals have the ability to produce material that can, from its inception, be located in the Official Record, the Public Record and the Historical Record, depending on the roles they hold at any particular place or time and the capacity in which they are generating material.

The importance of the Official Record

The Official Record is important for many reasons. Taking just three examples, it is a ledger of past activity and a guide to future practice for those who work within states, a resource to explore and exploit to further the knowledge and understanding of academics and journalists and a potential source of confirmation for those who feel wronged by state activity. Yet access to the Official Record can be closely guarded, with large disparities existing between the portions of the Public Record stemming from states (i.e., the totality of information, documents and statements placed into the public realm by states and/or leakers) and the Official Record.

In the arena of national security these disparities can, often for legitimate reasons, be particularly pronounced. Allusions to national security (and related terms), for instance, are often used to justify the withholding of documents requested via freedom of information processes. Conversely, calls for states to open their archives are common amongst campaigns seeking atonement for past injustices (whether real or perceived), in the arena of national security or otherwise.

In short, the importance of the Official Record lies in its diversity, its ability to capture at least one (often more) version(s) of events and to document policies, procedures and actions, as well as the trust a myriad of actors place in it and its capacity to provide insights into the size, scale and scope of state action. As we shall see, in the arena of national security as elsewhere, these facets of the Official Record feed into, and influence, the consideration of events.

How to 'read' the Official Record

The Official Record is an important primary resource (for many, *the* key such resource) on state activity. However, rather than being an objective collection of events and information (if such a ledger is possible), the Official Record is, by its very nature, a social construct that reflects the times and places in which it is constructed and maintained. The importance of individual opinions and perceptions as well as terminology and emphasis should also be taken into account. Similarly, interpretations of who can access which parts of the Official Record (and when they are able to) are contested.

This is not to suggest that the Official Record is always (or even generally) constructed in a manner deliberately designed to deceive or confuse (though sometimes this is the case), nor that one should shy away from engaging with it (quite the opposite is true). However, the Official Record needs to be read with both the sceptical eye that should be applied to any primary material and, as much as is possible, an awareness of context. If these standards are maintained, and we hope you will agree that all volume contributors have done this even if you disagree with the particularities of their analysis and conclusions, then critically engaging with the Official Record, as opposed to accepting the version of reality any one part of it purports to reflect, can provide novel empirical insights and conceptual developments.

Notes

1 US National Archives, *Disposal of Records (44 U.S.C. Chapter 33)* (2019). Available at: https://www.archives.gov/about/laws/disposal-of-records.html#def (Accessed 21 March 2019).

2 UK National Archives, *The Public Records System* (2020). Available at: www.nationalarchives.gov.uk/information-management/legislation/public-records-act/pra-faqs/ (Accessed 7 January 2020).

3 D. Cox, 'Burn after Viewing: The CIA's Destruction of the Abu Zubaydah Tapes and the Law of Federal Records', *Journal of National Security Law & Policy* 5:1 (2011), 131–78, 133.

4 For examples of the Official Record mistakenly entering the public domain see: P. Adam, 'Classified Ministry of Defence Documents Found at Bus Stop' (2021), BBC. Available at: https://www.bbc.co.uk/news/uk-57624942 (Accessed 4 May 2022); D. Connett, 'Classified Details of Army's Challenger Tank Leaked via Video Game' (2021), *Guardian*. Available at: https://www.theguardian.com/uk-news/2021/jul/18/classified-details-of-armys-challenger-tank-leaked-via-video-game (Accessed 4 May 2022).

Acknowledgements

Any book is a collective endeavour, and this volume is no different. That said, any errors or misinterpretations can be chalked up to ourselves and our authors.

Most obviously, we need to thank the authors who have contributed their time and valuable research to this volume. Thanks for responding to our every question with good humour, and for sticking with a project that, at multiple points, felt stuck in the weeds. Likewise, thanks to the team at Manchester University Press. It's been a journey, but we got here.

We both have long-running associations and connections to Kingston University, and, in particular, the sadly now defunct Politics Department and its undergraduate politics, international relations and human rights programmes. Colleagues from that department, as well as the more recently formed Department of Criminology, Politics and Sociology, have been crucial in providing encouragement for this project since its inception in 2019.

In particular, Peter would like to thank Binh, Felix and the rest of my wonderfully large family. A special thank you is due to Linda Fenge, who made me believe I could be an academic. Huge credit to Robert, for being a fantastic co-editor and long-time collaborator. I am lucky enough to have a very patient circle of friends who have put up with me talking incessantly about politics for years, and I imagine they expect that to continue.

Robert would like to thank Rebecca, Noah and Leon and the rest of his family for their support. He would also like to thank Pete for his patience and the endless hours he has put into this project. Looking forward to many more collaborations.

Finally, to all those who try to shine light in the darkness, you have our thanks and appreciation. We hope this volume does so in its own small way.

Introduction: The Official Record, oversight, national security and democracy

Peter Finn and Robert Ledger

On Monday 28 January 2013 the public gallery audio feed of proceedings at the US Military Commission Court located at Guantánamo Bay, Cuba, was replaced by white noise. The feed, which operated at a forty-second delay, was cut off as Defence Attorney David Nevin was informing the Judge, Army Colonel James Pohl, that his legal team was to present a motion arguing for the preservation of what remained of the CIA's post-9/11 detention sites. Within the Military Commission courtroom presiding judges, along with a security officer, are able to hit a 'kill switch' cutting the feed if classified information is mentioned: thus keeping it out of the public domain. However, neither Pohl nor the security officer hit the switch in this incident, nor were they aware anyone else had access to a kill switch. Moreover, the information being discussed was already in the public domain (or, in the parlance of this volume, already formed part of both the Public Record and the Historical Record).[1] A military escort initially 'advised reporters that the episode was a glitch, a technical error', whilst Pohl ordered the unplugging of the external kill switch and stated that '[i]f some external body is turning the commission [feed] off based on their own views of what things ought to be, with no reasonable explanation, then we are going to have a little meeting'.[2] Following the incident Joanna Baltes of the Justice Department, the prosecutor responsible for classified information, presented the court with a statement that labelled 'the hidden-hand controlling the court audio system "the OCA," an acronym for Original Classification Authority', and stated that the OCA 'reviews [a] closed-circuit feed [...] to ensure classified information is not inadvertently disclosed'.[3] Six months after the incident, Nevin told the court that '[w]e recently learned that [the OCA] was the CIA, that CIA was controlling that location of the feed', an allegation not denied by the US military or the CIA.[4] Commenting on the incident, Laura Pitter of Human Rights Watch stated it was a '"whoa moment" for the court', as it raised the possibility that Pohl was not in control of censorship imposed on his courtroom.[5] Similarly, Carol Rosenberg, the only reporter to have covered Guantánamo Bay full-time since it began being used as a detention site, has asked: '[h]ave you ever heard of a court where the judge doesn't even know or is not in control of what the public can hear or know?'[6]

Rosenberg's question is important. Especially if one is focusing on events at Guantánamo or particularly interested in the openness of judicial proceedings. However, the audio feed's cutting also raises broader questions about the Official Record, secrecy and (the suppression of) information held by governments. Should, for instance, the CIA legitimately have had the ability to censor information within the court at Guantánamo without the presiding judge knowing they had the ability to do so? What is the relationship between the Official Record and potential crime scenes such as the CIA sites? Does the fact that the proceedings occurred in a military court rather than a civilian court alter answers to these questions, and if so why? Did this episode fit broader patterns of the (illegitimate?) suppression of information and documents pertaining to national security operations? Where does oversight fit into this picture, how should it be formulated and how much power should overseers have? Moreover, can such events be interpreted conceptually to arrive at insights with broader applicability? What do these insights, and the empirical material upon which they are based, tell us about the relationship between the Official Record, national security and oversight in a democratic context? Finally, what counts as the Official Record in this instance (just the information pertaining to the CIA sites, documents and information pertaining to the OCA/CIA's authorisation to have access to the kill switch, transcripts and recordings of interactions between Nevin and Pohl, Pohl's statement after the kill switch had been externally pressed)? These are the types of questions around which the case studies in this volume oscillate. However, dealing with the final question here, as stated in the Preface, this volume, drawing from relatively expansive state definitions, defines the 'Official Record', as opposed to the Public Record, as the sum total of records or information made or received by a state in connection with the transaction of public business, regardless of whether such records or information are in written form. For clarity this volume subsumes the judiciary, and thus information collated, and documents created, as a result of legal cases, within this definition.

Work operating at the intersection of the Official Record, oversight and national security in the context of democracy, which is where this volume fits intellectually and is the focus of this Introduction, often engages with aspects of such questions and can be found in a number of disciplines and subdisciplines including international relations, history, political theory, law and intelligence and terrorism studies. Such work centres on broad-ranging topics, including whistle-blowing, oversight, specific eras such as the War on Terror, freedom of information legislation and processes, institutional actors such as the US presidency and the UK's Government Communications Headquarters (GCHQ) and the creation, control and preservation of the Official Record. It is written from a variety of perspectives, ranging from relatively sympathetic to state reasoning and rhetoric, to overtly critical work composed with an emancipatory goal in mind, along with numerous points on the spectrum between the two. Beyond the academy significant contributions have been made by journalists and campaigners, whilst primary material and first-hand accounts of those involved in policy and legal processes provide interesting, often tantalising, insights into the dichotomous (democratic?) relationship between the Official Record, oversight and national security.

Across seven chapters this volume illustrates the important role the Official Record can play in the historiography and interpretation of national security policies; the contested nature of such interpretations and the attention that should be paid to who (individually and institutionally) shapes the Official Record; and when and how others gain access to it; and how democratic governance influences or alters the behaviour of those who create, collate and otherwise influence it. Building on the Preface, across five sections this introduction grapples with the Official Record's creation, control, and preservation, the ability of individuals to feed into the creation of the Official Record, the Public Record and the Historical Record, touches on the tension between democratic openness and the secrecy, required at least some of the time, inherent in many national security operations and considers the role of oversight, leaking and whistle-blowers with relation to this tension.

Firstly, it grapples with the construction, control, and preservation of the Official Record. Secondly, the role played in the construction of the Official Record, the Public Record, and the Historical Record by individuals, as well as the complexity inherent in the management of the Official Record as it crosses state boundaries, is explored. In particular, this is done via material connected to the Mueller investigation, which will be discussed with regard to the rubric introduced in the Preface. In the third section, additions made to the rubric will be used to conceptualise the place and scope of oversight over different parts of the Official Record. The fourth section explores how the Official Record is constructed, managed, and released into the public domain in the US, the UK, and Canada. This Introduction closes by signposting the overall volume.

The creation, control and preservation of the Official Record

Who constructs, controls and preserves the Official Record, and who has access to it, are key to documenting and understanding events. Moreover, as correctly highlighted by a volume focused on exploring Canadian intelligence and the Covid-19 pandemic produced with impressive speed in the pandemic's early stages, the creation and consideration of an Official Record of events can feed into lessons-learned exercises, helping a state understand how operations are 'adapted' in stressful situations, and 'where it succeeded and failed'.[7] Yet, partly because of the Official Record's potential to contain evidence of controversial policies and malfeasance, its construction, control and preservation, and thus what lessons can be learnt, are inherently contested: with those seeking greater openness arguing 'sunlight is [...] the best of disinfectants',[8] and others who, not always unreasonably, urge stricter control because, to their mind, sound government arises when advice and policy can be formulated with a degree of secrecy. Indeed, as Ian Cobain states, '[i]t is not difficult to see that a degree of secrecy is required by government'.[9] Yet Cobain has documented 'many examples of [UK] state secrecy that went far beyond the understandable and expected precaution of national security'. Cobain concludes that UK 'government [secrecy is] [...] not just an occasional necessity but the fiercely protected norm'.[10] Backing up Cobain's thesis, a recent book details a fifth column of domestic Second World War Nazi sympathisers by drawing on documents released in a remarkably 'haphazard fashion' between 2000 and 2017. According to Tim Tate, the book's author, the 'haphazard' nature of the documents' release ensured that this 'story was hidden for far too long behind a wall of official secrecy'. Demonstrating the effect of this lack of co-ordination and delay, Tate illustrates that they caused key scholars to dismiss such a column as a 'myth'. Beyond debunking this myth, the documents also illustrate the use of 'sometimes ethically dubious methods of investigating and diffusing the dangers of Nazi sympathisers' that appear precursors to UK policies of the War on Terror era.[11] Significantly, and as we shall see in this volume's chapter by Louise Kettle on the Iraq War, debates about the control and access of information pertaining to aspects of UK national security policy relate as much to contemporary operations as they do to the events explored by Tate.

Beyond influencing historiography, access to the Official Record can influence judicial proceedings and the ability of those seeking recompense for potential wrongdoing to gain justice. MI6 documents found in Libya during the collapse of the Muhammar Qaddafi regime, for example, provide 'compelling evidence of British involvement in a number' of US rendition operations that fed into judicial proceedings that ultimately saw the UK government apologise to Abdul Hakim Belhaj and Fatima Bouchar, a married couple subjected to a UK-facilitated rendition to Libya.[12] Yet the pendulum can swing both ways. As Christine Sixta Rinehart's chapter on US citizens killed by US drones shows, the fact that states create the Official Record allows them to construct it in a manner amenable to the outcomes sought by particular bodies or individuals: in this instance via a US Justice Department white paper that allowed the CIA to circumvent the due process afforded US citizens in the US Constitution.

How then, to approach such a contentious quagmire of interdependent issues? Moreover, what should count as a democratic state's Official Record (and who gets to decide)? Some documents, such as diplomatic dispatches and the final versions of official reports, are relatively easy to quantify, although whether, how and when they should enter the public domain is, of course, another question. Yet what about the preparatory material and evidence that feeds into such documents or otherwise informs government action? Douglas Cox, for instance, has explored how the CIA is able to destroy files labelled, somewhat counterintuitively, as a 'non-record' if they are no longer deemed necessary along with those that 'duplicate' material in other documents.[13] Moreover, via the consideration of a broad range of material, this volume illustrates the need to keep an open mind about how the Official Record is constituted. This range of material raises important questions: who gets to decide what counts as a (non-)record, what would count as duplicate material, and what exactly is the relationship to the Official Record and oversight in the context of a democratic society, to highlight just a few issues?

Big questions no doubt, but things can become more perplexing still. In the preface to an oral history of the Bill Clinton presidency, for example, Russell Riley asserts that 'much that is historically important within every White House is never written down', a situation exacerbated by the 'hostile investigative climate' fostered in the 1970s and 1980s by the Watergate and Iran-Contra scandals. Indeed, by the 1990s 'careful record keeping in the White House' had become a 'dangerous habit'. Thus, while constructing his oral history Riley had 'Clinton associates' confirm 'over and over' that '[t]he twin perils of leaks and subpoenas chilled virtually every form of serious internal writing'.[14] Indeed, the National Security Adviser Sandy Berger stated 'I did not keep notes, nor did most of my colleagues',[15] with the Deputy National Security Adviser James Steinberg confirming that he behaved similarly because 'every time anybody took notes, they ended up ... being subpoenaed'.[16] In the UK, meanwhile, the Prime Minister Tony Blair was criticised for conducting government business informally and away from the formal discussions that would be officially recorded, via so-called 'sofa government'.[17] Likewise Blair's successor, Gordon Brown, who was fiercely protective of the policy-making process, was similarly notorious for failing to commit anything of substance to paper.[18] How then, as academics, should we account for such tactical gaps in the Official Record, especially when those who left them are sometimes explicit that they exist to ensure they were not caught up in legal proceedings? Given that Berger and Steinberg were National Security Adviser and Deputy National Security Adviser respectively, and the central role that UK prime ministers play in formulating and commanding foreign policy, these questions appear as pertinent to the consideration of national security as other policy areas.

Nevertheless, beyond such senior circles, the problem appears the opposite: with a tendency to collect more material than could ever be effectively analysed. Discussing the Vietnam War, for instance, Hannah Arendt argued '99½ per cent' of classified material should not have been labelled as such. According to Arendt the insights gleaned from such material were restricted to the small number able to access it – a group that, somewhat ironically, was likely too small to ever fully process, understand or analyse the material.[19] That the (over)classification and collation of vast troves of data continues apace was borne out by the numerous programmes revealed in the classified documents leaked in 2013 by Edward Snowden. Just one NSA programme named FAIRVIEW, for instance, collected over two hundred million records of telephone and internet activity per day in a thirty-day period beginning in December 2012, 'for a thirty-day total of more than six billion records'.[20] Crucially, FAIRVIEW was part of a broader NSA apparatus, often with significant assistance provided by its UK equivalent GCHQ, that had the explicit goal to 'collect it all' by monitoring 'all parts of the internet and any other means of communication'.[21]

To their supporters NSA and GCHQ legally plug intelligence gaps by effectively collecting data of telephone and internet traffic. Summarising this argument, Benjamin Wittes, Editor in Chief of the Lawfare site, amusingly opines, '[a]s we used to say in grade school, "Duh!" *That's why we have a signals intelligence agency.*'[22] Yet, to Mark Ellis, Executive Director of the International Bar Association, the NSA and GCHQ have presided over a data collection system of Orwellian proportions and 'engaged in systematic fear mongering and efforts to create an environment of constantly heightened security. [...] [Thus altering] the very lexicon of security and surveillance.' Looking to the future, Ellis asks: '[i]f we accept this shift today, what will be acceptable thirty years from now? How far is too far?'[23] Whether one feels sympathy for the stance of Wittes or Ellis probably relates to broader feelings about, and trust in, government action. Yet, at the least, Arendt's reflections and the capacity for surveillance detailed by the Snowden documents should likely cause reflection about the quantity of information being collected and classified, how such collation and classification can be legally accounted for and how (democratic) accountability and oversight can and/ or should monitor such vast data-collection enterprises.

Beyond scope and scale there is also the question of what information, exactly, should be collected, and by whom. In the late 1990s, and given fresh impetus by the SARS outbreak of 2004, the Canadian government, for instance, developed an ability to 'rapidly gather and disseminate epidemic intelligence' via the Global Public Health Intelligence Network (GPHIN) that, according to Kelley Lee and Julianne Piper, was 'a ground-breaking initiative'. Yet, as Lee and Piper demonstrate, '[w]ithin a decade, however, GPHIN's role would become less prominent, and was [...] downgraded by the Canadian government. Technologic new data platforms, and a shift in the political climate away from multilateralism led to the sidelining of GPHIN.'[24] According to Adrian R. Levy and Wesley Wark, this left GPHIN a 'toothless cog' that 'failed – or, more charitably, had little chance of success from the outset' at the start of the Covid-19 pandemic.[25] For these reasons, as well as balancing elite access and over collection, those deciding what to collect must seek a sweet spot that targets useful information.

Individuals, complexity, and the Official Record

A particularly intriguing facet of the discussion of the Official Record is the dynamic relationship between this ledger of state activity, the Public Record and the Historical Record, and the ability of individuals to produce material that, from its inception, could be included in one, two or three of these categories, with the number for some material increasing from one to three for material initially located only within the Official Record that later becomes public and, thus, also becomes part of both the Public Record and the Historical Record. As noted in the Preface, this dynamic can be seen in material related to a US government investigation into Russian interference in the 2016 US presidential election.

As explored in detail in Chapter 7, Robert Mueller was appointed as Special Counsel and tasked with heading an investigation into potential Russian interference in May 2017 (hereafter, the Mueller investigation). In this role Mueller generated a range of documents. Some documents, such as a Statement of Offence document pertaining to Paul Manafort filed on 14 September 2018, were not redacted (i.e. it had no material that was blacked out), from the start, thus making it part of the Official Record, the Public Record and the Historical Record from its first placement into the public domain (though if one wants to be really pedantic, it could be noted that prior to release this Statement of Offence was only part of the Official Record).[26] Other documents featured redactions while also providing details. The *Report on the Investigation into Russian Interference in the 2016 Presidential Election* (generally known as the Mueller report, for instance, provided a large amount of detail but did have some material redacted. This meant that some parts of the report, as with the Paul Manafort Statement of Offence, were located, within the Official Record, the Public Record and the Historical Record, whilst redacted portions were, and as of February 2023 remain, solely part of the Official Record.[27]

Moreover, after stepping down as Special Counsel and writing as a private citizen rather than a government employee, Mueller penned an op-ed for *The Washington Post* in an attempt to counter claims about the innocence of Roger Stone after Trump commuted a 40-month sentence in prison he was due to serve. Stone, who (as per the Mueller report) worked as an adviser to the Trump campaign was 'convicted in November 2019 of obstructing a congressional investigation into whether the Trump campaign colluded with Russia to win the 2016 election.[28] In his op-ed Mueller highlighted that, despite Trump having commuted his sentence, Stone 'was prosecuted and convicted because he committed federal crimes', and 'remains a convicted felon'.[29] Finally, since the Mueller investigation ended, a series of documents stemming from it have been released into the public domain. An illustrative set, released in January 2020, made interesting reading as much for what they did show as what they did not. Stretching to more than 350 pages, these documents, which chronicle interviews with key witnesses, were heavily redacted in places, with many pages having very little detail left. As such, the release of these documents saw some material moving from the Official Record into both the historic and public records, while some material within them was kept within the Official Record.[30]

Between May 2017 and November 2019 Mueller, and the investigation he led, created materials that were placed fully into the official, public and historical records from the outset, generated a two-volume report that was likewise placed into the official, public and historical records, though in partly redacted form, and created a welter of documents that, after being fully held within the Official Record, after the investigation has ceased operating, have started to be released into the official, public historical records, though in heavily redacted form. Whereas, as a private citizen who had stepped down from leading the investigation, Mueller penned an op-ed for the *Washington Post* that immediately became part of the public and historical records, but will never form part of the Official Record. In short, material created by Mueller, and the investigation he led, illustrates the dynamic and ever shifting relationship between the Official Record, the Public Record and the Historical Record, as well as the ability of individuals to produce material for all three, depending on the roles they hold at any particular place or time.

Yet, how to embed accountability mechanisms such as the Mueller investigation within a democracy is a multifaceted problem. Firstly, national security operations are ever evolving, both technologically and in thematic and geographic focus. As a result oversight and accountability mechanisms, be they judicial processes or parliamentary committees, must be nimble enough to adapt to adjustments in technological and political spheres, and the interconnected threats (real, imagined or deliberately inflated) that these spheres are said to create, almost in real time. Secondly, states collect and create vast amounts of data in myriad forms (including pictures, videos, audio, metadata and interview transcripts). Collecting, storing, classifying, organising, tabulating and analysing such a variety of information and documents is obviously a gargantuan task that will cut across numerous bureaucratic silos fraught with opportunities for game playing, manipulation and the destruction, sidelining or (deliberate?) misinterpretation of information.[31] Thirdly, and as we shall see in Chapter 7 when looking at the Mueller investigation, an important part of the material collected via said operations is the documenting of the official operations and records of one state within the Official Record of another state. As the CIA Director Mike Pompeo bluntly put it in 2017, the agency is 'in the business of stealing secrets', with John Brennan, one of his predecessors, clarifying the previous year that '[w]e uncover. We discover. We reveal. We obtain. We elicit. We solicit – all of that.'[32] Thus the Official Record of one state will contain material pertaining to that state's operations, as well as that drawn from, or pertaining to, the operations and Official Record(s) of other states.

An illustration of how complex this situation can become is found in a summation of the operation surrounding the Embassy of the Soviet Union (admittedly, not a democracy) in Denmark in the mid-1960s as it related to two members of the KGB (a Soviet intelligence body), Yelana Gordievsky and her husband Colonel Oleg Gordievsky (later a UK agent):

> The Danes routinely monitored Soviet embassy personnel, but lacked the resources for round-the-clock surveillance. Some of the telephones inside the embassy were bugged. KGB technicians, meanwhile, had successfully penetrated PET [the Danish Security and Intelligence Service] radio networks, and a listening post within the embassy routinely picked up messages passing between Danish surveillance teams. Yelana Gordievsky was [...] listening to these messages and translating them into Russian. [...] [Oleg] Gordievsky was referred to in PET radio messages as 'Uncle Gormsson', a reference to a tenth-century King of Denmark.[33]

As a result, at a single embassy in a single city, a complex situation ensued, with one state intermittently monitoring the embassy personnel, and some phone calls, of a second state. Whilst the second state had, as a result of its penetration of the first state's security and intelligence service, the ability to collect, in the form of said service's messages, fragments of the first state's Official Record. These messages were then translated into another language, where they passed into the second state's Official Record. In a quirk, one of those translating messages was married to someone referenced, via codename, in these messages. Rather than just of intellectual interest, this situation had real world effects as the 'KGB could often work out the positioning of PET surveillance cars, and establish when its officers', such as Oleg, 'were free of surveillance'.[34]

More complicated still, if states are working in a coalition, it may sometimes be unclear where, or if, the Official Record of one state ends and that of another begins. This situation is likely compounded when, as with the NSA and GCHQ and the Canadian signals intelligence agency the Communications Security Establishment,[35] organisations have been working together for decades, and made almost incomprehensible when thinking about long-term co-operation between states in large formal groupings like the 31-member North Atlantic Treaty Organisation (NATO), which features the US, the UK and Canada among its founding members.[36]

Democracy, oversight, and the Official Record

Further compounding the complexity highlighted above is the fact that '[a]rguably, the idea of "democratic intelligence" is [...] oxymoronic' because '[w]hile the central tenets of democratic governance are transparent decision making and the acceptance of responsibility by' decision makers, 'the secrecy that pervades security intelligence', and more broadly the arena of national security, 'means that taking responsibility for' failures 'can often be avoided'.[37] As already touched on, oversight is often portrayed as a way to square this circle, with oversight bodies, whether formal parts of a state or external actors such as NGOs, portrayed as 'mediators' between a citizenry and a state's national security apparatus. Such mediators, it is posited, are key to upholding the rule of law and for the imposition of sanctions when laws are broken.[38] Thus mediation ensures that 'trust' between citizens and a state is maintained.[39]

With these tensions, and the need to engage in such mediation, in mind, this section turns to introducing extensions to the official, public, and historical record rubric introduced in the Preface. As seen in Figure 0.2, these extensions conceptualise the place and scope of oversight. In short, the additions illuminate the presence of a Core Zone of Oversight, a Zone of Oversight Contestation and a Peripheral Oversight Zone. In short it is shown that the further one moves from the parts of the Official Record located in the Public Record, a diminishing of the effect and reach of oversight occurs. Conversely, for those tasked with controlling the Official Record, as Mike Larsen and Kevin Walby note, there is a 'spectrum of means of disclosure' that affords differing degrees 'of control over the scope and timing of disclosure it affords to government officials'.[40] Yet, as we shall see, this section also illustrates

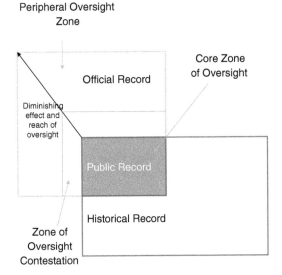

Peripheral Oversight
Zone

Core Zone
of Oversight

Official Record

Diminishing
effect and
reach of
oversight

Public Record

Historical Record

Zone of
Oversight
Contestation

Figure 0.2 Visualisation of the Official Record, the Public Record, and the
Historical Record with oversight zones applied

the possibility that any material located in the parts of the Official Record
covered by the Peripheral Oversight Zone can, via various means, move
into the public and historical records, and thus into the Core Zone of
Oversight. This essentially means that what counts solely as the Official
Record is not fixed, but rather is dynamic and contingent on the circumstances
present at any particular time and space.

As we shall see in this volume, the scope of oversight that occurs within
the Core Zone of Oversight is contested, yet the idea that oversight, whether
carried out by internal state bodies, the judiciary, or civil society and the
media, should occur with relation to material located within the Public
Record is relatively uncontested. The Zone of Oversight Contestation,
meanwhile, maps on to parts of the Official Record that can be conceptualised
as being part of a moveable border zone adjacent to, but not always within,
the Public Record. So there is disagreement about what exactly should be
subject to oversight in this border zone, the exact form and scope such
oversight should take and who should carry it out.

One way of illustrating the difference between the Core Zone of Oversight
and the Zone of Oversight Contestation can be seen in the different treatments
afforded to mainstream military personnel and special forces. In the UK,
for instance, parliamentary oversight of mainstream military operations
falls to the Defence Select Committee, with its website explaining that
it is 'appointed by the House of Commons to examine the expenditure,

administration, and policy of the Ministry of Defence and its associated public bodies'.[41] This means that such mainstream UK military personnel clearly fall within the Core Zone of Oversight. UK special forces, such as the Special Boat Service, however, do not fall within the committee's remit, nor that of any other parliamentary committee, essentially creating a lacuna in UK parliamentary oversight. Moreover, UK special forces, along with other bodies such as MI5 and GCHQ, are covered by a policy known as the 'neither confirm nor deny' policy, which means that the UK government will not comment on the activities of bodies covered by the policy (though there is a parliamentary committee that deals with intelligence matters).[42] Yet, illustrating the existence of a Zone of Oversight Contestation, the lack of parliamentary oversight of UK Special Forces is contested rather than settled, with parliamentarians (including Dominic Grieve MP,[43] when chair of the Intelligence and Security Committee in 2017, and Crispin Blunt MP,[44] former Chair of the Foreign Affairs Select Committee),[45] members of civil society and journalists[46] all questioning either the validity of the 'neither confirm nor deny' policy, the lack of parliamentary oversight or both.

Beyond material related to specific bodies or types of personnel there is also material related to other aspects of national security operations that, whilst it is generally accepted that some material and operations should be subject to oversight and/or in the public domain, there is disagreement about exactly what should be subject to oversight and/or in the public domain. This disagreement can be seen in US freedom of information requests placed by the American Civil Liberties Union (ACLU) pertaining to materials related to allegations of the mistreatment and torture of detainees held by US military forces (some by special forces, some by regular military personnel, some by, or with the involvement of, intelligence agencies) during the so-called War on Terror. The ACLU's requests led to protracted legal battles, with the US government arguing against disclosure. Over the course of 15 years, US courts variously sided with both sides at different points in a judicial battle that has led to the release of over six thousand documents.[47] In short this illustrates how what is and what is not in the public domain (and thus part of the Public Record and the Historical Record) is not fixed, but, at least in part, a product of an ongoing dichotomy between bodies and individuals tasked with oversight (some of which are themselves located within states) and states and the complex bureaucracies, and the individuals that staff them, present within states.

Finally, the Peripheral Oversight Zone maps on to material in the Official Record that is generally accepted as legitimately beyond the public domain. It could relate to information held by bureaucracies, such as mainstream military branches, that could be damaging to specific individuals, such as information that could reveal the identity of sources which, if revealed, could put them in danger, or information with the potential to cause great harm, such as the specifics of nuclear weapons programmes. However, there is always the possibility that such material could move either into the Zone of Oversight Contestation or, in certain circumstances, into the Core Zone of Oversight. The movement of materials could occur for numerous reasons, including the passage of time (some documents pertaining to national security operations are, at least in part, released into the public domain the further away one gets in time from an operation), via leaking, briefing (whether authorised or not),[48] or legal proceedings, by mistake,[49] or when such material or information is sought by an investigation or public inquiry.[50] As such, rather than containing materials that are guaranteed never to become public, the Peripheral Oversight Zone contains materials that are much less likely to enter the Public Record than those contained in the Zone of Oversight Contestation. Yet, as will be seen throughout this volume, because of the existence of whistle-blowers, human error, legal proceedings or an event, information or organisation(s) or policy(ies) becoming subject to an inquiry or investigation, there is no certainty of this. With this insight in mind, in the next section we now turn our attention to plotting how the Official Record is structured in the US, the UK and Canada. Beginning with the US, each country is dealt with in turn. Various routes that can see portions of the Official Record become part of the public and historical records are also highlighted.

The Official Record in the US, the UK and Canada

Classification and release processes related to portions of the Official Record pertaining to national security operations are complex and, despite some similarities, can differ between states. This section lays out the broad parameters of these classification and release processes in the US, the UK and Canada. Reflecting international norms, US Official Records processes divide material into three broad levels of classification: confidential, secret and top secret. A key operational division that impacts how information is stored within these three levels exists between intelligence and military forces. Intelligence organisations are governed by Title 50 of the US Code, whereas military organisations are governed by Title 10.[51] Under Title 50, secretive operations are labelled covert, whereas secretive Title 10 operations are labelled clandestine.[52] According to the Code of Federal Regulations, '[i]nformation or material' requiring 'protection against unauthorized disclosure' is classified 'depending upon [...] its significance'.[53] Regulations make clear these processes should not be used to 'conceal violations of law, inefficiency, or administrative error, or to prevent embarrassment to a person, organization, or agency, to restrain competition, or to prevent or delay the release of information that does not require protection in the interest of the national security'.[54] When information is passed to or from the US by another state, it must be treated with at least the same level of security by the receiving state as is required by the state providing information.[55] Each classification level contains a myriad of further categories, with separate protocols existing for intelligence information. Handling caveats that can cut across categories are also used, whilst documents can have a 'dissemination control' placed on them.[56] Documents related to intelligence can be labelled Sensitive Compartmented Information (SCI). According to the US Department of Homeland Security, the 'sensitivity' of SCI 'information requires that it be protected in a much more controlled environment than other classified information'.[57] Information not related to intelligence can be placed into a Special Access Program, which 'imposes safeguarding, need-to-know, and access requirements in excess of those normally required for information at the same classification level'.[58] Material from the US Official Record moves into the public and historical records via various official and unofficial means. Official means include freedom of information processes, rolling programmes of declassification and the publication of official reports. Unofficial means include leaking, whether of a single document to a journalist or the large-scale sharing of material via a group such as WikiLeaks, or the mistaken placement of material into the public domain.

Like the US, the UK segregates portions of the Official Record pertaining to national security information into three broad categories. In the UK these categories are official, secret and top secret.[59] Within these categories further classifications can be placed on documents via the use of a 'Caveat (e.g. OFFICIAL-SENSITIVE)' or 'Special Handling Instructions (e.g. CODE-WORDS or National Caveats)'. Such caveats and instructions are used to 'denote the need for further controls, particularly in respect of sharing'.[60] These processes are not enshrined in statute, but operate 'within the framework of domestic law'.[61] They incorporate provisions from legislation, including the 1989 Official Secrets Act and the 2000 Freedom of Information Act.[62] The Security Service (MI5), the Secret Intelligence Service (MI6) and the Government Communications Headquarters (GCHQ) allegedly pool 'intelligence material' in a 'covert' database named 'Scope'.[63] According to Gordon Thomas, only the heads of MI5, MI6, GCHQ, the Joint Terrorism Analysis Centre, the Prime Minister and the Foreign Secretary can access the database. The most secret category of documents MI6 deals with are supposedly known as 'Y-Category' documents, also known as 'locked boxes', which can be stored on the Scope database.[64] As noted above, significant portions of the UK's national security apparatus are covered by a policy, known as neither confirm nor deny, that has been adopted by governments of all political hues. This policy sees the UK refusing to comment on the operations of UK Special Forces, MI5, MI6 and GCHQ.[65] The neither confirm nor deny policy, which is embedded into legislation such as the 1989 Security Service Act, allegedly stems from the belief that 'secrecy is essential' for the bodies covered by it 'to perform [...] effectively'.[66] As with the US, materials from the UK Official Record can become public via numerous official and unofficial routes. Traditionally, some documents were released to the National Archives after thirty years, though between 2013 and 2022 this time lag has been reduced to twenty years.[67] The UK has a track record of dealing with controversial issues, whether related to national security or otherwise, via public inquiries. When focused on matters pertaining to national security, these inquiries can lead to significant amounts of material moving from the Official Record into the public domain.[68] Material from the UK Official Record also enters the public and historical records via numerous unofficial means such as leaking and, what one presumes was a mistake, by documents being left at a bus stop in Kent.[69]

Canada also separates information and materials pertaining to national security into three broad categories: confidential, secret and top secret. These categories operate on a sliding scale 'based on the gravity of injury [that may be] caused by unauthorized disclosure', with confidential information having the potential to cause 'simple injury', secret information 'serious injury' and top secret information 'exceptionally grave injury'.[70] It is possible to request material via the Access to Information Act, though there are exemptions and exclusions aimed at protecting the ability for public servants 'to provide full, free and frank advice to ministers' and 'the confidentiality of Cabinet deliberations', as well as 'the protection of personal information' (which relate to the Privacy Act) and, of particular interest here, 'national security considerations'.[71] Reflecting elsewhere, and the validity of these categories aside in many instances, access to parts of the Canadian Official Record has, it seems, been restricted for reasons beyond protecting national security. As Ann Cavoukian, writing while Information and Privacy Commissioner of Ontario, noted, in the case of Maher Arar (explored in Chapter 4) despite official refusals to make information public on the basis of allusions to national security, it later became clear the 'real reason had far less to do with national security than with covering up bureaucratic incompetence'.[72] Portions of the Canadian Official Record are subject to a 'neither confirm nor deny' policy found elsewhere.[73] As Chapter 4 will show, information and materials can move into the Public Record via public inquiries, with further official routes including documents being declassified under the Access to Information Act touched on above. That said, Canada does not currently have a framework for releasing documents akin to the UK thirty (now twenty) year rule, with Timothy Andrews Sayle and Susan Colbourn arguing that such a framework, 'with exceptions reserved for only the most sensitive of government secrets', 'would make it possible to write much more of Canada's recent history'. They conclude in frustration that '[a]t this rate, we'd even settle for a 50-year rule, just to see documents released to the public'.[74] Unofficial routes for information entering the public domain can include mistakes in the redaction process,[75] and in some cases the leaking of documents from other states that contain information about Canadian activities.[76] Now that the broad parameters of the classification and release processes in the US, the UK and Canada have been presented, the following section signposts the overall structure of this volume.

Chapters and contributors

In this volume we examine the competing tensions between political, legal, constitutional, military and intelligence constraints in democracies, and how these tensions can be understood through the Official Record. We do so via seven chapters that operate at the intersection of the Official Record, national security and democratic oversight. In so doing we touch on material stretching from the 1950s (and even further back in some cases) to the present day. Among other things we engage with some well-known case studies (the Mueller investigation), return to events that, while certainly worthy of significant attention, appear, thus far at least, to have 'slipped through the cracks of history', so to speak (the Pergau Dam scandal), consider constitutional rights and freedoms in the context of national security operations (the killings of Anwar al-Awlaki and Abdulrahman Al-Awlaki), examine historic events and policies in a new light (US assassination operations), scrutinise instances where the Official Record appears to contradict publicly stated policy (US Venezuelan policy) and survey events that have been the subject of official inquiries (the detention and rendition of Maher Arar and the Iraq War).

Beginning in the 1950s, Luca Trenta uses this volume's first chapter to explore the evolution of US assassination operations across the postwar period. Trenta draws from key documents including the Family Jewels, an early 1970s internal CIA report on actions that may have fallen outside the agency's charter, the Rockefeller Commission Report, which arose from attempts to investigate domestic CIA activities that violated its charter and the Church Committee Interim Report, which called for the establishment of a statute prohibiting assassination in 1975. In so doing he explores the evolution of US policy surrounding the assassination of foreign officials. By focusing on the discrepancy between the US government's rhetoric and practice, Trenta highlights efforts by multiple administrations to first preserve assassination as a policy option for the US government and later to circumvent and reinterpret the ban on assassination in ways that permitted the pursuit of desired policies.

In Chapter 2 attention shifts to the UK, where we examine the Pergau Dam scandal that, along with the Arms to Iraq scandal, almost brought down the government of the UK Prime Minister John Major. Drawing from a report by the UK parliament's Foreign Affairs Committee, we explore how the linking of UK government aid to Malaysia to the sale of military hardware arose from the privileging of a certain perception of the UK's national interest that was dominant within the government of Major's predecessor Margaret Thatcher. Moreover, we shall see how the Official Record documents the then UK Foreign Secretary Douglas Hurd's argument that the Pergau Dam was a matter of British prestige because Thatcher had made promises about the dam to her Malaysian counterpart and how such aid-for-arms deals were standard practice during the Thatcher era. Additionally, the chapter shows that the media tycoon Rupert Murdoch applied pressure to the editor of *The Sunday Times* to quash its reporting of the scandal because he had Malaysian media holdings.

In Chapter 3 our focus shifts to US policy towards Venezuela during the era of President Hugo Chávez (1999–2013). Officially the US sought positive relations with Venezuela, from which it imported significant quantities of oil but whose leader promoted a counterhegemonic Latin American movement against US power. By mining US diplomatic cables released by Wikileaks, Rubrick Biegon demonstrates that, in fact, the US actively sought to undermine Chávez's 'anti-American' project. Though the cables do not, and could not, offer the 'complete truth' behind Washington's Venezuela policy, Biegon utilises them to reveal a more complete picture of US goals, interests and actions during a time of tremendous upheaval in US–Latin American relations than shown by official pronouncements.

In Chapter 4 we explore the role Canada played in the capture, mistreatment and torture, and rendition to Syria of Canadian citizen of Syrian origin Maher Arar. Drawing on the Official Record, and in particular a Commission of Inquiry, this chapter will illustrate the role the information provided by the Canadian state played in the capture, detention and transfer of Arar to Syria, and a willingness to use information obtained whilst he was subject to abuse. It will further explore how oversight related to Arar's detention played out within the Canadian state, and how it can be traced through the Official Record.

In Chapter 5 Christine Sixta Rinehart explores the deaths of Anwar al-Awlaki and Abdulrahman al-Awlaki, two US citizens killed by US drone strikes in Yemen. In doing so she draws on documents as diverse as the US Constitution, a US Justice Department white paper, legal documents and US presidential executive orders to explore the killing of a father (Anwar), who was accused of being a top al-Qaeda member, and a son (Abdulrahman), who was not, who were killed just over two weeks apart in 2011. Though the US Constitution stipulates that US citizens be allowed prosecution within the US legal system, neither Anwar nor Abdulrahman was afforded due process of law by the US. In this chapter debates around the killings of Anwar and Abdulrahman are placed into their broader constitutional and legal context.

Chapter 6 sees Louise Kettle document the pressures in the UK that led to the formation of the Iraq inquiry (often referred to as the Chilcot inquiry, or less formally just as 'Chilcot', after the inquiry chair Sir John Chilcot) that explored the role of the UK in the, ultimately flawed, invasion and occupation of Iraq from 2003 to 2009. Kettle then documents how portions of the Official Record and Historical Record collected by the inquiry illustrate the existence of political-legal tensions surrounding the legal basis for the invasion in March 2003. This occurs with particular reference to correspondence involving the then UK Attorney General Lord Goldsmith and the then Foreign Secretary Jack Straw. The chapter also highlights the dynamics of these political-legal tensions revealed by materials placed into the Public Record by the Iraq Inquiry and the uniqueness of the inquiry in a UK context.

In the final chapter we turn to a process that dominated US political life between May 2017 and March 2019. Namely, the investigation of Special Counsel Robert Mueller into, firstly, co-ordination between the presidential campaign of Donald Trump and the Russian government and, secondly, Trump's attempts to influence Mueller's investigation. Among other documents the chapter draws from the report submitted by Mueller to the US Attorney General at the culmination of his investigation and a US Department of Justice Legal Opinion that argues against bringing criminal proceedings against sitting presidents. Thus this chapter documents both the real-time evolution of Mueller's investigation and the influence that the pre-existing Official Record had on his work.

This volume closes with the Afterword, where we return to themes touched on in the Preface and this introduction in light of the intellectual journey taken across the seven case-study chapters. We also signpost some of the many (many!) further avenues that exist for the study of the intersection of the Official Record, national security, oversight and democracy.

Notes

1 P. Finn (not one of the co-authors nor any relation), 'Guantanamo Judge declines to explain mysterious censoring' (2019), *The Washington Post*. Available at:

https://www.washingtonpost.com/world/national-security/guantanamo-judge-declines-to-explain-mysterious-censoring/2013/01/29/64cecc8c-6a25-11e2-af53-7b2b2a7510a8_story.html?utm_term=.ffe905d341c4 (Accessed 19 March 2019); Carol Rosenberg, 'Intercepted with Jeremy Scahill, The Secrets of American Power: The Unitary Executive Theory, Guantanamo Bay Prison, and Extraordinary Rendition' (2019), *The Intercept*. Available at: https://theintercept.com/2019/02/27/the-secrets-of-american-power-unitary-executive-theory-guantanamo-bay-prison-and-extraordinary-rendition/ (Accessed 19 March 2019).

2 James Pohl in C. Rosenberg, 'Strange Censorship Episode at Guantánamo Enrages Judge' (2013), *Miami Herald*. Available at: https://www.miamiherald.com/news/nation-world/world/americas/guantanamo/article3626139.html (Accessed 19 March 2019); C. Rosenberg, '9/11 Trial Lawyer: CIA Had Its Finger on Guantánamo's Mute Button' (2013), *Miami Herald*. Available at: https://www.miamiherald.com/news/nation-world/world/americas/guantanamo/article3649446.html (Accessed 19 March 2019).

3 Joanna Baltes in C. Munoz, 'Unseen Censor Can Black Out Broadcast of Guantánamo Tribunal Hearings' (2013), *The Hill*. Available at: https://thehill.com/policy/defense/280005-unseen-censor-can-black-out-broadcast-of-gitmo-hearings- (Accessed 19 March 2019); Rosenberg, '9/11 Trial Lawyer'.

4 David Nevin in Rosenberg, '9/11 Trial Lawyer'. In an interesting postscript, a similar incident occurred in 2017 when the feed from the courtroom was replaced by white noise without direction from within the court. The military blamed a 'glitch', potentially connected to a previous 'iteration' of technology, for the incident. C. Rosenberg, 'Pentagon Says Glitch Triggered Guantánamo Warcourt Kill Switch' (2017), *Miami Herald*. Available at: https://www.miamiherald.com/news/nation-world/world/americas/guantanamo/article183204551.html (Accessed 19 March 2019).

5 Laura Pitter in Rosenberg, 'Strange Censorship Episode'.

6 Rosenberg, 'Intercepted with Jeremy Scahill, The Secrets of American Power'.

7 Leah West, Thomas Juneau and Amarnath Amarasingam, 'Introduction', in Leah West, Thomas Juneau and Amarnath Amarasingam (eds), *Stress Tested: The COVID-19 Pandemic and Canadian National Security* (Calgary, AB: University of Calgary Press, 2021), 1–11, 9.

8 Louis Brandeis in A. Berger, *Brandeis and the History of Transparency* (2009). Available at: https://sunlightfoundation.com/2009/05/26/brandeis-and-the-history-of-transparency/ (Accessed 24 September 2019).

9 Ian Cobain, *The History Thieves* (London: Portobello Books, 2016), x.

10 Cobain, *History Thieves*, 292–3.

11 T. Tate, *Hitler's British Traitors* (London: Icon, 2018), xix–xxi, 392–3.

12 BBC, 'Abdul Hakim Belhaj: Libyan Rebel Commander who Got UK Apology' (2018), BBC. Available at: https://www.bbc.co.uk/news/world-africa-14786753 (Accessed 24 September 2019); Sam Raphael, Crofton Black and Ruth Blakeley, *CIA Torture Unredacted* (2019), 42–3. Available at: https://www.therenditionproject.org.uk/unredacted/the-report.html (Accessed 27 October 2023).

13 D. Cox, 'Burn after Viewing: The CIA's Destruction of the Abu Zubaydah Tapes and the Law of Federal Records', *Journal of National Security Law & Policy* 5:1 (2011), 131–78, 155–6.

14 Russell Riley, *Inside the Clinton White House: An Oral History*, Kindle Edition (Oxford: Oxford University Press, 2016), ix.

15 Sandy Berger in Riley, *Inside*, ix.

16 James Steinberg in Riley, *Inside*, ix.

17 Jon Davis and John Rentoul, *Heroes or Villains?: The Blair Government Reconsidered* (Oxford: Oxford University Press, 2019), 54–109.

18 Andrew Rawnsley, *The End of the Party: The Rise and Fall of New Labour* (London: Penguin, 2010), 69.

19 Hannah Arendt, *Crises of the Republic* (Harmondsworth: Pelican, 1973), 29–30.

20 Glenn Greenwald, *No Place to Hide* (London: Penguin, 2014), 104–5.

21 Greenwald, *No Place*, 169.

22 B. Wittes, 'Five In-Your-Face Thoughts in Defense of the NSA' (2013), *Lawfare*. Available at: https://www.lawfareblog.com/five-your-face-thoughts-defense-nsa (Accessed 24 September 2019). Emphasis in original.

23 M. Ellis, 'Losing Our Right to Privacy: How Far Is Too Far?', *Birkbeck Law Review* 2:1 (2014), 173–91, 190.

24 Kelley Lee and Julianne Piper, 'Reviving the Role of GPHIN in Global Epidemic Intelligence', in Leah West, Thomas Juneau and Amarnath Amarasingam (eds), *Stress Tested: The COVID-19 Pandemic and Canadian National Security* (Calgary, AB: University of Calgary Press, 2021), 177–92, 177–8.

25 A. Levy and W. Wark, 'The Pandemic Caught Canada Unawares: It Was an Intelligence Failure' (2021), Centre for International Governance Innovation. Available at: https://www.cigionline.org/articles/the-pandemic-caught-canada-unawares-it-was-an-intelligence-failure/ (Accessed 13 June 2022).

26 R. Mueller, *September 14th 2018 Statement of Offense of Paul Manafort* (2018). Available at: https://www.justice.gov/file/1094156/download (Accessed 27 October 2023).

27 R. Mueller, *Report on the Investigation into Russian Interference in the 2016 Presidential Election, Vol. I & II* (2019). Available at: https://www.justice.gov/archives/sco/file/1373816/download (Accessed 27 October 2023).

28 M. Singh, 'Trump Commutes Sentence of Roger Stone, Longtime Friend and Adviser' (2020), *Guardian*. Available at: https://www.theguardian.com/us-news/2020/jul/10/roger-stone-trump-commutes-prison-sentence (Accessed 18 May 2022).

29 R. Mueller, 'Roger Stone Remains a Convicted Felon, and Rightly So' (2020), *The Washington Post*. Available at: https://www.washingtonpost.com/opinions/2020/07/11/mueller-stone-oped/ (Accessed 18 May 2022).

30 R. Mueller, *Documents from the Investigation into Russian Interference in the 2016 Presidential Election*, released January 2020. Available at: https://edition.cnn.com/2020/01/02/politics/read-mueller-filings/index.html (Accessed 18 May 2022).

31 P. Finn, 'Freedom of Information Legislation and the Democratic Oversight Narrative', *Critical Military Studies* 7:3 (2021), 335–54.

32 E. Johnson, 'CIA Director: "We are Back in the Business of Stealing Secrets"' (2017), *Politico*. Available at: https://www.politico.com/story/2017/05/23/cia-pompeo-secrets-brennan-238748 (Accessed 26 September 2019).

33 Ben Macintryre, *The Spy and the Traitor* (London: Penguin, 2019), 29.

34 Macintryre, *The Spy*, 29.

35 Government of Canada, *History: Communications Security Establishment* (2020). Available at: https://www.cse-cst.gc.ca/en/culture-and-community/history (Accessed 14 June 2022).

36 NATO, *NATO Member Countries* (2023). Available at: https://www.nato.int/cps/en/natolive/nato_countries.htm (Accessed 21 April 2023).

37 Peter Gill and Mark Phythian, *Intelligence in an Insecure World*, third edition (Cambridge: Polity, 2018), 154.

38 D. Curtin, 'Overseeing Secrets in the EU: A Democratic Perspective', *Journal of Common Market Studies* 52:3 (2014), 684–700, 688–9.

39 A. Gurria, *Openness and Transparency – Pillars for Democracy, Trust and Progress* (2016). Available at: www.oecd.org/about/secretary-general/opennessandtransparency-pillarsfordemocracytrustandprogress.htm (Accessed 13 August 2016).

40 Mike Larsen and Kevin Walby, 'Introduction: On the Politics of Access to Information', in Mike Larsen and Kevin Walby (eds), *Brokering Access: Power, Politics, and Freedom of Information Process in Canada* (Vancouver: UBC Press, 2012), 1–29, 6.

41 UK Parliament, *UK Defence Select Committee* (2021). Available at: https://committees.parliament.uk/committee/24/defence-committee (Accessed 30 March 2021).

42 UK Intelligence and Security Committee of Parliament, *Homepage* (2022). Available at: https://isc.independent.gov.uk/ (Accessed 20 May 2022).

43 R. Kerbaj, 'ISC Watchdog Turns Eye on Special Forces' (2017), *The Times*. Available at: https://www.thetimes.co.uk/article/isc-watchdog-turns-eye-on-special-forces-6dnhm3xpc (Accessed 30 March 2021).

44 E. MacAskill, 'Special Forces Need to Face Scrutiny from Parliament, Say MPs' (2018), *Guardian*. Available at: https://www.theguardian.com/uk-news/2018/apr/24/special-forces-need-to-face-scrutiny-from-parliament-say-mps (Accessed 30 March 2021).

45 L. Walpole, 'Out from the Shadows: The Case for External Oversight of UK Special Forces' (2018), *Democratic Audit*. Available at: https://www.democraticaudit.com/2018/06/04/out-from-the-shadows-the-case-for-external-oversight-of-uk-special-forces/ (Accessed 30 March 2021).

46 R. Norton-Taylor, 'Why "neither confirm nor deny" has Become Untenable for British Spies' (2014), *Guardian*. Available at: https://www.theguardian.com/commentisfree/2014/jul/15/neither-confirm-nor-deny-british-spies-edward-snowden-revelations (Accessed: 30 March 2021).

47 American Civil Liberties Union, *The Torture Database* (2022). Available at: https://www.thetorturedatabase.org/search/apachesolr_search (Accessed 20 May 2022).

48 Meredith B. Lilly, 'The Prime Minister's Office (PMO)', in Stephanie Carvin, Thomas Juneau and Craig Forcese (eds), *Top Secret Canada: Understanding the Canadian Intelligence and National Security Community*, Kindle Edition (Toronto, ON: University of Toronto Press, 2020), 29–42.

49 See, for instance: D. Sabbagh, 'MI5 Involvement in Drone Project Revealed In Paperwork Slip-up' (2021), *Guardian*. Available at: https://www.theguardian.com/uk-news/2021/mar/06/mi5-involvement-in-drone-project-revealed-in-paperwork-slip-up?CMP=Share_AndroidApp_Other (Accessed 30 March 2021).

50 Global Public Health Intelligence Network (GPHIN) Independent Review Panel, *Letter to the Minister of Health from the External Review Panel* (2021). Available at: https://www.canada.ca/en/public-health/corporate/mandate/about-agency/external-advisory-bodies/list/independent-review-global-public-health-intelligence-network/final-report.html#a0 (Accessed 14 June 2022).

51 US Government, *Title 10, United States Code: Armed Forces* (2011). Available at: https://www.govinfo.gov/content/pkg/CPRT-112HPRT67344/pdf/CPRT-112HPRT67344.pdf (Accessed 9 June 2022); US Government, *Title 50, War and National Defense* (2011). Available at: https://www.govinfo.gov/content/pkg/USCODE-2011-title50/html/USCODE-2011-title50.htm (Accessed 9 June 2022).

52 Dana Priest and William M. Arkin, *Top Secret America: The Rise of the New American Security State* (London: Little Brown, 2011), 230.

53 US Government, *Code of Federal Regulations: 18 CFR 3a.11 – Classification of Official Information* (1982). Available at: https://www.law.cornell.edu/cfr/text/18/3a.11 (Accessed 9 June 2022).

54 US Government, *Code of Federal Regulations: 22 CFR 9.4 – Original Classification* (2022). Available at: https://www.law.cornell.edu/cfr/text/22/9.4 (Accessed 9 June 2022).

55 UK Cabinet Office, *Government Security Classifications May 2018* (2018). Available at: https://assets.publishing.service.gov.uk/government/uploads/system/uploads/attachment_data/file/715778/May-2018_Government-Security-Classifications-2.pdf (Accessed 9 June 2022), 6.

56 US Department of Defense, *Special Access Program (SAP) Security Manual: Marking* (2013). Available at: https://www.esd.whs.mil/Portals/54/Documents/DD/issuances/dodm/520507-V4p.pdf (Accessed 9 June 2022), 8.

57 US Department of Homeland Security, *Sensitive Compartmented Information Program Management* (2004). Available at: www.dhs.gov/xlibrary/assets/foia/mgmt_directive_11043_sensitive_compartmented_information_program_management.pdf (Accessed 9 June 2022), 3.

58 US Department of Homeland Security, *Special Access Program Management* (2009). Available at: www.dhs.gov/sites/default/files/publications/mgmt_directive_140-04_special_access_program_management.pdf (Accessed 2 October 2015), 2.

59 UK Cabinet Office, *Government Security Classifications May 2018*, 3–4.

60 UK Cabinet Office, *Government Security Classifications May 2018*, 30.

61 UK Cabinet Office, *Government Security Classifications May 2018*, 15.

62 UK Cabinet Office, *Government Security Classifications May 2018*, 15.

63 A. Gatton and R. Mendick, 'Mandelson Named in Spy Files on Oligarch' (2008), *The Evening Standard*. Available at: www.standard.co.uk/news/mandelson-named-in-spy-files-on-oligarch-6925129.html (Accessed 9 June 2022); D. Gardham and J. Kirkup, 'Lord Mandelson Admits Public were Misled over Relationship with Russian Oligarch' (2008), *The Daily Telegraph*. Available at: www.telegraph.co.uk/news/politics/georgeosborne/3255400/Lord-Mandelson-admits-public-were-misled-over-relationship-with-Russian-oligarch.html (Accessed 9 June 2022).

64 Gatton and Mendick, 'Mandelson Named'; Gordon Thomas, *Inside British Intelligence: 100 Years of MI5 and MI6*, Kindle Edition (London: JR Books, 2009), Loc. 626/1338 (n.p.).

65 GCHQ, *FAQs* (2019). Available at: https://www.gchq.gov.uk/information/faqs-1d0b4d5b (Accessed 9 June 2022); D. Lewis, 'Zero Six Bravo Proves that Too Much Secrecy Over Special Forces Is a Bad Thing' (2013), *The Spectator*. Available at: https://www.spectator.co.uk/article/zero-six-bravo-proves-that-too-much-secrecy-over-special-forces-is-a-bad-thing (Accessed 9 June 2022).; MI5, *Centenary History Policy on Disclosure* (2022). Available at: https://www.mi5.gov.uk/centenary-history-policy-on-disclosure (Accessed 9 June 2022); R. Norton-Taylor, 'Spies Chilled about Spooks but Military Heated over Memoirs' (2013), *Guardian*. Available at: www.theguardian.com/uk/2013/feb/14/britain-military-relaxed-about-spooks (Accessed 9 June 2022); R. Norton-Taylor, 'Why "neither confirm nor deny" Has Become Untenable for British Spies' (2014), *Guardian*. Available at: www.theguardian.com/commentisfree/2014/jul/15/neither-confirm-nor-deny-british-spies-edward-snowden-revelations (Accessed 9 June 2022).

66 MI5, *Centenary History*.

67 UK National Archives, *20-Year Rule* (2022). Available at: https://www.nationalarchives.gov.uk/about/our-role/transparency/20-year-rule/ (Accessed 8 June 2022).

68 Baha Mousa Inquiry, *The Report of the Baha Mousa Inquiry, Vol. 1* (2011). Available at: https://assets.publishing.service.gov.uk/media/5a74e74be5274a3cb28681be/1452_i.pdf (Accessed: 27 October 2023).

69 P. Adams, 'Classified Ministry of Defence Documents Found at Bus Stop' (2021), BBC. Available at: https://www.bbc.co.uk/news/uk-57624942 (Accessed 8 June 2022).

70 Department of Justice Canada, *Department of Justice Guidelines on Security for Domestic Legal Agents: Protected Information and Assets* (2021). Available at: https://www.justice.gc.ca/eng/abt-apd/la-man/security-securite/a.html#:~:text=There%20are%20three%20security%20clearance,Confidential%2C%20Secret%20and%20Top%20Secret.&text=Government%20of%20Canada%20information%20and,categorized%20as%20Protected%20or%20Classified (Accessed 8 June 2022).

71 Treasury Board of Canada Secretariat, *The Access to Information Act* (2019). Available at: https://www.canada.ca/en/treasury-board-secretariat/services/access-information-privacy/access-information-act.html (Accessed 8 June 2022).

72 Ann Cavoukian, 'Foreword', in Mike Larsen and Kevin Walby (eds), *Brokering Access: Power, Politics, and Freedom of Information Process in Canada* (Vancouver: UBC Press, 2012), xii–xv, xv.

73 C. Linnitt, 'CSIS "can neither confirm nor deny" Spying on Me (Or You for That Matter)' (2015), *The Narwhal*. Available at: https://thenarwhal.ca/csis-can-neither-confirm-nor-deny-spying-me-or-you-matter/ (Accessed 9 June 2022).

74 S. Colbourn and A. T. Sayle, 'Canadians Will Be Glad to Know' (2021), *Policy Options*. Available at: https://policyoptions.irpp.org/magazines/november-2021/access-to-information-act-is-a-shambles/ (Accessed 9 June 2022).

75 C. Tunney, 'Federal Government Mistakenly Sent "sensitive" Information to Lawyer – and Now Wants It Back in the Box' (2021), CBC. Available at: https://www.cbc.ca/news/politics/cbsa-ircc-national-security-redactions-1.5942306 (Accessed 9 June 2022).

76 G. Weston, 'Snowden Document Shows Canada Set Up Spy Posts for NSA' (2013), CBC. Available at: https://www.cbc.ca/news/politics/snowden-document-shows-canada-set-up-spy-posts-for-nsa-1.2456886 (Accessed 9 June 2022); US National Security Agency, *NSA Intelligence Relationship with Canada's Communications Security Establishment Canada* (2013). Available at: https://www.cbc.ca/news2/pdf/nsa-canada-april32013.pdf (Accessed 28 October 2023).

1

'The Scarlet A': Assassination and the US Official Record from the Cold War to 9/11

Luca Trenta

In a National Security Planning Group meeting on 14 March 1986 members of the administration of US President Ronald Reagan debated how to deal with the Libyan leader Muhammar Qaddafi. 'Our forces should plaster him and the military targets,' stated Secretary of State George Shultz. When some officials objected to this recommendation, Shultz added that it would have been better if Qaddafi was 'put in a box'.[1] By 1986 the Reagan Administration had developed political and legal instruments to target and kill terrorists and leaders of states supporting terrorism (like Qaddafi). These instruments had been developed in spite of the existence of a ban prohibiting agencies of the US government (and their proxies) from engaging in assassination. In peacetime assassination refers to the killing of a foreign official for political reasons. In wartime, not every killing is an assassination. Assassination requires the use of treacherous means and/or a breach of trust.[2]

This chapter focuses on the place of assassination in US foreign policy and language, as well as in its Official Record. Documents, often in extract form, key to the chapter can be found in the Document Appendix. These documents are *Alleged Assassination Plots Involving Foreign Leaders*, a 1975 Interim Report of the Senate Select Committee to Study Governmental Operations with Respect to Intelligence Activities (hereafter **Document 1**), the *Family Jewels Directive* from 1973 (hereafter **Document 2**), the *Final Report of the Rockefeller Commission* from 1975 (hereafter **Document 3**), minutes from a 1975 National Security Council meeting documenting the views of Henry Kissinger (hereafter **Document 4**), three US bans on assassination from the Ford, Carter and Reagan administrations (hereafter documents **5A, 5B** and **5C**), an extract from National Security Decision Directive 138 from 1984 (hereafter **Document 6**) and the 1989 *Hays Parks Memorandum* (hereafter **Document 7**). As with other chapters, the extracts from certain documents are chosen to reflect broader points or themes. While some of the references to these documents in this chapter refer to the material in the Document Appendix, some refer to material elsewhere in these documents. To gain a greater understanding of the documents, readers are encouraged to seek out the full documents.

The chapter starts with an analysis of the 1950s and 1960s by exploring the individuals targeted and the language used by the US government. Utilising **Document 1**, it highlights the pervasiveness of both assassination and of circumlocutory language, innuendos and euphemisms to describe assassination operations. It also showcases efforts by US officials to distance the US government from assassination, tampering with the Official Record. The next section explores the so-called 'season of inquiry.' It highlights the Family Jewels Directive (**Document 2**) and the folly attributed to an assassination ban by Henry Kissinger during a 1975 National Security Council meeting (**Document 4**), looks at the Rockefeller Commission with the aid of **Document 3**, at the Church Committee's Interim Report on assassination (**Document 1**) and at the Ford Administration's reaction through the publication of Executive Order 11905 that included a ban on assassination (**Document 5A**). Section four discusses how the vagueness of the ban enabled the Reagan Administration to reinterpret it in ways that permitted the pursuit of its preferred policies, drawing on **Document 5C** and **Document 6**. Finally, through engagement with, among other material, **Document 7**, the influence of the Reagan Administration's interpretations of the ban in the late 1980s and 1990s is explored. The chapter concludes these political and legal developments permitted the removal of assassination from the language of US foreign policy and opened the way for the proliferation of so-called 'targeted killings'.

Through a documentary analysis the chapter highlights how multiple administrations worked to preserve assassination as a policy option while engaging in a concerted effort to remove assassination from the Official Record and prevent its exposure in the public and historical records. Needless to say, this poses challenges for historians and researchers. While archives do provide documentary evidence and windows into the Official Record, they represent a necessarily limited and biased window. Furthermore, in the case of assassination, US officials altered documents and destroyed evidence, afraid of being branded with the Scarlet A of assassination. Scholars, then, as Patrice McSherry has noted, 'must use care, judgement, and experience and apply knowledge and expertise to draw plausible, if sometimes tentative, conclusions'. They should piece together patterns and fragments of evidence, triangulating archival material with other available sources.[3] Through this process the analysis will show that assassination – like torture[4] – is something 'un-American'; something the US government does not do, except when it does.

The 'golden age' of assassination: poison, proxies and plausible deniability

On 10 August 1962 the Special Group (Augmented) within the administration of President John F. Kennedy met to discuss the situation in Cuba and the US government's campaign of harassment and sabotage against Fidel Castro's government, also known as Operation Mongoose. During the meeting the Secretary of Defence Robert McNamara asked that the group explicitly 'consider the elimination or assassination of Fidel'. Taken aback by the Secretary's suggestion, William Harvey, the CIA man in charge of operations in Cuba, replied that such options should not have been discussed in that forum. After the meeting Harvey reviewed the exchange with CIA Director John McCone. The Director called McNamara to warn him against future explicit references to assassination. McNamara's suggestion never made it into the minutes of the meeting. In the aftermath of the meeting General Edward Lansdale – then in charge of operations against Cuba – wrote a memorandum assigning the CIA several tasks, including the 'elimination of leaders'. Once again Harvey was incensed. He told Lansdale's assistant that he (Harvey) 'would write no document pertaining to this and would participate in no open meeting to discuss it'.[5] The request to eliminate leaders was excised. These developments became part of the Public Record only through revelations during the Church Committee's investigations.[6]

Document 1 provides a detailed, if incomplete, account of the US government's involvement in assassination during the early Cold War. It describes involvement in the assassination of five foreign officials: the Congolese Prime Minister Patrice Lumumba, the Cuban leader Fidel Castro, the Dominican leader Rafael Trujillo, the South Vietnamese Prime Minister Ngo Dinh Diem and the Chilean Commander in Chief of the Army, General René Schneider. The report also discusses the development, during the early 1960s, of a generalised 'executive action' (assassination) capability within the CIA.[7] We now know that, in the same years, the US government was involved in assassination attempts against other leaders: Zhou Enlai of China, Sukarno in Indonesia, a senior military figure in Iraq in 1960 (either leader Abdul Karim Kassem or Colonel Mahdawi) and Gamal Abdel Nasser in Egypt (although this was mostly a British operation).[8]

Policy-makers, however, took care to distance themselves from such a distasteful practice as assassination. Assassination was rarely mentioned explicitly. There are, of course, exceptions. Henry Dearborn, State Department and CIA official in the Dominican Republic during the last days of Trujillo's reign, for example, had a penchant for explicit calls for assassination. 'Political assassination,' he wrote in one telegram to Washington, 'is ugly and repulsive, but everything must be judged in its own context.'[9] More often, however, senior US officials discussed assassination through circumlocutory language, innuendos and omissions. These were particularly prominent when the meetings included the President.

Certainly, explicit discussions of assassination, let alone presidential orders to assassinate, were unlikely to be put to paper. The closest the Public Record comes to a Presidential request for assassination comes indirectly from Gordon Gray, Special Assistant for National Security Affairs to President Dwight D. Eisenhower. During a meeting to discuss the situation in the Congo, Gray reported 'the President "had expressed extremely strong feelings on the necessity for very straightforward action in this situation"'. The meeting concluded with the participants agreeing 'that planning for the Congo would not necessarily rule out "consideration" of any particular kind of activity which might contribute to getting rid of Lumumba'.[10] When officials broke character, as we have seen in the case of McNamara, efforts were made to remove assassination from the Official Record, as well as to scold those who had dared include it in the first place.

Furthermore US officials also tampered with the Official Record to distance the government from assassination. For example, in 1959, the CIA, through one of its men in Havana, arranged for an assassination attempt against Raul Castro, through an aeroplane accident. After the plane had departed, and it was clearly too late to abort, a cable was sent from Headquarters to Havana, asking the CIA official not to pursue the attempt.[11] A similar pattern emerged in cases surrounding the assassination of Trujillo and Diem. The former CIA Director Richard Bissell agreed that this sort of telegram represented a 'save your ass document'. In his view: '[a]n important purpose of the cable was for the record to minimize or to counter charges of US association with an assassination attempt'.[12]

In the early Cold War policy-makers generally took care that no direct instructions made it on to the Official Record. They spoke in euphemisms. Their language blurred the extent of authorisations, the lines of responsibility and the boundaries between what had been authorised and what was not permissible. Minute-takers tended to skip controversial discussions altogether and, when controversial instructions made it into documents, these were physically destroyed.[13] Beyond language, officials also intervened to distance the US government from allegations that it had been involved in assassination. These techniques, beyond obscuring the Official Record, also opened the door for denials, justifications and severe episodes of collective 'amnesia', just in case information began to seep into either the public or the historical records.

The 1970s: From the Family Jewels to the ban on assassination

If the 1950s and 1960s had represented a golden age for covert action and assassination, the 1970s turned into one of the darkest times for CIA covert warriors. In 1972 Congress questioned the morality and effectiveness of assassination and targeted killings. During Congressional Hearings on the US Government Assistance Program in Vietnam, William Colby, then working for the CIA, was asked to explain the workings of the Phoenix Program. The Phoenix Program aimed at arresting, rallying or killing members of the Viet Cong infrastructure, that is South Vietnamese civilians who played a – more or less voluntary – role in supporting the Viet Cong. The aseptic term used at the time was 'neutralization' and Colby rejected accusations that the Phoenix Program engaged extensively in 'assassination'. The numbers he presented, however, were staggering. The Program had killed approximately 22,000 people in its five years of existence, often on the basis of the flimsiest of evidence.[14]

Congress's attention to and scrutiny of the CIA increased because of the Watergate scandal and its aftermath. When suspicions emerged that the CIA had been directly involved in the Watergate break-in, the CIA Director James Schlesinger signed a directive (**Document 2**) commanding senior officers to compile a report of current or past CIA actions that might have fallen outside the Agency's charter.[15]

The documents were later collected in the so-called 'Family Jewels' and are now part of both the Public Record and the Historical Record as well as the Official Record. Part of the Family Jewels was leaked to the journalist Seymour Hersh. Hersh published a *New York Times* story titled 'Huge CIA Operation Reported in US against Anti-War Forces, Other Dissidents in Nixon Years' on 22 December 1974. After the story emerged, the National Security Adviser Henry Kissinger and the Chief of Staff Donald Rumsfeld asked Colby to compile a report on the activities included in the 'jewels'. Having seen Colby's explosive report, Kissinger wrote to Ford that, of the activities discussed, few were 'illegal', whilst 'others – though not technically illegal raise profound moral questions [...] A number, while neither illegal nor morally unsound, demonstrated very poor judgment.'[16] Ford decided to appoint a Presidential Commission, headed by Vice President Nelson Rockefeller, to investigate improper activities conducted by the CIA within the US.

US government documents make clear that the White House, from the start, aimed at containing the scandal, at protecting the intelligence community and at preserving the power of the presidency. This was evident in the mandate and composition of the Commission.[17] In the Commission, the Executive Director David Belin took charge of the investigation on assassination attempts. He compiled an 86-page draft chapter mentioning the assassination of Lumumba and Sukarno but analysing in detail the plots against Castro and Trujillo, since they originated within the US and, hence, belonged more explicitly within the Commission's remit.[18]

Once a full draft of the Commission report was completed, it was sent to the White House for review. Dick Cheney, at the time Deputy Assistant to the President, took charge of editing the report. Most of the edits aimed at blurring the CIA's responsibilities and at toning down sections that denounced the illegality of CIA's activities. More importantly, however, Cheney also decided to completely exclude Chapter 20 on the assassination of foreign leaders from the final (published) report. The published report (**Document 3**) also included an explicit lie. It stated that the Commission's staff did not have time to investigate the allegations surrounding assassination plots.[19] Only after declassification did Belin's chapter and his papers became publicly available. At the time some of that material was passed to the Church Committee.

While giving an appearance of collaboration, the White House stonewalled the Church Committee's investigation. Several strategies were adopted. The White House kept a tight leash on Congressional testimonies while Colby and the CIA released documents only selectively and strategically.[20] **Document 1** highlights how testimonies from former policy-makers and CIA officials were characterised by frequent cases of 'amnesia'.[21] When **Document 1** was ready, a battle between Congress and the executive ensued as the administration made a last-ditch effort to prevent publication.[22] This effort to keep assassination and revelations regarding US government plots off the public record failed, but the executive relented only when Senator Church threatened to resign.

In its Recommendations section the Committee established clear criteria regarding the type of activity prohibited. Killing, attempting to kill or conspiring to kill were all prohibited. The report recommended the prohibition of 'political' killings and defined 'political motivation' as the killing of a foreign official for his or her political views, actions or statements. It made clear that due to the 'reality of international politics' the label of 'foreign official' applied not only to officials of a foreign government but also to officials of an insurgent force, an unrecognised government or a political party. The prohibition, the Committee clarified, did not apply in a state of declared war or during a use of force in accordance with the War Powers Resolution.[23] The Committee did not intend the ban to apply in every foreseeable circumstance, but it identified only two extreme exceptions: 'a Hitler' or a situation of 'grave national emergency', like the one confronted by President Abraham Lincoln during the American Civil War.[24]

Document 1 also acknowledged that the CIA had established internal directives to prohibit assassination. The report, however, also stated that these measures were not sufficient. The Report called for a law or a statute prohibiting assassination.[25] This would have made decisions regarding assassination a potential object of public debate and Congressional oversight. Within the Ford Administration, the Attorney General Edward Levi agreed with the Committee and advised Ford to support Congressional efforts at legislation.[26] Ford and Kissinger, however, feared that a law would constrain the power of the Presidency and would undermine the intelligence community, as well as the conduct of US foreign policy. As seen in **Document 4,** during a National Security Council meeting, for instance, Kissinger stated: 'It is an act of insanity and national humiliation to have a law prohibiting the President from ordering assassination.' Ford agreed.[27]

The administration prevented the development of Congressional legislation through the approval of Executive Order 11905. This executive order only mildly reformed the intelligence community and contained a ban on assassination (**Document 5A**). The ban read: 'No employee of the United States Government shall engage in, or conspire to engage in, political assassination.' Contrary to the Church Committee's recommendations, the ban did not specify what type of activities were prohibited, who could be targeted and under what circumstances. The details were left strategically vague to avoid too tightly constraining future presidents.

The Carter Administration tried to work with Congress to develop legislation to reform the intelligence community. Eventually, the administration settled for a revised executive order 12036, which contained a new version of the ban seen in **Document 5B**. Carter's ban read: 'No person employed by or acting on behalf of the United States Government shall engage in, or conspire to engage in, assassination.' The available evidence suggests that the administration did not consider assassination an option. The administration also included officials, like Vice President Walter Mondale, who had played a prominent role in the Congressional inquiries into the actions of previous administrations.

The ban under Reagan: From assassination to 'neutralization'

Challenges to the ban emerged as soon as the Reagan Administration came to power. After heated internal debate the administration published its own Executive Order 12333 (still on the books today). While the structure is similar to the Carter order, the language of the order made clear that regulating and constraining the intelligence community was not a primary aim. The language of restrictions – prominent in Carter's order– disappeared. Intelligence activities needed only to avoid explicit illegality.[28] This opened the possibility that the CIA might simply request favourable legal opinions to legalise previously controversial or prohibited policies. The order also contained a new ban on assassination (**Document 5C**). The ban read: 'No person employed by or acting on behalf of the United States Government shall engage in, or conspire to engage in, assassination.' In Reagan's order Section 2.12 also added that: 'No agency of the Intelligence Community shall participate in or request any person to undertake activities forbidden by this Order.'

From the start, however, the restraints imposed by the ban conflicted with the administration's priorities.[29] The CIA Director William Casey pushed for an expansion of the CIA's powers, especially in the realm of counter-terrorism. In this effort he obtained a favourable legal opinion from General Counsel Stanley Sporkin. First, contrary to the Church Committee's interpretation, the opinion stated the ban on assassination applied only to heads of state. Secondly, it stated that killings conducted in counter-terrorism operations could not be considered assassination.[30] Building on this opinion, the administration developed broader political instruments for the pre-emptive targeting of terrorists. Oliver North, working at the National Security Council (NSC), drafted a new counter-terrorism directive in the shape of **Document 6**. The Directive recommended that the administration should have adopted a policy of 'pre-emptive neutralization'.[31] The word 'neutralization', as we have seen, has often accompanied US policies of assassination and targeted killing (e.g. Phoenix). It clearly represents a euphemism like those identified in **Document 1**. While its practice was acceptable, the word 'assassination', as Noel Koch (Assistant Secretary of Defence for International Affairs and the Pentagon's counter-terrorism chief) recalled, was still taboo in meetings of US government officials and in the documents they produced.[32] The more aseptic 'neutralization', however, was acceptable.

In the Reagan years one of the main counter-terrorism targets was the Libyan leader Muhammar Qaddafi. On 5 April 1986 a bomb exploded at the La Belle Discotheque in Berlin, killing US servicemen. The US identified Libya as the culprit. The administration, however, had set its sight on Qaddafi even before the attack. Building on **Document 6** and on counter-terrorism co-operation, the US was also able to rely on Mossad's intelligence to track with precision Qaddafi's location.[33] On 14 April the US launched Operation El Dorado Canyon, a night-time bombing raid on Qaddafi's headquarters and residences. The attack and the selection of Qaddafi's residences as a permissible target seemingly violated the ban on assassination. Qaddafi was a head of state and was being targeted for political reasons. In press conferences and public statements, however, US officials denied that the intent of the raid was the killing of Qaddafi.[34] In spite of the administration's denial, several sources agree the raid amounted to assassination.[35]

More importantly, Abraham Sofaer, White House Legal Counsel, made the administration's position clear in Congressional hearings. He argued that the strike against Qaddafi represented a self-defensive and pre-emptive military measure. In his view such a measure did not require notification to Congress (it was outside of War Power Resolution requirements) and, more importantly, could not be considered assassination even if the target of the strike was a head of state. With this opinion, in other words, the administration had established a far-reaching exception to the ban on assassination. No operation taken in self-defence, even pre-emptive self-defence, could amount to assassination, regardless of the target.[36]

By the end of the Reagan Administration, the United States had conducted or supported assassinations in the context of both unconventional warfare and counter-terrorism. Furthermore, the administration had developed legal (Sporkin's and Sofaer's opinions) and political (**Document 6**) instruments that permitted the use of assassination in US foreign policy. To be sure, none of these policies explicitly named 'assassination' or explicitly suspended the ban. These policies more accurately 'evacuated' assassination from US discourse and practice, while permitting activities that amounted to assassination in all but name. Assassination did not appear in the US Official Record and, when accusations of involvement in assassination emerged in the public sphere, they were shut down through reinterpretations of the ban and its meaning.

Narcos, dictators and terrorists: The ban on assassination before 9/11

This process continued during the administration of George H. W. Bush. Debates over the ban emerged in three main areas: the so-called 'war on drugs', US involvement in coups and the targeting of foreign leaders. These debates highlighted the importance of the precedents established in the Reagan years and the weakened status of the ban. They established new legal and political instruments to conduct assassination, while removing the term from the practice of US foreign policy.

In the realm of counter-narcotics, as Mark Bowden reported, by mid-1989 US officials were calling for the direct targeting of drug-traffickers and the Justice Department Office of Legal Counsel was working on making this policy option legal.[37] The administration started considering the killing of narco-traffickers. Debates within the NSC raised the possibility that these killings might violate the ban on assassination. Most officials involved, however, agreed that, since the targeting of terrorists was legal (on the basis of Reagan-era precedents), drug-traffickers and drug lords did not deserve more protection. The term 'narco-terrorist' was frequently used in internal debate to blur the distinction between the two categories. As one official put it: 'Certainly drug cartel leaders fall into the same camp as terrorist leaders – in fact, they don't even have the political cachet of terrorists'.[38] These developments combined with the US effort to undermine the Panamanian leader Manuel Noriega.

In late 1989 the US became involved in a coup plot to overthrow Noriega, led by Major Moises Giroldi. From the start US officials were suspicious of Giroldi's chances. As Bob Woodward put it, the US government felt that 'getting rid of Noriega was something to do on a US timetable; not a half-baked coup with a half-baked coup leader'.[39] After a one-day delay, the coup went ahead on 3 October and, without US support, it quickly collapsed. News of the failed coup exposed the administration to domestic criticisms. The reasons for the failure of the coup are multiple and beyond the purposes of this chapter. What is certain is that the administration built on this failure to reshape the meaning and further constrain the remit of the ban on assassination.

Firstly, the CIA Director William Webster called explicitly on the President and Congress to renegotiate the meaning of the ban on assassination. As Webster put it, '[t]he United States does not engage in selective, individual assassination [...] But the United States has other important overriding concerns about security and protecting democracy [...] And when despots take over, there has to be a means to deal with that short of making us to be hired killers.'[40] By November 1989 the CIA had drafted and submitted to Congress a new interpretation of the ban on assassination. The interpretation established that the US involvement in a coup that led to the death of a foreign official did not necessarily violate the ban on assassination.[41] As we have seen, however, cases like this represented the bulk of cases examined in **Document 1**. Seemingly, this interpretation also violated Section 2.12 of Reagan's order, which was, arguably, still in force. Secondly, Hays Parks – from the Office of the Judge Advocate General of the Department of the Army – prepared a memorandum clarifying the meaning of assassination and the ban's remit (**Document 7**). According to Parks in **Document 7**, **Document 5C** applied only to 'selected foreign officials', with **Document 7** also stating that a use of force in (pre-emptive) self-defence against a terrorist or terrorist organisation did not constitute a violation of the ban on assassination but a legitimate use of force.[42] These conclusions clearly built on the precedents set during the Reagan years.

The reinterpretation of the ban pushed by Webster helped the administration in its confrontation with Saddam Hussein. An episode at the time, however, made clear that, while political and legal instruments had been put in place for the assassination of terrorists and foreign officials, assassination still represented something the US government could not discuss publicly.

As the campaign against Saddam was being ramped up, the Air Force Chief General Michael Dugan was interviewed by the *Washington Post* and *Los Angeles Times*. Dugan publicly admitted that '[t]he Joint Chiefs of Staff have concluded that US military air power – including a massive bombing campaign against Baghdad that specifically targets Iraqi President Saddam Hussein – is the only effective option to force Iraqi forces from Kuwait if war erupts'. Dugan also added that, since Saddam's regime was heavily centralised, it might crumble if the leader was removed. As he put it: '"if and when we choose violence, he [Saddam] ought to be the focus of our efforts"' – a military strategy known as decapitation'.[43] The admission cost Dugan his job. And yet, although Dugan was fired, the first air raids of operation Desert Storm struck the Saddam regime military and security infrastructure targets, as well as targets that could help in fomenting a coup and might lead to the dictator's killing like 'frequented locations and personal compounds'.[44] By the end of the Bush Administration the US government could kill terrorists and 'narco-terrorists' in more or less pre-emptive self-defence, participate in coups that might lead to the death of foreign officials and target foreign leaders' infrastructure.

Assassination, counter-terrorism and regime change remained prominent topics in the Clinton years. While failed plots against Saddam Hussein again raised the question of whether the CIA could support a coup that might lead to the killing of a foreign leader, most of the debate during the Clinton Administration surrounded the hunt for Osama Bin Laden. As the 9/11 Commission Report and memoirs of participants detail, some CIA officials were concerned that kill or capture operations against Bin Laden might be viewed as assassination and expose the CIA to scandal. Members of the administration, however, worried about the broader consequences of a strike against Bin Laden. Concerns included civilian casualties, the political fallout of a failed mission and the security of CIA assets and agents.[45]

The complexity of these decisions is reflected in the Administration's and in President Clinton's approach to the Memoranda of Notification (MON) giving the CIA authority to target Bin Laden. While these remain classified, the 9/11 Commission and work exploring the conduct of the Commission suggest that – at least on one occasion – Clinton gave the CIA an explicit, written order to kill Bin Laden. As the Commission's Executive Director, Philip Zelikow, who saw the text of the MON, put it, it contained a 'kill authority;' there were 'no euphemisms in the language'.[46] To be sure, in other memoranda of notification, the language was more fudged, thus increasing both the US government's plausible deniability and CIA confusion regarding the extent of its authority.

The administration's position on assassination and the ban, however, built on arguments and legal precedents established under its predecessors. Firstly, the administration relied on an argument regarding the targeting of infrastructure. Discussing the Reagan Administration's strike on Qaddafi, Judge Sofaer had stated that Qaddafi's position as the leader of a country did not make him immune from targeting when present at a legitimate military target. As Vlasic asserted, this argument established an important precedent that permitted the conduct of assassination as long as it was presented as the targeting of a military target rather than a specific individual who might be present at that target.[47] The Clinton Administration used this justification after it conducted missile strikes on the city of Khost in Afghanistan in August 1998. As the National Security Council spokesman David Leavy put it, 'the terrorist group's "Infrastructure" and "command and control" are "justifiable targets" and such "infrastructures" are often "human"'.[48] Secondly, and beyond the convoluted nature of this argument, the administration accepted the precedent set in **Document 6** and in **Document 7** regarding the legitimacy of (pre-emptive) strikes in self-defence against terrorists. As the 9/11 Commission Report summarised, '[t]he administration's position was that under the law of armed conflict, killing a person who posed an imminent threat to the United States would be an act of self-defense, not an assassination'.[49]

This justification, based on the notion that strikes against imminent threats are legitimate, combined with an expanded understanding of 'imminence' would inform the US government targeted killing and drone programme in the aftermath of 9/11.[50] By then, however, the word assassination had been completely replaced by the more aseptic 'targeted killing', and US officials made public and repeated efforts to distinguish one practice from the other.[51]

Conclusion

The chapter has discussed the place of assassination in the practice, language and Official Record of US foreign policy. Firstly, it has detailed the evolution of the discourse surrounding assassination. It has been suggested that in the early Cold War, while the practice of assassination was considered permissible, officials refrained from adopting explicit language and instead relied on euphemisms and circumlocutory language. This was particularly true when the aim was to shield presidents from controversial decisions. This process was accompanied by extensive 'massaging' of the Official Record to remove inconvenient outbursts and to distance the US government from assassination plots. Secondly, the chapter has traced the origins and evolution of the ban on assassination. It has suggested that the ban emerged not as a genuine concern for the reform of the intelligence community but as part of an executive (Presidential) effort to stifle Congressional oversight and prevent legislation in the same area.

The analysis has traced the approach to the ban adopted by multiple administrations. It has suggested that, starting in the Reagan years, when a conflict emerged between the ban and the pursuit of US foreign policy, the ban was set aside and/or reinterpreted to permit the controversial policies. Multiple administrations developed legal and political arguments and linguistic sleights-of-hand to reinterpret the ban and redefine its remit. This also permitted administrations to remove assassination from the language of foreign policy. In particular, US officials developed and refined a multiplicity of arguments to permit the killing both of terrorists and of leaders of states supporting terrorism, thus allowing them to avoid discussing the Scarlet A of assassination.

This process was accompanied by public denials that assassination was the explicit intent of US operations. It is in this context that the Official Record with its deceptions and omissions plays a prominent role. As the chapter has detailed, US officials made every effort to evacuate assassination and discourses surrounding assassination from the language and the documents of policy-making. While Kissinger's outburst and Shultz's policy recommendation to put Qaddafi 'in a box' could almost be considered smoking guns, the aim remains that of carefully sifting through the Historical Record to piece together a series of 'exhibits' or 'fingerprints'.

Document appendix

1) Extract from: Senate Select Committee to Study Governmental Operations with Respect to Intelligence Activities, *Alleged Assassination Plots Involving Foreign Leaders*, Interim Report (1975), 6–7
2) James R. Schlesinger, *Family Jewels Directive* (9 May 1973)
3) Extract from: Rockefeller Commission, *Final Report* (1975), xi
4) NSC Meeting, minutes, Henry Kissinger's view of assassination (15 May 1975)
5) The US ban on assassination as featured in:
   A: *Executive Order 11905* (Ford Administration)
   B: *Executive Order 12036* (Carter Administration)
   C: *Executive Order 12333* (Reagan Administration)
6) Extract from: *National Security Decision Directive 138* (1984)
7) Extract from: *Hays Parks Memorandum* (1989)

1) **Extract from: Senate Select Committee to Study Governmental Operations with Respect to Intelligence Activities,** *Alleged Assassination Plots Involving Foreign Leaders,* **Interim Report (1975), 6-7**

To put the inquiry into assassination allegations in context, two points must be made clear. First, there is no doubt that the United States Government opposed the various leaders in question. Officials at the highest levels objected to the Castro and Trujillo regimes, believed the accession of Allende to power in Chile would be harmful to American interests, and thought of Lumumba as a dangerous force in the heart of Africa. Second, the evidence on assassinations has to be viewed in the context of other, more massive activities against the regimes in question. For example, the plots against Fidel Castro personally cannot be understood without considering the fully authorized, comprehensive assaults upon his regime, such as the Bay of Pigs invasion in 1961 and Operation MONGOOSE in 1962.
[...]

While we are critical of certain individual actions, the Committee is also mindful of the inherent problems in a system which relies on secrecy, compartmentation, circumlocution, and the avoidance of clear responsibility. This system creates the risk of confusion and rashness in the very areas where clarity and sober judgment are most necessary.

2) **James R. Schlesinger,** *Family Jewels Directive* **(9 May 1973)**

Central Intelligence Agency - Office of the Director, 9 May 1973

Memorandum for all CIA employees

1. Recent press reports outline in detail certain alleged CIA activities with respect to Mr. Howard Hunt and other parties

   [...]

2. All CIA employees should understand my attitude on this type of issue. I shall do everything in my power to confine CIA activities to those which fall within a strict interpretation of its legislative charter. I take this position because I am determined that the law shall be respected and because this is the best way to foster the legitimate and necessary contributions we in CIA can make to the national security of the United States.
3. I am taking several actions to implement this objective:
   - I have ordered all the senior operating officials of this Agency to report to me immediately on any activities now going on, or that have gone on in the past, which might be construed to be outside the legislative charter of this Agency.

–   I hereby direct every person presently employed by CIA to report to me on any such activities of which he has knowledge. I invite all ex-employees to do the same. Anyone who has such information should call my secretary (extension 6363) and say that he wishes to talk to me about "activities outside CIA's charter".

[...]

Any CIA employee who believes that he has received instructions which in any way appear inconsistent with the CIA legislative charter shall inform the Director of Central Intelligence immediately.

James R. Schlesinger
Director

3) **Extract from: Rockefeller Commission, Final Report, (1975), xi**

D. Alleged plans to assassinate certain foreign leaders

Allegations that the CIA had been involved in plans to assassinate certain leaders of foreign countries came to the Commission's attention shortly after its inquiry was under way. Although it was unclear whether or not those allegations fell within the scope of the Commission's authority, the Commission directed that an inquiry be undertaken. The President concurred in this approach.

The Commission's staff began the required inquiry, but time did not permit a full investigation before this report was due. The President therefore requested that the materials in the possession of the Commission which bear on these allegations be turned over to him. This has been done.

4) **NSC Meeting, minutes, Henry Kissinger's view of assassination (15 May 1975)**

Colby: Then. I talked about Radio Free Europe. And then at the end I got to assassination. I described the delicacy of the problem and how little of this sort of thing the U. S. has really done. There were attempts against Castro, in the early 1960s but our information is very scarce [...] Then they wanted to know whether we had ever had any of our own agents assassinated, you know, the Green Beret stuff. I told them we never do that. I also told them that our policy and our orders are very clear: we will have nothing to do with assassination: Church ended by saying that is not enough. That to be certain we need more than orders [...] We need to have a law which prohibits assassination in time of peace.

President: Who was in the meeting?

Colby: All of the senators.

Kissinger: It is an act of insanity and national humiliation to have a law prohibiting the President from ordering assassination.

5) Three iterations of the US ban on assassination as featured in *Executive Order 11905* (Ford Administration), *Executive Order 12036* (Carter Administration), and *Executive Order 12333* (Reagan Administration)

Document 5A: *EO11905*

(g) Prohibition of Assassination. No employee of the United States Government shall engage in, or conspire to engage in, political assassination.

Document 5B: *EO12036*

2-305. Prohibition on Assassination. No person employed by or acting on behalf of the United States Government shall engage in, or conspire to engage in, assassination.

Document 5C: *EO12333*

2.11 *Prohibition on Assassination.* No person employed by or acting on behalf of the United States Government shall engage in, or conspire to engage in, assassination.

2.12 *Indirect Participation.* No agency of the Intelligence Community shall participate in or request any person to undertake activities forbidden by this Order.

6) **Extract from:** National Security Decision Directive 138 (**1984**)

The Director of Central Intelligence, in consultation with the Secretaries of State, Treasury, and Defense and the Attorney General, shall:

- Enhance foreign collection, analysis, and dissemination of information on state-sponsored terrorist organizations and anti-Western international terrorist movements/ groups including relationships with hostile intelligence services. This effort shall include a prioritization of those terrorist organizations (whether or not state-sponsored) which are most threatening to the U.S. and an assessment of their potential vulnerabilities.
- Develop, in coordination with other friendly security services, capabilities for the pre-emptive neutralization of anti-American terrorist groups which plan, support, or conduct hostile terrorist acts against U.S. citizens, interests, and property overseas.
- Develop a clandestine service capability, using all lawful means, for effective response overseas against terrorist acts committed against U.S. citizens, facilities, or interests.

- Provide a new Finding on combatting terrorism which includes, inter alia, lawful measures to:
  - Increase cooperation with the security agencies of other friendly governments. (S)
  - Unilaterally and/or in concert with other countries neutralize or counter terrorist organizations and terrorist leaders.
  - Develop an information exploitation program, aimed at disrupting and demoralizing terrorist groups.

7) **Extract from:** Hays Parks Memorandum (**1989**)

Memorandum of Law Subject: Executive Order 12333 and assassination

1. Summary. Executive Order 12333 prohibits assassination as a matter of national policy, but does not expound on its meaning or application. This memorandum explores the term and analyzes application of the ban to military operations at three levels: (a) conventional military operations; (b) counterinsurgency operations; and (c) peacetime counterterrorist operations. It concludes that the clandestine, low visibility or overt use of military force against legitimate targets in time of war, or against similar targets in time of peace where such individuals or groups pose an immediate threat to United States citizens or the national security of the United States, as determined by competent' authority, does not constitute assassination or conspiracy to engage in assassination, and would not be prohibited by the proscription in EO 12333 or by international law.

Notes

1 National Security Planning Group (NSPG), 'Memorandum of conversation, NSPG on Libya, March 14 (1986)', in *Digital National Security Archives, Collection: CIA Covert Operations, from Carter to Obama, 1977–2010*. Available at: https://www.thereaganfiles.com/19860314-nspg-129-libya.pdf (Accessed 28 October 2023).

2 M. Schmitt, 'State-Sponsored Assassination in International and Domestic Law', *Yale Journal of International Law* 17:2 (1992), 609–85.

3 Patrice McSherry, *Predatory States* (New York: Rowman and Littlefield, 2005), xxviii.

4 Fitzhugh Brundage, *Civilizing Torture* (Cambridge, MA: Belknap Press, 2018).

5 105–William K. Harvey, *Operation Mongoose Memorandum* (1962). Available at: https://history.state.gov/historicaldocuments/frus1961-63v10-12mSupp/d290 (Accessed 28 October 2023).

6 Senate Select Committee to Study Governmental Operations with Respect to Intelligence Activities (hereinafter, SSCIA), '*Alleged Assassination Plots Involving Foreign Leaders*,' *Interim Report* (1975), 168. Available at: https://www.cia.gov/

readingroom/docs/CIA-RDP83-01042R000200090002-0.pdf (Accessed 28 October 2023).

7 SSCIA, *Interim Report*.

8 SSCIA, *Interim Report*; Stephen Kinzer, *Poisoner in Chief* (New York: Henry Holt, 2019); Stephen Kinzer, Interview with the author, Skype, 14 February 2021.

9 Dearborn to Department of State, Telegram, 22 March (1961). In Colección Bernardo Vega, National Archives of the Dominican Republic.

10 SSCIA, *Interim Report*, 13.

11 Peter Kornbluh, 'CIA Assassination Plot Targeted Cuba's Raul Castro' (2021), National Security Archives. Available at: https://nsarchive.gwu.edu/briefing-book/cuba/2021–04–16/documents-cia-assassination-plot-targeted-raul-castro (Accessed 6 February 2023).

12 SSCIA, *Richard Bissell Testimony, 22 July* (1975), in Digital National Security Archives, Covert Operations II, 138. Available at: https://www.proquest.com/dnsa/docview/1679073923/2628DDBC019E40C9PQ/5?accountid=14680 (Accessed 10 November 2023).

13 CIA Inspector General, *Report on Plots to Assassinate Fidel Castro, 23 May* (1967), JFK Release. Available at: https://www.archives.gov/files/research/jfk/releases/104-10213-10101.pdf (Accessed 28 October 2023).

14 US House of Representatives, '*US Assistance Programs in Vietnam,*' *22nd Report, Committee on Government operations, 17 October* (1972), 46. Available at: https://www.cia.gov/readingroom/docs/CIA-RDP74B00415R000200100010-4.pdf (Accessed 28 October 2023).

15 John Prados, *The Family Jewels* (Austin: University of Texas Press, 2014).

16 Henry Kissinger, 'Colby Report', *Memorandum to President Ford,* 25 December 1975, Richard Cheney Files, Box 5, Intelligence Subseries, Folder Intelligence – Appointment of CIA Director, Folder Intelligence – Colby Report, Gerald Ford Presidential Library.

17 L. Trenta, '"An Act of Insanity and National Humiliation": The Ford Administration, Congressional Inquiries and the Ban on Assassination', *Journal of Intelligence History* 17:2 (2018), 121–40.

18 J. Prados and A. Jimenez-Bacardi, 'Gerald Ford White House Altered Rockefeller Commission Report in 1975; Removed Section on CIA Assassination Plots' (2016), National Security Archives. Available at: https://nsarchive.gwu.edu/briefing-book/intelligence/2016–02–29/gerald-ford-white-house-altered-rockefeller-commission-report (Accessed 6 February 2023).

19 Commission on CIA Activities within the United States, *Report to the President, 6 June* (1975), Gerald Ford Presidential Library. Available at: https://www.fordlibrarymuseum.gov/library/document/0005/1561495.pdf (Accessed: 6 February 2023), xi.

20 Trenta, 'An Act of Insanity'.

21 SSCIA, *Interim Report*.

22 Trenta, 'An Act of Insanity', 136.

23 SSCIA, *Interim Report*, 283–4.

24 SSCIA, *Interim Report*, 285–6.
25 SSCIA, *Interim Report*, 283.
26 Trenta, 'An Act of Insanity'.
27 Trenta, 'An Act of Insanity', 137.
28 John Oseth, *Regulating U.S. Intelligence Operation* (Lexington: University of Kentucky Press, 1985).
29 For a detailed discussion of the administration's effort to challenge the ban see: L. Trenta, 'Death by Reinterpretation: Dynamics of Norm Contestation and the US Ban on Assassination in the Reagan Years', *Journal of Global Security Studies* 6:4 (2021). https://doi.org/10.1093/jogss/ogab012,
30 Joseph Persico, *Casey* (New York: Penguin, 1991), 429.
31 Ronald Reagan, *National Security Decision Directive 138 – Combatting Terrorism* (1984). Available at: https://fas.org/irp/offdocs/nsdd/nsdd-138.pdf (Accessed 6 February 2023).
32 David Martin and John Walcott, *Best Laid Plans* (New York: Simon and Schuster, 1988), 65.
33 Persico, *Casey*, 498.
34 Joseph Stanik, *El Dorado Canyon* (Annapolis, MD: Naval Institute Press, 2003).
35 B. Woodward, *Veil* (New York: Pocket Books, 1988); S. Hersh, 'Target Gaddafi', *The New York Times* (1987). Available at: https://www.nytimes.com/1987/02/22/magazine/target-qaddafi.html (Accessed 8 November 2023).
36 Trenta, 'Death by Reinterpretation'; M. Vlasic, 'Cloak and Dagger Diplomacy: The US and Assassination', *Georgetown Journal of International Affairs* 1:2 (2000), 95–104, 101.
37 Mark Bowden, *Killing Pablo* (New York: Atlantic Books, 2012), 107
38 Frank Greve, 'US Weighs Assassination of Foreign Drug Traffickers', *Philadelphia Inquirer* (1989). Available at: https://www.proquest.com/docview/1834333384/1F92C0DBB85643C8PQ/1?accountid=14680 (Accessed 10 November 2023).
39 Bob Woodward, *The Commanders* (New York: Touchstone Books, 1991), 120.
40 Stephen Engelberg, 'C.I.A. Seeks Looser Rules on Killings During Coups', *The New York Times* (1989). Available at: https://www.nytimes.com/1989/10/17/world/cia-seeks-looser-rules-on-killings-during-coups.html (Accessed 8 November 2023).
41 D. B. Ottaway and D. Oberdorfer, 'Administration Alters Assassination Ban', *Washington Post* (1989). Available at: https://www.washingtonpost.com/archive/politics/1989/11/04/administration-alters-assassination-ban/8a89e8a0-8f3e-4ce2-b34d-dd33b2403ec2/?itid=sr_1 (Accessed: 8 November 2023).
42 Hayes Parks, *Memorandum of Law: Assassination*, Department of the Army (1989). Available at: https://nsarchive2.gwu.edu/IMG/assassinations.pdf (Accessed 6 February 2023).
43 Woodward, *The Commanders*, 291.
44 Leif Mollo, *The United States and Assassination Policy: Diluting the Absolute*, Naval Postgraduate School, Thesis (2003). Available at: http://hdl.handle.net/10945/6164 (Accessed 6 February 2023), 18.

The killing of Saddam during the Gulf War might not have violated the ban. It seemingly also conformed to the Church Committee's distinction between wartime and peacetime.

45 George Tenet, *At the Center of the Storm* (New York: Harper Collins, 2007); 9/11 Commission, *9/11 Commission Report* (2004), 113. Available at: www.9-11commission.gov/report/911Report.pdf (Accessed 29 October 2023).

46 Philip Shenon, *The Commission* (New York: Twelve, 2009), 357–8.

47 Vlasic, 'Cloak and Dagger', 101.

48 Vlasic, 'Cloak and Dagger', 102.

49 9/11 Commission, *Report*, 132.

50 N. Erakat, 'New Imminence in the Time of Obama: The Impact of Targeted Killings on the Law of Self-Defense', *Arizona Law Review* 56 (2014), 195–248.

51 L. Trenta, 'The Obama Administration's Conceptual Change: Imminence and the Legitimation of Targeted Killings', *European Journal of International Security* 3:1 (2018), 69–93.

2

How public inquiries and scandals reshaped UK foreign and aid policy

Robert Ledger

The 1994 Pergau Dam inquiry shone a spotlight on policy practices that embarrassed a number of Conservative politicians and angered the British public,[1] ultimately leading to a cleaving of the Overseas Development Administration (ODA) from the Foreign and Commonwealth Office (FCO) and a change in the law regarding 'tied aid' in British overseas development policy. The Foreign Affairs select committee demonstrated the interplay between the oversight role of the UK Parliament, the Official Record and government policy-making. The 1996 Scott report into the Arms to Iraq scandal, likewise, showed the opacity of ministerial accountability and arms sales, adding to calls for more open government and freedom of information legislation.

Among other elements of the Official Record, this chapter draws on a report from the Foreign Affairs Committee titled *Public Expenditure: The Pergau Hydro-electric Project, Malaysia, The Aid and Trade Provision and Related Matters. Volume 1* (hereafter **Document 1**) that placed significant details related to the Pergau Dam scandal into the Public Record. It also draws from a 26 February 1996 speech from the Labour Party MP, and later Foreign Secretary, Robin Cook in a parliamentary debate about the Scott inquiry, which examined arms sales by UK firms to Saddam Hussein's Iraq before the 1990–91 Gulf War. Hereafter, the speech from Cook will be referred to as **Document 2**. As with other chapters, the extracts for **Document 1** and **Document 2**, which can be found in the Document Appendix, are chosen to reflect broader points or themes. While some of the references to these documents in this chapter refer to material in the Document Appendix, some refer to material elsewhere in these documents. Readers are encouraged to seek out the full documents. In general terms, this chapter aligns with, and provides evidence to back up, the assertion of Peter Riddell, who, speaking of oversight in a UK context such as parliamentary committees and public inquiries, argues that:

From my own observation, the most important impact has come from the public hearings, questioning of ministers, civil servants and others. This has forced ministers to produce more detailed answers than are required on the floor of the House [...] This has broadened the debate. The committees have also tackled controversial matters, such as monetarism, the Pargau dam [*sic*] and aid to Malaysia, London's health service, the future of the BBC, the operation of the Child Support Act, and various privatization measures in ways that would never have happened before 1979.[2]

Drawing from underutilised aspects of the official and public records, as well as academic work, this chapter explores the intersection between the Westminster Select Committee system and scandals stemming from two UK deals with Malaysia and Iraq. This chapter first introduces Westminster select committees, highlighting key points in their history and development. Next, elements of UK arms and trade policy under the premierships of Margaret Thatcher and John Major are documented. Attention then moves, in turn, to the Pergau Dam and Arms to Iraq scandals. The final section documents the impacts these two scandals had on UK foreign and aid policy. These impacts include the increased ability of those outside of government to understand how these aspects of UK foreign policy were developed, greater pressure for a more ethical approach to foreign policy and open government and, for more than two decades,[3] the bureaucratic separation of aid from the broader foreign policy apparatus. Illustrating the broader importance of the Pergau Dam and Arms to Iraq scandals, this chapter touches on broader UK policy with relation to, for instance, the 'Al-Yamamah' arms deal with Saudi Arabia and engagement with the Chilean state led by Augusto Pinochet.

UK select committees: history and development

From 1979 select committees began their rise to prominence in British politics and as an alternative means of scrutinising policy-makers and government. It was also the year Thatcher took office as UK Prime Minister, although the two developments are for the most part coincidental. In fact parliamentary committees already existed in some form in the UK but their salience increased in the 1960s and 1970s, in particular under the influence of the Labour politician and Leader of the House of Commons 1966–68, Richard Crossman.[4] A report conducted between 1976 and 1978 by the obliquely named Procedure Committee recommended a system of formal select committees, decoupled from the House of Commons, to scrutinise the major government departments.[5] This was duly implemented. A formalised system of select committees had been a Conservative manifesto commitment in 1979 and, although Margaret Thatcher was not vocal on the issue, the new Conservative Leader of the House of Commons Norman St John Stevas was an advocate of parliamentary reform.[6]

Initially, 12 select committees were set up, including the Foreign Affairs Select Committee (FAC), which is one of the subjects of this chapter. This was quickly expanded to 14 and in the years since has generally shifted to reflect the departmental organisation of a particular government. As well as holding hearings, calling witnesses and generating reams of reports (on average four hundred per parliament between 1979 and 2005),[7] select committees have (in part via such reports) provided an important addition to the British Official Record.

Analysis of select committees has ranged somewhere on a scale between influential at one end and limited at the other and mirrors a general view of how effective Parliament is at holding the executive to account. A number of writers have described select committees as relatively ineffectual.[8] Andrew Defty, for instance, views the establishment of the Intelligence Select Committee in 1994 as a significant step towards more accountability but remains sceptical of its ability to restrain government.[9] For some the tangible impact of select committees is difficult to gauge.[10] A study by Meghan Benton and Meg Russell, however, attempted to quantify the influence of select committees and was far more upbeat about their significance. They found that, out of the hundreds of reports and policy suggestions made by the committees, some 40 per cent of recommendations were fully or partially accepted.[11] Benton and Russell conceptualised the impact of select committees in eight ways: direct government acceptance of committee recommendations; influencing policy debate; spotlighting issues and altering policy priorities; brokering policy disputes; providing expert evidence; holding government and outside bodies accountable; exposure; and generating fear of likely exposure.[12] Crucially, select committees rarely focus their recommendations on flagship policies or manifesto commitments, but concentrate on less known areas. In this way they are also more likely to exert an impact, as we shall see with the example of aid and the Pergau Dam.

1980s UK arms sales and aid policy under Thatcher and Major

The Thatcher governments have often been framed as ideologically driven, particularly by liberal economic ideas. It is better to view 'Thatcherism', however, as a number of broad principles (and sometimes prejudices), most of which were superseded by, as the Conservative Party and Thatcher saw it, British national interest. This is not unusual in itself, particularly from a right-leaning government. What was more noteworthy was how this manifested itself as the Thatcher government promoting British business, including military hardware, overseas. The Prime Minister was the embodiment of this shift, presenting herself as arms salesperson in chief, particularly in the Middle East. Over the course of the 1980s the Conservatives increasingly sought to boost jobs and profits for British companies in the course of foreign policy. It was this convergence that would ultimately lead to the focus of the FAC on the Pergau Dam project.

An early indicator in the change of approach of the Thatcher government came with its attitude towards Chile. The year after Augusto Pinochet's 1973 coup in Chile, and amid reports of dire human rights abuses, Harold Wilson's government placed an embargo on military sales to the country. In late 1979, months after taking office, the Thatcher government approved a change of approach, in principle, leading to Foreign Secretary Lord Carrington conducting a review of the embargo,[13] followed by a defence ministry delegation to Santiago, which 'the Chileans will clearly expect [...] to be a forerunner of arms sales'.[14] By April 1980 the Foreign Office had reversed its opinion of the embargo in its report on the matter, stating: 'Chile's human rights record remains bad but is no worse than many other countries. With the revival of the Chilean economy, there is a good deal of potential business to be sought.'[15] The Chancellor of the Exchequer Geoffrey Howe signed off on the change in policy soon afterwards and by the summer the government was back in the market to sell arms to authoritarian regimes across the globe.[16] Often initiated by in-person meetings with Margaret Thatcher herself, the British government conducted a great deal of business for UK defence contractors over the decade, including with Jordan, Oman, UAE, Qatar, Indonesia and Thailand.[17] Despite claims to the contrary, archival research reveals how the Foreign Office sought arms sales to Saddam Hussein's Iraq during the country's bloody eight-year war with Iran between 1980 and 1988.[18] Iran was actually already using British hardware, bought during the pre-revolutionary period, meaning that the UK was in effect seeking to arm both sides.[19]

Perhaps the most notorious example of the era was the 1985 multi-billion-pound 'Al-Yamamah' deal involving British Aerospace.[20] Margaret Thatcher considered this agreement to be particularly well-deserved and was 'proud' of the business she had brought to the British defence industry.[21] That much of this business had been conducted with unsavoury regimes was never deemed relevant. Thatcher's official biographer Charles Moore wrote that her 'attitude to these matters was simple, arguably simplistic. Her view was that if countries wanted to be armed, better that they should be armed by the British.'[22] This point leads to another, that Britain was essentially in competition with its other NATO allies to supply arms to dictatorships. If Britain did not sell weapons to them, then Germany or France would step into the breach. Indeed, regarding aircraft sales to Iraq in 1981 Carrington wrote to Thatcher, 'I fear we could end up by letting the market go to the French and American aircraft and there are naughty suggestions that the Germans would not mind selling Leopard [tanks] while holding us up on Tornado [aircraft]'.[23] Nevertheless, it should be noted that while arms sales were and are the kind of subject that animates some journalists and academics, there is little evidence that the British public was concerned about these practices during the 1980s, especially against the backdrop of the Cold War. Aggressive arms sales, using overseas development funds as leverage, after the Cold War had ended, however, was to prove a different matter.

The first Thatcher government primarily focused on defeating inflation, an approach that involved severe cuts in public expenditure. The aid budget saw significant cuts and the task was made easier by moving the Overseas Development Ministry, whose budget was due to rise more in percentage terms than any other Whitehall department under Labour, within the FCO as the rebranded Overseas Development Administration (ODA). Whereas British governments in the 2000s and 2010s aimed to meet the aid spending target of 0.7 per cent of GDP – the UN target had already been in place for almost two decades in the early 1980s – the Thatcher government felt no compunction to reach this level. After hitting almost 0.5 per cent of GDP in the late 1970s the figure declined to less than 0.3 per cent during the Thatcher era and to 0.26 per cent when the Conservatives left office in 1997.[24]

However, the focus of the Pergau Dam inquiry was the expansion of a facility started under Labour: the Aid and Trade Provision (ATP), a subsidy to UK companies seeking contracts in developing countries.[25] The Overseas Development Ministry had developed ATP in an attempt to boost exports and contracts for struggling British firms. The Conservatives also increased the 'tying' of aid with certain conditions, linking assistance with the purchase of British goods and services.[26] The Thatcher government brought these elements – tied aid, ATP, assertive arms sales – together in its foreign policy with Malaysia.

Pergau Dam inquiry and report

The Malaysian government had been seeking to finance a prestige hydroelectric dam project, the Pergau Dam, for several years when the British approached with an offer of assistance in the late 1980s.[27] The UK government had in fact been trying to rebuild relations with Malaysia for most of the decade after a falling-out over a change to education visas that led to Kuala Lumpar adopting a 'Buy British Last' policy. The Thatcher government saw an opportunity in 1988 when Secretary of State for Defence George Younger visited Malaysia, securing a protocol for an arms package.[28] This was also the point when problems began, later uncovered by the FAC. Younger's protocol implied 'aid for arms' (British subsidies on top of an aid package to build the Pergau Dam) as a sweetener to the deal, which 'horrified' the Permanent Secretary at the ODA, Tim Lankester.[29] The linkage was compounded by Margaret Thatcher's subsequent meeting with the Malaysian Prime Minister Mahathir Mohamad in 1989. After a consortium of construction companies had applied for the ATP subsidy late in 1988, Thatcher made an offer to Mahathir that the consortium, if granted the contract, would build the dam with ATP support worth £200 million. This was diplomacy using all the economic incentives the Prime Minister had at her disposal.

The problem, however, was that the ODA did not initially acquiesce in the strategy. A report it conducted in 1990 concluded that the Pergau Dam was neither an effective use of development funding nor appropriate for ATP. The ODA thought, after conducting its research, that Pergau Dam was 'uneconomic' and would mean that Malaysian energy consumers would pay higher electricity prices over the space of three decades than for alternative sources of energy, such as gas-fired turbines.[30] This was not the news the government wanted to hear, and ultimately, in April 1991, after Thatcher had left office, the ODA was overruled and the project and the funding sources through ATP were given the green light. Construction of the Pergau Dam, or Stesen Janaelektrik Sultan Ismail Petra to give the dam its official title, began that year and was completed in 2000. And that would have been the end of the matter had it not been for the FAC, as well as a series of articles on Pergau Dam run by, of all places, the Murdoch-owned press, notably *The Sunday Times*.

In October 1993 the UK National Audit Office released some details of the Pergau Dam project and its funding.[31] This was then taken up by the Public Accounts Committee (PAC), which criticised the ODA in its report in March 1994.[32] Whereas the audit office and the PAC were primarily interested in how public money was spent and if a weapons deal had encroached upon the aid budget, the FAC then took up the matter with a broader remit, investigating government policy more generally. As the FAC conducted its inquiry and compiled a report in early 1994, the story was picked up by the press.[33]

The Sunday Times and its editor Andrew Neil took a particular interest in the Pergau Dam deal and an 'arms-for-aid' arrangement. Neil explained in his memoirs how he first investigated the details of the deal and the links between aid and commercial interests. The newspaper then broadened its investigation, claiming that the scandal had revealed an unlawful use of aid (invoking the 1980 Overseas Development Act), that public funds earmarked for overseas development were in actual fact being used as sweeteners to secure arms contracts, enriching British companies seeking to secure both arms and construction contracts. The paper then 'widened the attack against the British and Malaysian governments by showing a well-established pattern of using our overseas aid budget to clinch arms deals'.[34] Neil himself was by now attracting the ire of the Malaysian government and his boss Rupert Murdoch. Indeed, the Pergau Dam affair was becoming an international scandal and a major embarrassment for the British government and UK–Malaysian relations.[35] Neil was sacked by Murdoch soon afterwards. The Chancellor of the Exchequer at the time, Ken Clarke, claimed in his memoirs that Mahathir had phoned Murdoch directly to demand Neil's firing.[36] Mahathir was offended by the allegations of corruption published in *The Sunday Times* and issued an embargo on UK business with Malaysia.[37] Murdoch, for his part, was attempting to gain access to South East Asian television markets. This side show was another disturbing feature of the whole Pergau Dam episode.[38]

Ultimately, however, the FAC conducted a far-reaching inquiry and made the most valuable entry to the Public Record on the matter, although even this was too narrow for anti-corruption campaigners.[39] Yet, under growing pressure over the Pergau Dam scandal, the Major government faced calls for a public inquiry. In February 1994 the government announced to Parliament that it would co-operate on the issue with the FAC, which took on responsibility for the probe. It was one example of how select committees can sometimes be at the centre of better-known cases, not just niche areas. Nevertheless, the appearance of the matter in the press put more pressure on the government to co-operate than if the project had been investigated against less background noise.

The cast of characters assembled for the FAC hearings was impressive: the Foreign Secretary Douglas Hurd, who was also in the role when the project was signed off, the former Foreign Secretary Geoffrey Howe, who had been in charge of the FCO when the crucial 1988 memorandum of understanding had been signed, the ODA Minister Lynda Chalker, the ODA Permanent Secretary Tim Lankester, who subsequently wrote a book about the affair, the former foreign policy adviser to both Margaret Thatcher and John Major, Charles Powell, and the Secretary of State for Defence in 1988, George Younger, all appeared in front of the committee. It was perhaps the most high-profile select committee hearing to date. Margaret Thatcher, for her part, did not give evidence and never spoke about the Pergau Dam scandal in public or issued any kind of statement.

The FAC published its report (**Document 1**) in July 1994 and the verdict was damning towards Conservative aid policy as well as other elements of its foreign and defence policy and practices. The select committee hearings appeared to show politicians and officials who never thought they would have to answer for the minutiae of this seemingly low-profile policy and the associated backroom deals. There was understandable focus on the 'arms-for-aid' element of the original 1988 agreement. Former Conservative ministers were evasive about the precise details but conceded, as **Document 1** shows, 'conditional linkage' between aid and arms. Further scrutiny fell on Thatcher's undocumented assurances during her meeting with Mahathir in 1989. Douglas Hurd said that, because the Prime Minister had given her word, continuing the project was a matter of British prestige,[40] a point emphasised by Charles Powell.[41] As **Document 1** shows, Geoffrey Howe also said there was a 'moral obligation' to continue and the British 'couldn't go back on their word'.[42] More specifically it was claimed Powell had 'pressurised' the ODA to come to a decision on the viability of the dam before Thatcher's 1989 meeting,[43] while Hurd confirmed he had overruled ODA Minister Chalker's, and the ODA's opposition, to the project. Hurd lamented his role in the affair in his memoirs.[44]

Following the report, the Pergau Dam affair was debated in the House of Commons several times in late 1994 and early 1995. Hurd was compelled to make a statement about its findings, although his attempts to claim the furore was essentially a misunderstanding caused by 'temporary linkage' of arms and aid in 1988 (that is to say by his predecessors) was a masterclass in circumvention.[45] The backbench Labour MP Jim Marshall summed up the mood: 'The Pergau dam affair shows all that is wrong with the way that Britain gives its aid to some of the less poor countries of the world. To me, and I am sure to many other hon. Members, the affair still leaves a nasty taste in the mouth. Despite protestations to the contrary, it will always, to me and to others, be associated with aid for arms.'[46]

Scott report

During the same period, a protracted investigation – the Scott inquiry, or *Report of the Inquiry into the Export of Defence Equipment and Dual-Use Goods to Iraq and Related Prosecutions* to give the report its full name – examined arms sales by UK firms to Saddam Hussein's Iraq before the 1990–91 Gulf War. The Prime Minister John Major commissioned Lord Justice Scott to look into exports of 'dual-use' items, that is to say goods sold nominally for one purpose that could be used as weapons, in 1992 after the trial of three executives of the machine-tools company Matrix Churchill collapsed.[47] The trial, which aimed to prove that the company had knowingly sold machine tools that would later be used as shell fuses in Iraq, collapsed after evidence by the Trade Minister between 1986 and 1989, Alan Clark. Newspaper reports claimed that the government had acted duplicitously and in conjunction with Matrix Churchill to hide the practice of dual-use sales. Indeed Matrix Churchill had defended itself against allegations of misuse of export licences by saying that the government was well aware of its actions.[48]

The Scott inquiry held public hearings into defence and dual-use sales to Iraq in 1993–1994 but a report was not published until February 1996, after delays and requests for further evidence. The inquiry heard testimony from officials like the Cabinet Secretary Robin Butler and leading Conservative politicians of the era such as John Major, Margaret Thatcher, Michael Heseltine, Kenneth Clarke, Geoffrey Howe and Douglas Hurd. The UK government's policy between 1980 and 1988 was not to sell lethal weapons to either Iran or Iraq, but Heseltine, Clarke and others said that the stance was relaxed in 1988.[49] The change caused particular outrage in the British media with the hindsight that Saddam invaded Iraq's tiny oil-rich neighbour Kuwait in August 1990.[50] In fact, as we have seen, archival research shows that the UK's posture on arms sales to the Middle East, including Iran and Iraq, had been problematic over an extended period. The eventual report declared that, regarding arms sales to Iraq, the government had failed to disclose a 'more liberal policy on defence sales to Iraq' to Parliament.[51] In addition the report made a number of suggestions on ministerial accountability and the conduct of inquiries themselves.[52]

The inquiry highlighted the problems of ministerial culpability in the British system of governance, in particular citing the not insignificant task of trying to trace accountability with arms sales.[53] The report demonstrated the British state's tendency to classify increasing numbers of documents and a trend towards secrecy.[54] After the Scott Report's publication, the government faced a hostile reception from the UK media and opposition parties. The Labour MP Robin Cook, who went on to become Foreign Secretary in the early New Labour years, excoriated the Conservatives in a memorable performance in the House of Commons (an extended extract of this speech is found as **Document 2** in the Document Appendix):

> Tonight Parliament has the opportunity to insist that Ministers must accept responsibility for their conduct in office and to assert that the health of our democracy depends on the honesty of Government to Parliament [...] If they vote to reject those principles, however, they will demonstrate not only that the two Ministers who have been most criticised in the Scott report should leave office, they will convince the public that this is an arrogant Government who have been in power too long to remember that they are accountable to the people, and that the time has come when the people must turn them all out of office.[55]

The Major government won the resulting House of Commons motion by one vote. However, as suggested by the tenor of **Document 2**, the Scott report was another heavy blow to a teetering Tory administration, appearing to show that the party had run out of steam in government and had crossed ethical lines once too often in foreign affairs.

In fact, calls had been growing for more open government before the publication of the Scott report. The Major government had set out the basis for reform in its 1994 white paper titled 'Open Government'.[56] Nevertheless, a private member's bill, the 'Right to Know' bill, introduced by the Labour MP Mark Fisher in 1993, received insufficient backing in Parliament.[57] In opposition Labour saw an opportunity to present itself on the side of transparency and proposed more far-reaching changes such as freedom of information legislation, initially published in 1997 as 'Your right to know: the Government's proposals for a Freedom of Information Act', as well as an overhaul of the UK's aid department and policy on arms sales.[58]

Impact of scandals

Media coverage of the Pergau Dam scandal and the Scott report inevitably died down. Nevertheless, the scandals merged with other aspects of negative coverage of the Major government. While **Document 1** was a valuable addition to the Official Record, the Scott report provided further insight into the government's approach to foreign and defence policy. Apart from questions of policy-related impropriety, the Major government was engulfed in a series of scandals regarding individual ministers, some of which were tabloid fodder, others more serious, such as the 'cash for questions' row.[59] Taken together these events developed into a narrative that, in the 1990s, the Conservatives were engaged in 'sleaze'. The government staggered on to the May 1997 general election and was swept away by Tony Blair's New Labour landslide victory. The ramifications of Conservative foreign policy, including overseas development, could be seen almost immediately in the Labour government's attempts to make a sharp break from the kind of approach revealed in **Document 1** and the Scott report, and critiqued by Cook in **Document 2**. As Blair's first Foreign Secretary, Cook outlined the new government's 'ethical foreign policy' just days after taking office.[60] The ethical dimension of New Labour's foreign policy would run into particular trouble after the events of 9/11 and the subsequent 'War on Terror'. Changes to aid policy, however, would be more durable.

In line with its Labour predecessors, the government moved aid policy into a standalone department, the Department for International Development (DfID), outside the FCO. Clare Short, one of the most un-New Labour politicians still in the higher echelons of the party, was made head of the department and elevated to cabinet rank. Short's approach was aligned with the lessons of the 1994 FAC inquiry. ATP and tied aid ended and legislation was even passed to make tied aid or reciprocal arrangements like aid-for-arms, as seen in the Pergau Dam scandal, illegal.[61] Short restructured the focus of aid away from commercially based national interest and gave NGOs more salience in both the decision-making process and facilitation of British aid. Labour increased aid as a proportion of GDP to approaching 0.7 per cent by the time it left office and boosted the reputation of UK overseas development. When Blair left office in 2007 (similar sentiments were expressed about Gordon Brown when he stepped down in 2010) many of the retrospectives of New Labour's period in power were highly critical of much of its foreign policy, particularly the 2003 invasion of Iraq. What almost everyone agreed on, however, was that overseas development under New Labour had been a (for the most critical, almost only) success.[62]

The Pergau Dam and Scott inquiries also provided impetus to freedom of information legislation. The 1997 Labour manifesto declared that '[u]nnecessary secrecy in government leads to arrogance in government and defective policy decisions. The Scott Report on arms to Iraq revealed Conservative abuses of power. We are pledged to a Freedom of Information Act, leading to more open government, and an independent National Statistical Service.' Tony Blair himself came to regret the 2000 Freedom of Information Act but the reforms must be seen against the backdrop of Conservative sleaze in the 1990s and public inquiries into secrecy in foreign policy.[63]

Conclusion

The Pergau Dam scandal was an unusually high-profile example of a select committee inquiry. Yet a number of similarly well-known committee hearings subsequently dwarfed the Pergau Dam inquiry. The FAC hearings on the invasion of Iraq and presence (or lack) of weapons of mass destruction in 2003, for instance, was one particular case study that attracted intense media scrutiny. Tony Blair's Director of Communications Alastair Campbell, who was at the centre of the furore both in the lead-up to and aftermath of the invasion, attended the hearings. Campbell – by this time at war with the BBC over whether he had 'sexed-up' a dossier in 2002, exaggerating the threat posed by Iraq – saw the committee as an opportunity to put his side of the story across publicly. Campbell wrote in his diary:

> The *Independent on Sunday* had a story with quotes from Eric Illsley [Labour MP on the FAC] that they were going to go for me personally re the Iraq

dossier and I felt the best thing for me to do was to go to give evidence and get my retaliation in first. I was sure of my ground, so why not?[64]

Nevertheless, Campbell's willingness to appear in front of the select committee demonstrated both the 'expression' function played by this arm of Parliament (Campbell wanting to 'set the record straight') and its scrutinising role, as we have seen with the Pergau Dam and Scott inquiries. For the most part, however, select committees provide a role more in keeping with other aspects of Benton and Russell's framework, primarily oversight and technocratic advice and recommendations. They are also an unusual forum in Parliament as one of the few arenas to question officials, protagonists from the private sector and outside experts. Perhaps the most influential select committee reports, for instance, have been on subjects such as health, notably the health select committee's 2005 report *Smoking in Public Places*, which acted as a forerunner to the 2007 ban.[65]

Despite sceptics viewing public inquiries as a relatively ineffective instrument unable to hold policy-makers to account, the Pergau Dam and Scott inquiries show how they can play a valuable scrutinising role. The foreign-policy examples featured in this chapter revealed how behind-closed-door deals were coaxed out into the open by public inquiries, revealing details perhaps better suited to spy novels – arms deals and alleged corruption in far-flung locations – and ensuring previously opaque issues entered the public domain and Official Record.

Document appendix

1) Extract from: Foreign Affairs Committee, Public Expenditure: *The Pergau Hydro-electric Project, Malaysia, the Aid and Trade Provision and Related Matters*. Vol. I. Report together with the Proceedings of the Committee (House of Commons, 1994)
2) Extract from: Robin Cook, House of Commons Hansard, HC Deb 26 Feb 1996, Vol. 272, cols 589–694

1) Extract from: Foreign Affairs Committee, Public Expenditure: *The Pergau Hydro-electric Project, Malaysia, the Aid and Trade Provision and Related Matters*, Vol. I, Report together with the Proceedings of the Committee (House of Commons, 1994)

Defence exports and aid provision

4. While we understand the position that the Defence Secretary found himself then to be in during the discussions with the Malaysians we

find the form of words agreed was wholly inappropriate in as much as they were capable of an interpretation quite contrary to declared Government policy on links between aid and arms. Whether the amendment to the Protocol came about as the result of negotiation as Lord Younger told us, or a wholesale acceptance of the Malaysian proposal as recalled by Sir Nicholas Spreckley, it certainly appears to us to include, at the very least, the 'moral obligation' identified by Lord Howe.

5. We conclude that, whatever the intentions of those round the negotiating table, the relevant words of the Protocol could bear the interpretation that the UK Government accepted the principle of a conditional linkage between aid and arms in so far as that the UK was prepared to discuss the detail of such a linkage in later talks in the context of the Memorandum of Understanding. In the light of subsequent events it is clear to the Committee that the Secretary of State for Defence should not have signed an undertaking to bring to bear the resources of his Department in order to secure an aid package, without first seeking the approval of the ODA and the FCO.

6. We conclude that the British Government did take steps to remove the possibility that the March 1988 Protocol may have created conditional linkage between the sale of arms and the provision of aid. In designing the steps to be taken the Government had in mind the reasonable aim of causing as little damage as possible to the progress that had already been made in negotiating the defence sales. However, it appears to us that it was not unreasonable for the Malaysian Government to have viewed the letters of 28 June and 8 August 1988 as tacit consent to their request for a sum, equivalent to a specified proportion of the value of the defence sales package but calculated on a totally different basis, to be made available to support civil projects. Although the UK Government attempted to break any linkage or entanglement expressed in the Protocol between an arms deal and an aid package, the aim and effect of the three letters was to assure the Malaysian Government that the arms deal and an aid package would nevertheless both proceed in parallel.

2) Extract from: Robin Cook, House of Commons Hansard, HC Deb 26 Feb 1996, Vol. 272, cols 589-694

This is not just a Government who do not know how to accept blame: they are a Government who know no shame. That is an appropriate judgment from which to approach how we should each vote tonight. Last week, I again heard the Deputy Prime Minister on the 'Today' programme, gently remonstrating with the presenter, as is his style. He said: You keep looking at it in terms of will the Government be defeated. That isn't the way to look at it. You ought to rejoice we live in a democracy. I must confess that I was a bit surprised to hear that subconscious echo of his old opponent in the invitation to us all to rejoice – but, once again, I find myself in agreement. Conservative Members should heed his advice. They should not think of tonight's vote in terms of whether it is a defeat for the Government; they should look on it as a vote that will decide the quality of the democracy in which we live. They should remember Sir Richard's summing-up. In his final chapter, he said: 'A failure by Ministers to meet the obligations of Ministerial accountability undermines the democratic process'. The first function of Parliament is to hold the Government to account. The first duty of hon. Members is to defend the rights of Parliament against any Government who threaten those rights. That is why Parliament cannot allow the current Government to ignore the findings of the Scott report: hon. Members were designedly misled, and Ministers consistently failed in their duty of accountability to the House.Of course the hon. Members on the other side of the Chamber were elected as Conservative Members, but that does not lessen their obligation to defend the rights of Parliament. On the contrary, there was a time when insisting on individual responsibility and upholding the sovereignty of Parliament would have been seen as conservative values.

Tonight Parliament has the opportunity to insist that Ministers must accept responsibility for their conduct in office and to assert that the health of our democracy depends on the honesty of Government to Parliament. That is what we shall vote for tonight. Of course Conservative Members have enough votes to defeat us. If they vote to reject those principles, however, they will demonstrate not only that the two Ministers who have been most criticised in the Scott report should leave office, they will convince the public that this is an arrogant Government who have been in power too long to remember that they are accountable to the people, and that the time has come when the people must turn them all out of office.

Notes

1 The Pergau Dam affair ranked unfavourably among the other 'Sleaze' scandals of the era in this article by *The Independent* in 1995: *The Independent*, 'Sleaze: The List' (1995), *The Independent*. Available at: www.independent.co.uk/life-style/sleaze-the-list-1592762.html (Accessed 18 March 2023).

2 Peter Riddell, *Parliament under Pressure* (London: Weidenfeld & Nicolson, 2000), 213.

3 In 2020 the Department for International Development, which was created in 1997 by the Labour Government, was folded into the Foreign, Commonwealth & Development Office.

4 Lucinda Maer, Oonagh Gay and Richard Kelly, *The Departmental Select Committee System*, House of Commons Library (Research Paper 9/55, 15 June 2009), 2; Philip Norton, 'The House of Commons at Work', in Bill Jones and Philip Norton (eds), *Politics UK* (London: Routledge, 2014), 316.

5 Norton, 'House', 316; P. Dunleavy and C. Gilson, 'The House of Commons' Select Committees Are Now More Independent of Government. But Are They Any Better Informed?' (2010), *LSE British Politics and Policy Blog*. Available at: https://blogs.lse.ac.uk/politicsandpolicy/the-house-of-commons%E2%80%99-select-committees-are-now-more-independent-of-government-but-are-they-any-better-informed/ (Accessed 18 March 2023).

6 Maer et al., *Departmental*, 2, 34.

7 Norton, 'House', 317.

8 M. Russell and P. Cowley, 'The Policy Power of the Westminster Parliament: The "Parliamentary State" and the Empirical Evidence', *Governance* 29:1 (2016), 121–37, 123, 131.

9 A. Defty, 'Coming in from the Cold: Bringing the Intelligence and Security Committee into Parliament', *Intelligence and National Security* 34:1 (2019), 22–37.

10 Maer et al., *Departmental*, 36.

11 M. Benton and M. Russell, 'Assessing the Impact of Parliamentary Oversight Committees: The Select Committees in the British House of Commons', *Parliamentary Affairs* 66:4 (2013), 772–97, 780.

12 Benton and Russell, 'Assessing', 788–9.

13 Records of the Foreign and Commonwealth Office, National Archives, Kew, London (hereafter FCO), FCO 7/3753, Keith Joseph, *Letter to Margaret Thatcher*, 17 January (1980).

14 FCO 7/3753, British Embassy, *Note to FCO*, 26 February (1980).

15 FCO 7/3753, FCO, *Report to Margaret Thatcher*, 14 April (1980).

16 FCO 7/3753, Sir Geoffrey Howe, *Note to FCO*, 21 July (1980).

17 Records of the Prime Minister's Office: Correspondence and Papers, 1979–1997, National Archives, Kew, London (hereafter PREM), PREM 19/529, Margaret Thatcher, *Letter to King Hussein, 30 March* (1981); Amir of Qatar, *Letter to Margaret Thatcher, 27 February* (1981); Foreign Affairs Committee, *Public Expenditure: The Pergau Hydro-electric Project, Malaysia, The Aid and Trade Provision and Related Matters*, Vol. I. *Report together with the Proceedings of the Committee* (House of Commons, 1994), 13, 20–1 (hereafter FAC).

18 PREM 19/529, Lord Trenchard at Ministry of Defence, *Letter to Margaret Thatcher*, 23 March (1981).

19 PREM 19/529, Lord Carrington, *Note to Margaret Thatcher*, 26 March (1981).

20 D. Leigh and R. Evans, 'The al-Yamamah Deal' (2007), *Guardian*. Available at: www.guardian.co.uk/world/2007/jun/07/bae15 (Accessed 24 April 2020).

21 Charles Moore, *Margaret Thatcher: The Authorized Biography*, Vol. 2: *Everything She Wants* (London: Allen Lane, 2015), 289.

22 Moore, *Thatcher*, Vol. 2, 282.

23 PREM 19/529, Lord Carrington, *Note to Margaret Thatcher*, 26 March (1981).

24 Full Fact, *UK Spending on Foreign Aid* (15 February 2018). Available at: https://fullfact.org/economy/uk-spending-foreign-aid/ (Accessed 13 March 2022); Gordon Brown, *My Life, Our Times* (London: Bodley Head, 2017), 137.

25 J. Toye, 'The Aid and Trade Provision of the British Overseas Aid Programme', in Anuradha Bose and Peter J. Burnell (eds), *Britain's Overseas Aid since 1979. Between Idealism and Self Interest* (Manchester: Manchester University Press, 1991), 97–8.

26 Oliver Morrissey, Brian Smith and Edward Horesh, *British Aid and International Trade* (Buckingham: Open University Press, 1992), 100.

27 For a more in-depth critique of the affair, see: Robert Ledger, 'The Road to Pergau Dam: Aid Policy, Ideology and the Thatcher Government', *Diplomacy & Statecraft* 30:1 (2019), 50–69.

28 Tim Lankester, *The Politics and Economics of Britain's Foreign Aid: The Pergau Dam Affair* (London: Routledge, 2013), 58.

29 Lankester, *Pergau*.

30 In his 2013 book about the affair, the then ODA Permanent Secretary Tim Lankester reappraised the project, writing that the economic case against Pergau Dam became less clear-cut with the hindsight of fuel prices. Lankester, *Pergau*, 143.

31 National Audit Office, *Pergau Hydro-Electric Project* (House of Commons, 18 October 1993). Available at: www.nao.org.uk/pubsarchive/wp-content/uploads/sites/14/2018/11/Pergau-Hydro-Electric-Project.pdf (Accessed 1 March 2023).

32 Lankester, *Pergau*, 101.

33 Andrew Neil, *Full Disclosure* (Basingstoke: Macmillan, 1996), 424–5.

34 Neil, *Full Disclosure*, 426.

35 John Darnton, 'Britain Accused of Tinkering on Malaysian Dam' (1994), *The New York Times*. Available at: www.nytimes.com/1994/03/04/world/britain-accused-of-tinkering-on-malaysian-dam.html (Accessed 22 April 2020).

36 Ken Clarke, *Kind of Blue* (London: Pan Macmillan, 2016), 389.

37 C. Blackhurst, 'Murdoch Fired Editor of Sunday Times to Protect TV Interests' (1996), *The Independent*. Available at: www.independent.co.uk/news/murdoch-fired-editor-of-sunday-times-to-protect-tv-interests-1358587.html (Accessed 13 March 2023).

38 The Malaysian Defence Minister between 1991 and 1995 was the future Prime Minister Najib Razak, now disgraced due to the 1MDB corruption scandal.

39 World Peace Foundation, *The Pergau Dam 'Arms for Aid' Scandal*, The Fletcher School, Tufts University. Available at: https://sites.tufts.edu/corruptarmsdeals/the-pergau-dam-arms-for-aid-scandal/ (Accessed 13 March 2023).

40 FAC, 23.

41 FAC, 23.

42 FAC, 5–18.

43 FAC, 29.

44 Douglas Hurd, *Memoirs* (London: Little Brown, 2004), 495.

45 Douglas Hurd, House of Commons Debate (hereafter HC Deb), 13 December 1994, Vol. 251, col. 773.

46 Jim Marshall, HC Deb 25 January 1995, Vol. 253, col. 275.
47 Fiona M. Watson, *The Scott Inquiry: Approaching Publication*, Research Paper 96/16, House of Commons Library, 25 January 1996. Available at: https://researchbriefings.files.parliament.uk/documents/RP96–16/RP96–16.pdf (Accessed 1 March 2023).
48 BBC, 'Q&A: The Scott Report' (27 April 2004), BBC. Available at: http://news.bbc.co.uk/2/hi/programmes/bbc_parliament/3631539.stm (Accessed 28 February 2023).
49 Watson, 'The Scott Inquiry'.
50 For a sense of the media's 'sleaze' narrative against the Conservatives in the 1990s, see: Andy K. Hughes, *A History of Political Scandals: Sex, Sleaze and Spin* (Barnsley: Pen & Sword, 2013), 47–8.
51 BBC, 'Q&A'.
52 V. Bogdanor, 'The Scott Report', *Public Administration* 74:4 (1996), 593–611.
53 C. Foster, 'Reflections on the True Significance of the Scott Report for Government Accountability', *Public Administration* 74:4 (1996), 567–92.
54 Adam Tomkins, *The Constitution after Scott: Government Unwrapped* (Oxford: Oxford University Press, 1998), 185.
55 Robin Cook, HC Deb 26 Feb 1996, Vol. 272. cols 589–694.
56 Tomkins, *Constitution*, 113.
57 Mark Fisher, HC Deb 19 Feb 1993, Vol. 219, cols 583–654.
58 Tomkins, *Constitution*, 103.
59 Donald Macintyre, 'The Cash-for-Questions Affair: Major Rocked as Payments Scandal Grows: Minister Resigns over "cash for questions" PM Reveals He Knew of Allegations by Harrods Owner Three Weeks Ago' (1994), *The Independent*. Available at: www.independent.co.uk/news/the-cash-for-questions-affair-major-rocked-as-payments-scandal-grows-minister-resigns-over-cash-for-1444057.html (Accessed 23 April 2020).
60 Guardian, 'Robin Cook's Speech on the Government's Ethical Foreign Policy' (1997), *Guardian*. Available at: https://www.theguardian.com/world/1997/may/12/indonesia.ethicalforeignpolicy (Accessed 23 April 2020).
61 Clare Short, HC Deb 6 March 2001, Vol. 364, col. 188; BBC, 'Government Ends Tied Aid' (2000), BBC. Available at: http://news.bbc.co.uk/2/hi/uk_news/1064978.stm (Accessed 23 April 2020).
62 K. Watkins, 'Those who Focus on New Labour in Gordon Brown's Memoir Neglect His International Legacy' (2018), *New Statesman*. Available at: www.newstatesman.com/politics/uk/2018/01/those-who-focus-new-labour-gordon-brown-s-memoir-neglect-his-international (Accessed 23 April 2020).
63 Maurice Frankel, 'The Roots of Blair's Hostility to Freedom of Information' (2010), *Open Democracy*. Available at: www.opendemocracy.net/en/freedom-of-information/roots-of-blairs-hostility-to-freedom-of-information (Accessed 1 March 2023).
64 Alastair Campbell, *The Diaries: The Blair Years* (Reading: Arrow Books, 2008), 706 (entry for 21 June 2003).
65 Benton and Russell, *Assessing*, 787.

3

Containing Hugo Chávez: Insights from the WikiLeaks cables

Rubrick Biegon

The Venezuelan President Hugo Chávez was the talisman of Latin America's Pink Tide, the wave of left-wing governments that took power in the region in the 2000s. Chávez was widely viewed as the most influential figure in its radical wing, which spanned socialist and anti-neoliberal currents along with more moderate, social democratic forces. Not only was Chávez the first Pink Tide leader to come to power (following his election in 1998), he became emblematic of the pan-Latin American and 'anti-US' features of the region's transformation. A strident nationalist, Chávez viewed his self-styled Bolivarian revolution (named after South American independence hero Simón Bolívar) as a means of countering the hegemony of the United States in its traditional 'backyard'.

The US was compelled to respond to the counter-hegemony of the new left.[1] This meant containing Hugo Chávez and his movement, a challenge made more acute by his attempts to wield Venezuela's massive oil reserves as a geopolitical 'weapon'. In 2002 Chávez was briefly overthrown in a coup backed by the George W. Bush Administration. In subsequent years the Bush White House took a hard line against Chávez. When he won re-election in 2006, however, Washington changed tack, implementing a more circumspect approach. This involved an attempt to isolate Chávez diplomatically, counter or co-opt his message and 'drive a wedge' between his government and that of other left-leaning states in the region. It also meant blocking the spread of *chavismo*, the ideology of the Venezuelan project.

This chapter explores US relations with Latin America during the period of the Chávez presidency, with a focus on Venezuela. It begins with a discussion of the WikiLeaks archive, explores the methodology adopted for the chapter and notes some troubling actions of WikiLeaks as an organisation. Next it explores US foreign policy towards Chávez. In the final section it traces the relationship between Chávez and *chavismo* as shown in the leaked diplomatic cables released by WikiLeaks. Particularly in the final section, there are discussions of the broader politics and diplomacy of Latin America.

Extracts of documents, and in particular cables from the WikiLeaks archive, can be found in the Document Appendix. The documents in this appendix are: extracts from testimony of General James T. Hill, Commander, US Southern Command, given to a 2004 hearing of the House Armed Services Committee (hereafter **Document 1**), extracts from a 2006 US diplomatic cable leaked by WikiLeaks with the title *Is Chavez Losing It?* (hereafter **Document 2**), extracts from a 2007 US diplomatic cable leaked by WikiLeaks with the title *Iran-Russia-Venezuela Triangle Threatens Regional Stability* (hereafter **Document 3**) and extracts from a 2008 US diplomatic cable leaked by WikiLeaks with the title *President Jose Manuel Zelaya Rosales: Personal* (hereafter **Document 4**). As with other chapters, document extracts are chosen to reflect broader points or themes. While some of the references to these documents in this chapter refer to material in the Document Appendix, some refer to material elsewhere in these documents. To gain a greater understanding of the documents, readers are encouraged to seek out the full documents.

As shown in this chapter, efforts to contain Chávez and his movement can be traced through the documentary record of US foreign policy. To gain a more complete picture of the dynamics of this containment process, we need to examine not only the Official Record but also the Public Record, a distinction set out in the Preface. The former encompasses efforts to manage the views and expectations of various audiences, domestic and international, elite and non-elite. In contrast the Public Record includes information placed in the public domain by states *and* leakers. A comprehensive reading of WikiLeaks cables enriches more traditional modes of documentary analysis, expanding the coverage of primary material and allowing for critical engagement with US national security policy.

WikiLeaks as an archive

In 2010 WikiLeaks released over 251,000 secret, classified and confidential diplomatic cables from US embassies, consulates and interest sections around the world. Known as 'Cablegate', the release of these materials created a trove of primary documents unparalleled in the study of international politics. 'A multi-national media organization and associated library [...] founded by its publisher Julian Assange in 2006', WikiLeaks 'specializes in the analysis and publication of large datasets of censored or otherwise restricted official materials involving war, spying and corruption', and has 'published more than 10 million documents and associated analyses'.[2] The organisation has generated considerable controversy, and its reputation may influence views on whether to consult and/or cite WikiLeaks documents.[3]

With some exceptions,[4] the WikiLeaks cables have been underutilised in International Relations and political science research.[5] This chapter fore-grounds the significance of these materials for the scholarly study of American foreign policy without discounting accompanying methodological challenges. Cablegate opened a panorama on to the 'actual' positions held by policy-makers on many of the key issues of the 2000s, within the State Department and via embassies' consultations with other actors and agencies. In contrast to on-the-record statements and public-facing documents, these materials provide an unfiltered, behind-the-scenes account of official viewpoints. Whether used to corroborate existing findings or open new avenues of inquiry, leaked documents can strengthen the rigour of social science research and augment the originality of scholarly projects.

The critical 'reading' and incorporation of WikiLeaks cables raises a number of considerations. As a sample of a wider population (composed mostly of undisclosed cables), it is difficult to gauge the *representativeness* of those documents provided to WikiLeaks.[6] 'Because of its size, the WikiLeaks archive makes it almost impossible for a single scholar to read it all'.[7] The collection of documents comprising 'Cablegate' has its own peculiarities, to be sure, but this is true of all archives, which 'vary significantly' and which 'differ in terms of rules of access, politics, internal practices, and other parameters'.[8] Archival work involves interpretation.[9] 'As with all sources and methods, it is prudent to ask what other types of information may usefully complement this (archival) approach and what are the limitations of documentary records?'[10] WikiLeaks cables should be analysed and tri-angulated in conjunction with other sources of information.

Working with leaked documents carries unique challenges, including potential ethical issues. WikiLeaks is not a 'neutral' actor in world politics, but an organisation with an agenda. It has sometimes released documents in a careless and haphazard way.[11] The cable dump 'drew the rebuke of five human rights organizations, including Amnesty International, because, they felt, civilian sources were not adequately protected'.[12] Although WikiLeaks later implemented a scheme to address this, its seriousness should be acknowledged. However, these issues do not preclude the use of WikiLeaks data for scholarly research. 'There is nothing new about whistle-blowing itself [...] nor is there anything new about the ethical issues over harm and collateral damage that [WikiLeaks'] approach to transparency raises'.[13] Once released, the cables are part of the public and historical records, and are thus widely accessible.

Because of the controversies surrounding the organisation (and especially its targeting of the US diplomatic corps), Cablegate generated an 'integrated, cross-system attack on WikiLeaks, led by the US government with support from other governments, private companies, and online vigilantes'.[14] This facilitated the development of 'mirror sites' designed by concerned 'netizens' to keep the information online. In the research for this chapter I accessed relevant documents through the WikiLeaks website.[15] As general practice, I searched for cables by keyword and groups of keywords (e.g. 'Chávez', 'Venezuela' and 'populism'). I focused on embassies in Latin America, citing the most relevant examples where appropriate. These are identified in the notes using their State Department identification number, subject heading and date of transmission. In Documents 2–4 in the Document Appendix, this chapter contains selections from several illustrative examples.

The detail found in the cables can furnish scholarly accounts with a granular, textured analysis. In providing an 'internal perspective', they deliver 'critically important insights' into the thinking of US foreign policy and national security elites.[16] The cables illuminate the 'rich tapestry of political life'[17] at the heart of US diplomacy and national security policy. 'Documents, of course, do not speak for themselves but only acquire significant meaning when situated within a context set by vigorous analytical and methodological assumptions'.[18] Ultimately this type of leaked material enables what Robert E. Goodin and Charles Tilly define as contextual political analysis. Building on their approach, this chapter assumes that politics and its study are inherently process-based phenomena, meaning the political analyst must be highly attuned to (various kinds of) context. Modes of triangulation can be useful in drawing out context-based insights.[19] By examining leaked primary sources alongside other kinds of documentary evidence, the analyst gains a more complete picture of political processes under investigation.

US foreign policy towards Hugo Chávez

When Hugo Chávez was elected in 1998, Washington was nominally supportive of his reformist government. As he moved towards an anti-neoliberal posture and established closer relations with Cuba, however, the US adopted an adversarial stance. The George W. Bush Administration supported a (brief and unsuccessful) military coup against Chávez in 2002. Following the attempted ouster, the opposition, backed by the US, sought the collapse of the government through street protests and strikes or lockouts in the country's all-important petroleum sector.[20] Surviving the crises, Chávez pushed forward a nationalist agenda that challenged the neoliberal Washington consensus. The popularity of '*chavista*' social programmes contributed to his re-election in 2006 and allowed him to 'radicalise' the Bolivarian revolution, which he equated with twenty-first-century socialism. The Bolivarian vision emphasised counter-hegemonic co-operation as the charismatic Chávez, utilising Venezuela's oil wealth, forged alliances to undermine Washington's long-standing geopolitical dominance in Latin America.

As the Pink Tide gained traction, Chávez gained partners. Analysts saw the regional trend as comprising two distinct lefts. A moderate and largely market-oriented left, as expressed in governments in Brazil, Chile and Uruguay, could be contrasted with a more radical, statist variant, associated with Chávez, Bolivia's Evo Morales and Ecuador's Rafael Correa.[21] In the international relations of the Western hemisphere, however, these differences were muted. Progressive governments of all stripes sought greater autonomy from Washington, including through the creation of new pathways to intra-Latin American co-operation. For Venezuela the most important initiative was the Bolivarian Alliance for Our Americas (ALBA), which began as a joint project with Cuba before its expansion into a trade and investment pact with as many as 12 member states. It included the Petrocaribe and Petrosur programmes, which aimed at fostering socio-economic development and co-ordination through the energy sector. Venezuela also supported initiatives led by moderate governments. These included the Union of South American Nations (UNASUR) and the Community of Latin American and Caribbean States (CELAC), two multilateral bodies championed by Brazil that excluded the US. This new regionalism diminished the centrality of the Organisation of American States (OAS) to hemispheric diplomacy, signalling the further erosion of US hegemony.[22]

For Washington, Venezuela's leadership of the radical left was concerning, as was its influence over the Pink Tide's moderate strands. However, the inability of the anti-Chávez opposition and its allies in the Bush Administration to depose Chávez led to a shift in strategy. The confrontational posture seemed only to play into Chávez's anti-imperialist image. Washington would develop a more diplomatic approach, at times ambiguous in its strategic disposition. Under the guidance of Thomas Shannon, who served as Assistant Secretary of State for Western Hemisphere Affairs from 2005 to 2009, Washington sought to accommodate elements of Latin America's new left. US policy-makers adopted the language of 'social justice' in an effort to co-opt the progressive message.[23] Although officials continued to criticise the 'false populism' of certain leaders, they tended to avoid naming Chávez or directly condemning his government. The Obama Administration maintained this 'softer' posture. At the Summit of the Americas in 2009 Obama called for a 'new era of partnership'. Acknowledging the ill-effects of the legacy of interventionism, he pledged a 'new chapter of engagement' characterised by 'mutual respect and common interests and shared values'.[24] 'Partnership' would become an important watchword in the Obama Administration's efforts to reset US policy in the region.[25]

There was an obvious tension in the public presentation of US policy towards Venezuela over the course of the Bush and Obama presidencies, as reflected in official documents and statements. On the one hand, as seen in **Document 1**, the Chávez government was depicted as a national security threat. On the other hand, officials maintained they would not 'impose [an] ideological litmus test on potential partners in the region' and sought 'productive relationships with governments from across the political spectrum'.[26] Throughout the Chávez years Venezuela remained one of the largest suppliers of crude oil to the American market.[27] But there were concerns that Chávez's socialism could damage US-based international oil companies.[28] Potential disruptions in the sector could threaten national security, particularly as Chávez sought to diversify Venezuela's export markets by brokering deals with China.

As illustrated by the 2004 Congressional testimony of General Hill of the US Southern Command (SOUTHCOM) seen in **Document 1**, for the US military the 'radical populism' of Chávez constituted a clear threat. By catalysing anti-American sentiment Chávez could mobilise movements across the Andean region. Hill advocated action to address threats to US interests in Bolivia, Colombia and Ecuador. National security concerns related to populism persisted into the era of renewed 'partnership' under Obama. Monographs and reports from the Strategic Studies Institute, a research body within the US Army, reflected the widespread view that Chávez was a threat to the US not only because of his personality, his ideology or Venezuela's oil resources but because his influence could spread.[29] The Congressional Research Service summarised the sources of 'friction' between Washington and the Chávez government, which it traced to 'concerns about human rights, Venezuela's military arms purchases, its relations with Cuba and Iran, and its efforts to export its brand of populism to other Latin American countries'.[30] In this context US foreign policy did not acquiesce to this new political reality, but sought to check and limit *chavismo*. Although the term was rarely used in official discourse, Chávez and his movement needed to be *contained*. This meant that the US recognised the limits placed on its own power by the existence of an adversarial actor, even as it sought to manage the status quo, bending a complex reality towards its long-term interests.

Chávez and *chavismo* in the WikiLeaks cables

The similarities across the Bush and Obama administrations illustrate the force of structural and material factors in US policy towards its Latin American neighbours.[31] Both presidents viewed Bolivarian socialism as a clear challenge to the US. Among other things, leaked diplomatic cables provide a way of tracing the continuities in US policy, which are often obscured by wider attention to matters of presidential style. Despite the disturbances over various forms of populism, there was little outward sense that US policy could, or should, contain and/or rollback Chávez's regional movement. Below the surface, however, WikiLeaks cables from the 2000s paint a detailed picture of Washington's aims and anxieties. As a 2004 cable from the embassy in Caracas stated bluntly (quoting an interlocutor): 'regional and international containment is the only realistic policy toward Chavez', and 'without clear US leadership, there will be no containment whatsoever'.[32]

WikiLeaks materials provide a unique angle partly because they were 'obviously not intended for public disclosure', as demonstrated by the 'blunt, entertaining, and offensive language' found in many of the documents.[33] Connecting personalities to political trends and events, the cables contain sketches of key figures in the Pink Tide milieu, including Chávez himself. As suggested in **Document 2**, a 2006 cable, the radical rhetoric of Chávez may have been only partly strategic. Personal issues provided an opportunity to take advantage of his volatility to 'drive a wedge' between his government and its would-be partners, including through 'creative outreach'. A similar character sketch featured in **Document 4** of Honduran President Manual Zelaya, ousted in a coup in 2009, shows the extent to which his connections to Venezuela drew the ire of US officials. **Document 4**, a 2008 cable, reveals, for instance, that President Bush personally conveyed his 'strong opposition' to Zelaya's intention to join Petrocaribe. The cable suggested that Zelaya's 'old-fashioned nationalism' indicated that he was 'not a friend' of the US. It disparaged Zelaya as a 'throwback' and a 'caricature of a land-owner *caudillo*' (strongman) before likening him to a 'rebellious teenager' and would-be 'martyr'. The cables provide similar insights into various figures associated with the 'radical' left, including, most prominently, Evo Morales and Rafael Correa.[34] The documentary record oscillates in the depictions of these leaders; at times they are astute political operators to be taken seriously, cunning in their attempts to undermine US interests; elsewhere they are merely corrupt, almost comical leaders bereft of any meaningful political platform. More importantly, however, the cables illustrate that US unease went well beyond the personal proclivities of the Pink Tide's most well-known provocateurs.

Indeed, the cables showed an abiding apprehension over the spread of *chavismo*, populism, Bolivarianism, twenty-first-century socialism and the programmes and institutions associated with Venezuelan foreign policy, including ALBA and its initiatives. This contrasts with the official face of US policy in the late 2000s and early 2010s, overlapping the Bush and

Obama administrations. One cable from 2009, following Obama's inauguration, indicated that US officials were sceptical of overtures by the Venezuelan government to 'turn the page' and improve bilateral relations. However, it noted that 'the arrival of a new administration in Washington [...] provide[d] an excellent opportunity to reach out to [nationalist] voters and change the conventional wisdom' that Chávez 'stands up to the "'empire"'.[35] **Document 3**, a 2007 cable, meanwhile, documents conversations with interlocutors from other countries, showing how US policy dovetails with the interests of local elites in the region.

Unsurprisingly, developments in South America's resource-rich Andean region drew particular attention. The source of much of Latin America's illicit narcotics trade, the complex political realities of the Andes can be traced to inequalities that span myriad socio-economic and ethnic divisions. The region was – and remains – home to 'ungoverned spaces' and diverse oppositional forces, from vibrant social movements to armed non-state actors. As **Document 1** illustrates, for US officials this provided the kind of environment that Chávez could deftly exploit. A confidential cable from 2008, meanwhile, noted that the FARC (the Revolutionary Armed Forces of Colombia, a Marxist guerrilla organisation) appeared to be incorporating Bolivarian ideas into its messaging, such as 'unifying Latin America through socialism'.[36] Andean leaders like Morales and Correa were understood as protégés of Chávez. The spread of populism directly threatened Washington's economic agenda, including trade liberalisation, 'free-market growth' and 'responsible macroeconomic and fiscal policy'.[37] Venezuela's ability to finance developments across the region's energy sector was closely monitored.[38]

Security issues were also important. This included co-operation with US counter-narcotic efforts in the region, often tied to trade and investment benefits for compliant partners through the US Andean Trade Preferences Act.[39] Amidst protests, Washington protected the viability of its Defense Co-operation Agreement (DCA) with Colombia, which gave the US military access to several bases in the country. This included diplomatic efforts to calm the controversy sparked by the signing of the DCA, which was opposed by other South American states then attempting closer co-operation through the UNASUR-based South American Defense Council.[40] In Ecuador the US sought to preserve its access to the Manta airbase, its largest in South America. By letting the agreement with the US Department of Defense lapse in 2009, the Correa government effectively expelled the US military from a 'Forward Operating Location'. As per **Document 3**, the (ostensible) security implications of *chavismo* extended well beyond the Andean region, fuelled by an 'anti-American ideology' that resonated outside the hemisphere and connected 'radical populist governments' in Latin America to adversaries like Russia and Iran. When the Chávez government angled for a seat on the United Nations Security Council in 2006, the State Department leaned on partners to vote against Caracas.[41]

ALBA was a major flashpoint in the US–Venezuela rivalry. It represented a means not only of spreading the ideas of *chavismo* but of connecting them to concrete social and economic policies. For example the US embassy in Lima highlighted 'Venezuelan proselytizing in Peru' through health and education programmes funded by ALBA.[42] Initially downplayed in US diplomatic discourse, at least as reflected in the cables,[43] by 2010 officials were characterising ALBA as an 'increasingly vocal and coordinated grouping that demands attention in international fora, both inside and outside the Hemisphere'.[44] In assessing the rhetoric and policies of Evo Morales, one cable detected 'a coordinated ALBA script'.[45] As ALBA expanded into the Caribbean, the region was increasingly seen through the lens of geostrategic competition between the US and Venezuela. One cable argued that in addition to investment associated with ALBA and Petrocaribe, 'Chavez's most significant influence [was] in providing a blueprint for populist demagoguery', allowing leaders in the region, such as Dominica's Prime Minister Roosevelt Skerrit, to style their politics 'self-consciously after Chavez'.[46]

Although the cables provide insight into US perceptions, interests and aims with respect to Chávez and his movement, they do not offer as much when it comes to the *means* by which Chávez was to be contained. Naturally the focus was generally on diplomatic tools as opposed to other instruments of statecraft. This is not to say that the cables are mute on core strategic themes. For instance it is clear the US sought to contain Chávez by 'isolating' him from other leftist and centre-left figures. One cable recounting a meeting between Thomas Shannon and Evo Morales stated: the US 'should engage with [Morales's] government and call its bluff at each turn. We can use such engagement to bring other allies into the effort, and to try to drive a wedge between Chavez and Morales'.[47]

The ability of US officials to pressure foreign leaders on an individual basis is an underappreciated facet of American foreign policy. In respect to the aforementioned Zelaya, the deposed president of Honduras, one cable stated: 'In several instances when Zelaya has threatened our interests [...] we have approached him in a direct and discreet way and articulated our core interests. In these instances he has not crossed our red lines'. The cable noted that the embassy had worked with prominent opposition politicians who would later be involved in the coup. 'Above all', it added, 'we have avoided taking our disagreements public, which only makes Zelaya more difficult'.[48] In such a scenario, the analytical utility of leaked portions of the Official Record becomes ever more apparent.

Visits from high-profile officials were seen as a crucial means of shoring-up key allies, including the governments of Colombia and Peru.[49] Many cables reference activities of US embassies without offering much detail. Embassies exert influence through their ability to disseminate (mis)information in a manner consistent with US interests; to 'spread the word'[50] about the actions of adversaries and thus frame policies in a particular light. For instance, in regards to the controversy over the Manta airbase, noted above, which drew an international anti-basing conference to Ecuador in 2007, the embassy in Quito stated that it was 'taking proactive steps to counter the conference's anti-US base and anti-US military propaganda campaign'. The cable referred to 'public diplomacy efforts', 'paid media placements', private meetings and an 'aggressive communications plan'.[51] The deployment of humanitarian assistance in the region was also linked to efforts by the US military to improve its image and 'create a more favorable climate for possible renegotiation of the Manta' agreement.[52] More broadly US policy sought to encourage sympathetic civil-society actors to criticise not only Chávez but also the policies associated with his movement.[53]

Conclusion

This chapter has investigated secret and confidential cables published by WikiLeaks to analyse efforts by the US to contain the international influence of the Venezuelan President Hugo Chávez. Over the course of his presidency, and until his death in 2013, Chávez promoted a counter-hegemonic movement against US power, becoming Washington's most prominent geopolitical adversary in Latin America. Officially the US sought positive relations with Venezuela (which remained a major source of US petroleum imports), as well as its leftist-populist partners, including Bolivia and Ecuador. Beneath the veneer of normal diplomatic relations, however, the US worked to undermine the Bolivarian project. The political complexities of this effort can be read across the official and public records.

By delving into WikiLeaks materials to analyse the details of US foreign policy toward Venezuela, this chapter highlighted the value of working with leaked diplomatic documents, while also acknowledging some potential pitfalls. Against the limitations of the Official Record, the cables provide for a more nuanced, granular understanding of US diplomacy. The cables do not – and cannot – offer the 'complete truth' behind Washington's policy toward Venezuela, but they can – and do – reveal a more complete picture of US goals, interests and actions during a time of tremendous upheaval in US–Latin American relations. In underscoring the challenges associated with relying on this type of material, the chapter has reinforced the need to triangulate between sources and modes of textual and documentary analysis present in the official and public (and thus also historical) records.

Document appendix

1) Extracts from: United States Congress, *Testimony of General James T. Hill, Commander, United States Southern Command, Hearing of the House Armed Services Committee: 'Fiscal Year 2005 National Defense Authorization Budget request'*, March 24 (2004)
2) Extracts from: WikiLeaks Cable. *'Is Chavez Losing It?'*, 3 May. Reference ID: 06CARACAS1169 (2006)
3) Extracts from: WikiLeaks Cable. *Iran-Russia-Venezuela Triangle Threatens Regional Stability*, 13 November. Reference ID: 07BRASILIA2132 (2007)
4) Extracts from: WikiLeaks Cable. *President Jose Manuel Zelaya Rosales: Personal*, 15 May. Reference ID: 08TEGUCIGALPA459 (2008)

1) **Extracts from: United States Congress, *Testimony of General James T. Hill, Commander, United States Southern Command, hearing of the House Armed Services Committee: 'Fiscal Year 2005 National Defense Authorization budget request'*, March 24 (2004)**

The security picture in Latin America and the Caribbean has grown more complex over the past year. Colombia's considerable progress in the battle against narcoterrorism is offset by negative developments elsewhere in the region, particularly in Haiti, Bolivia, and Venezuela. These developments represent an increasing threat to U.S. interests. We face two primary types of threats in the region: an established set of threats detailed in previous years and a nascent set likely to raise serious issues during this year. On the traditional front, we still face threats from narcoterrorists and their ilk, a growing threat to law and order in partner nations from urban gangs and other illegal armed groups, which are also generally tied to the narcotics trade, and a lesser but sophisticated threat from Islamic radical groups in the region. These traditional threats are now complemented by an emerging threat best described as radical populism, in which the democratic process is undermined to decrease rather than protect individual rights. Some leaders in the region are tapping into deep-seated frustrations of the failure of democratic reforms to deliver expected goods and services. By tapping into these frustrations, which run concurrently with frustrations caused by social and economic inequality, the leaders are at the same time able to reinforce their radical positions by inflaming anti-U.S. sentiment. Additionally, other actors are seeking to undermine U.S. interests in the region by supporting these movements.

[...]

Radical populism is another emerging concern in the region. Populism in and of itself is not a threat. Rather, the threat emerges when it becomes radicalized by a leader who increasingly uses his position and support from a segment of the population to infringe gradually upon the rights of all citizens. This trend degrades democracy and promises to concentrate power in the hands of a few rather than guaranteeing the individual rights of the many. Anti-American sentiment has also been used to reinforce the positions of radical leaders who seek to distract the populace from their own shortcomings. Anti-American sentiment also troubles our partner nations as well, as elected leaders must take into account the sometime very vocal views of their constituents. The threats and trends in the region paint a negative picture in many regards and certainly bear close scrutiny in the coming year. We will maintain vigilance. We will also continue our work with partner nations and the interagency to shore up stability and promote increasing security cooperation.

2) **Extracts from: WikiLeaks Cable.** *Is Chavez Losing It?*, 3 May. **Reference ID: 06CARACAS1169 (2006)**

Summary: Venezuelan President Hugo Chavez' rhetoric has always been radical. Yet, up until the last six to 12 months, he reserved his most extreme statements for domestic audiences. Lately, he has flown off the handle in front of international microphones. He has criticized regional counterparts who in the past he attempted to court. He has even lashed out at his own domestic supporters. Meanwhile, his claims that the United States is trying to assassinate him or to invade Venezuela have continued. Although there is some evidence that elements of the Venezuelan Government question his reactionary harangues, his most senior advisers mimic his radical rhetoric. Whether his attempts to circle the wagons around a smaller, more radical group of countries is a calculated strategy or a frustrated reaction to the region's refusal to embrace him as its leader is unclear. We do not know whether Chavez' job is getting to him, but his public antics are making him appear increasingly on edge. Whatever the cause, we can take advantage of his volatile behavior. Creative U.S. outreach to Chavez' regional partners will drive a wedge between him and them. Through his relationship with Iran, Chavez' appears to have begun to alarm countries untroubled by his anti-U.S. rhetoric on his own. As international attention – especially from us – feeds Chavez' ego, we need to be circumspect in choosing which of his outbursts to respond to.

3) **Extracts from: WikiLeaks Cable.** *Iran-Russia-Venezuela Triangle Threatens Regional Stability*, 13 November. **Reference ID: 07BRASI-LIA2132 (2007)**

Summary: Iran, Russia, and Venezuela are involved in an open and growing collaboration with a common purpose to make more arms available to radical populist governments and spread anti-American ideology in the region, according to the chairman of the Senate Foreign Relations and National Defense committee. He is 'truly concerned' and urges the USG to be more engaged 'before it is too late.' The chairman said presidential foreign policy adviser Marco Aurelio Garcia strongly recommended Ahmadinejad visit Brazil. Chairman Fortes surmised that Foreign Minister Celso Amorim was less receptive to the visit. Fortes noted that with the increasing wealth of oil-producing states, there are some that will support Russian arms purchases, and in conversation, the Deputy Minister alluded that perhaps Ecuador and even Brazil could become beneficiaries.

4) Extracts from: WikiLeaks Cable. *President Jose Manuel Zelaya Rosales: Personal*, 15 May. Reference ID: 08TEGUCIGALPA459 (2008)

Summary: Honduran President Jose Manuel 'Mel' Zelaya Rosales is a throwback to an earlier Central American era, almost a caricature of a land-owner & caudillo in terms of his leadership style and tone. Ever the rebellious teenager, Zelaya's principal goal in office is to enrich himself and his family while leaving a public legacy as a martyr who tried to do good but was thwarted at every turn by powerful, unnamed interests. Various public statements over his tenure suggest he would be quite comfortable as a martyr who tried but failed honorably in his attempt to seek out social justice for the poor. He is comfortable working with the Armed Forces and until recently with the Catholic Church, yet resents the very existence of the Congress, the Attorney General and Supreme Court. Over his two and a half years in office, he has become increasingly surrounded by those involved in organized crime activities.
[...]
Personally, I have found Zelaya to be gracious and charming, quite willing to tell me whatever he thinks I want to hear at that moment. For example, in the period June–August 2007, we must have met weekly, with his agenda focused on explaining his nomination of Jorge Arturo Reina (who lost his U.S. visa for past terrorist connections) as the UN Ambassador, his presence in Managua at Sandinista celebrations and his intentions with regard to Hugo Chavez. It was interesting to see how his explanations differed from meeting to meeting, almost as if he had no recollection of our exchange just a few days before.
   In the period May–June 2006, Zelaya pressed me hard to obtain President Bush's approval of his plan to join PetroCaribe. When he met in early June with President Bush who confirmed our strong opposition to his intention, Zelaya later told me that he was surprised that this item had been on our agenda. In short, over an almost three year period it has become crystal

clear to me that Zelaya's views change by the day or in some cases by the hour, depending on his mood and who he has seen last.

[...]

There also exists a sinister Zelaya, surrounded by a few close advisors with ties to both Venezuela and Cuba and organized crime.

[...]

I have found Zelaya's real views of the United States hidden not too very deeply below the surface. In a word, he is not a friend. His views are shaped not by ideology or personal ambitions but by an old-fashioned nationalism where he holds the United States accountable for Honduras, [*sic*] current state of poverty and dependency. Zelaya's public position against the Contra War and against the establishment of Joint Task Force Bravo at Soto Cano Air Force Base are manifestations of this underlying viewpoint.

Notes

1 Rubrick Biegon, *US Power in Latin America: Renewing Hegemony* (London: Routledge, 2017); Greg Grandin, *Empire's Workshop: Latin America, the United States, and the Rise of the New Imperialism* (New York: Metropolitan Books, 2006), 223–44.

2 WikiLeaks, *What Is WikiLeaks* (2015). Available at: https://wikileaks.org/What-is-WikiLeaks.html (Accessed 20 February 2020).

3 J. O'Loughlin, 'The Perils of Self-Censorship in Academic Research in a WikiLeaks World', *Journal of Global Security Studies* 1:4 (2016), 337–45.

4 See for example: Biegon, *US Power in Latin America*; R. Biegon, 'The United States and Latin America in the Trans-Pacific Partnership: Renewing Hegemony in a Post-Washington Consensus Hemisphere?', *Latin American Perspectives* 44:4 (2017), 81–98.

5 E. Hunt, 'The WikiLeaks Cables: How the United States Exploits the World, in Detail, from an Internal Perspective, 2001–2010', *Diplomacy & Statecraft* 30:1 (2019), 70–98; G. J. Michael, 'Who's Afraid of WikiLeaks? Missed Opportunities in Political Science Research', *Review of Policy Research* 32:2 (2015), 175–99; O'Loughlin, 'The Perils of Self-Censorship'. The lack of engagement among scholars evidently contributed to WikiLeaks' efforts to spearhead analysis of the cables through the publication of their own edited volume. See: Julian Assange, 'Introduction', in WikiLeaks (ed.), *The WikiLeaks Files: The World According to US Empire* (London: Verso, 2015).

6 M. Gill and A. Spirling, 'Estimating the Severity of the WikiLeaks U.S. Diplomatic Cables Disclosure', *Political Analysis* 23:2 (2015), 299–305.

7 Hunt, 'The WikiLeaks Cables', 73.

8 Diana Kapiszewski, Lauren M. MacLean and Benjamin L. Read, *Field Research in Political Science: Practices and Principles* (Cambridge: Cambridge University Press, 2015), 178.

9 Rhiannon Vickers, 'Using Archives in Political Research', in Peter Burnham (ed.), *Surviving the Research Process in Politics* (London: Pinter, 1997).

10 Peter Burnham, Karin Gilland Lutz, Wyn Grant and Zig Layton-Henny, *Research Methods in Politics*, second edition (London: Palgrave Macmillan, 2008), 208.

11 Y. Benkler, 'A Free Irresponsible Press: Wikileaks and the Battle over the Soul of the Networked Fourth Estate', *Harvard Civil Rights-Civil Liberties Law Review* 46 (2011), 311–97.

12 P. Ludlow, 'Wikileaks and Hacktivist Culture', *The Nation*, 4 October 2010, 26.

13 C. Hood, 'From FOI World to WikiLeaks World: A New Chapter in the Transparency Story?', *Governance: An International Journal of Policy, Administration, and Institutions* 24:4 (2011), 635–8, 636.

14 Benkler, 'A Free Irresponsible Press', 330.

15 WikiLeaks, *Public Library of US Diplomacy*. Available at: https://search.wikileaks.org/plusd/ (Accessed 20 February 2020).

16 Hunt, 'The WikiLeaks Cables'.

17 Charles Tilly and Robert E. Goodin, 'It Depends', in Robert E. Goodin and Charles Tilly (eds), *The Oxford Handbook of Contextual Political Analysis* (Oxford: Oxford University Press, 2006), 19.

18 Burnham et al., *Research Methods in Politics*, 212.

19 P. Howard, 'Triangulating Debates within the Field: Teaching International Relations Research Methodology', *International Studies Perspectives* 11:4 (2010), 393–408.

20 See for example: Richard Gott, *Hugo Chávez and the Bolivarian Revolution* (London: Verso, 2005), 223–55; Nikolas Kozloff, *Hugo Chávez: Oil, Politics, and the Challenge to the United States* (New York: Palgrave, 2006).

21 Steve Ellner (ed.), *Latin America's Pink Tide: Breakthroughs and Shortcomings* (Lanham, MD: Rowman & Littlefield, 2020); George Philip and Francisco Panizza, *The Triumph of Politics: The Return of the Left in Venezuela, Bolivia and Ecuador* (Cambridge: Polity, 2011).

22 The OAS has long served as Washington's favoured forum for regional diplomacy in the Americas. See for example: Biegon, *US Power in Latin America*, 117–36.; R. Biegon, 'The Normalization of U.S. Policy toward Cuba? Rapprochement and Regional Hegemony', *Latin American Politics and Society* 62:1 (2020), 46–72.

23 See for example: The White House, President George W. Bush, *Fact Sheet: Advancing the Cause of Social Justice in the Western Hemisphere*, 5 March 2007. Available at: https://georgewbush-whitehouse.archives.gov/news/releases/2007/03/20070305–4.html (Accessed 2 March 2020).

24 The White House, President Barack Obama, *Remarks by the President at the Summit of the Americas Opening Ceremony*, 17 April 2009. Available at: https://obamawhitehouse.archives.gov/the-press-office/remarks-president-summit-americas-opening-ceremony (Accessed 2 March 2020).

25 James G. Stavridis, *Partnership for the Americas: Western Hemisphere Strategy and U.S. Southern Command* (Washington, DC: National Defense University Press, 2010).

26 Nicolas Burns, *Under Secretary Burns: Promoting Peace and Prosperity in Colombia*, 22 October (2007). Available at: https://www.as-coa.org/articles/under-secretary-burns-promoting-peace-and-prosperity-colombia (Accessed 2 March 2020).

27 US Energy Information Agency, *Country Analysis Executive Summary: Venezuela*, 7 January (2019). Available at: https://www.eia.gov/international/content/analysis/countries_long/Venezuela/venezuela_exe.pdf (Accessed 2 March 2020).

28 Gott, *Hugo Chávez*; Kozloff, *Hugo Chávez*.

29 See for example: Max G. Manwaring, *Latin America's New Security Reality: Irregular Asymmetric Conflict and Hugo Chavez*, Strategic Studies Institute (August 2007); Steve C. Ropp, *The Strategic Implications of the Rise of Populism in Europe and South America*, Strategic Studies Institute (June 2005).

30 Mark P. Sullivan, *Venezuela: Political Conditions and U.S. Policy*, Congressional Research Service (28 July 2009). Available at: https://fas.org/sgp/crs/row/RL32488.pdf (Accessed 2 March 2020), ii.

31 Biegon, *US Power in Latin America*.

32 WikiLeaks, 04CARACAS3977, *Venezuela's Magnate Discusses Chavez and the Region*, 30 December (2004). On utilising the cables to gain insight into US containment of Venezuela, see also: Hunt, 'The WikiLeaks Cables', 80–1; and Dan Beeton, Jake Johnston and Alexander Main, 'Venezuela', in WikiLeaks (ed.), *The WikiLeaks Files*.

33 S. Pegg and E. Berg, 'Lost and Found: The WikiLeaks of *De Facto* State – Great Power Relations', *International Studies Perspectives* 17:3 (2016), 275.

34 Among many other examples, see: WikiLeaks, 06LAPAZ886, *Evo and His Advisory Circle (Part 1 of 3)*, 30 March (2006); WikiLeaks, 06QUITO2391, *Correa Takes the Lead, Could Win the First Round*, 27 September (2006); WikiLeaks, 07QUITO1483, *Radio Addresses Illuminate Correa*, 27 June (2007).

35 WikiLeaks, 09CARACAS257, *The Bolivarian Revolution Advances: What's Next?* 27 February (2009).

36 WikiLeaks, 08CARACAS802_a, *FARC Adopts Bolivarian Rhetoric*, 6 June (2008).

37 WikiLeaks, 06LIMA4698, *Scenesetter for CODEL Reid*, 15 December (2006).

38 WikiLeaks, 07BUENOSAIRES1514, *President Chavez's August 6 Visit to Argentina: Bonds, Energy, Bolivarian Fraternity*, 3 August (2007).

39 See for example: WikiLeaks, 09PARTO42805, *Secretary Clinton's April 18, 2009 Conversation with Ecuadorian President Rafael Correa*, 28 April (2009).

40 See for example: WikiLeaks, 09BOGOTA3527, *Colombia Debrief on UNASUR Meeting Generally Positive, but Venezuela Still an Issue*, 10 December (2009).

41 See for example: WikiLeaks, 06LIMA847, *Scenesetter for Visit of Secretary of State Condoleezza Rice, March 11–12, 2006*, 3 March (2006).

42 WikiLeaks, 07LIMA2000_a, *Bolivarian Influence in Puno*, 7 June (2007).

43 See for example: WikiLeaks, 08CARACAS118_a, *Not Much Substance at the VI ALBA Summit*, 30 January (2008); WikiLeaks, 08TEGUCIGALPA789_a, *Honduras Signs on to 'Bolivarian Alternative' Despite Wide Opposition*, 26 August (2008).

44 WikiLeaks, 10MANAGUA115, *Ortega and the US: New-found True Love or Another Still-born Charm Offensive*, 25 February (2010).

45 WikiLeaks, 10LAPAZ13_a, *Bolivia Steps up Anti-U.S. Rhetoric*, 21 January (2010).

46 WikiLeaks, 09BRIDGETOWN745_a, *Dominica Election Primer: The Bolivarian Candidate*, 4 December (2009).

47 WikiLeaks, 06LAPAZ195, *Morales-Shannon Meeting: President Recounts Personal, Political History*, 26 January (2006). On efforts to 'drive a wedge' between Chávez and other actors, see also **Document 2**.

48 WikiLeaks, 09TEGUCIGALPA181, *Scenesetter for Assistant Secretary Shannon's Visit to Honduras*, 17 March (2009).

49 See for example: WikiLeaks, 10LIMA29, *Scenesetter for Deputy Secretary Stienberg*, 7 January (2010).

50 See for example: WikiLeaks, 07HAVANA1052, *Cuban Nationalism and the Bolivarian Ideal*, 7 November (2007).

51 WikiLeaks, 07QUITO420, *International Conference for the Abolition of Foreign Military Bases to Be Held in Ecuador, March 5–9*, 23 February (2007).

52 WikiLeaks, 07QUITO1947, *USNS Comfort Visit to Ecuador*, 24 August (2007).

53 See for example: WikiLeaks, 05LIMA4983, *Countering Chavez in Peru*, 22 November (2005).

4

'Caveats were down': The Canadian Official Record and the treatment of Maher Arar

Peter Finn

In September 2002 the Canadian citizen of Syrian origin Maher Arar was detained at JFK airport in New York City. He was meant to be transiting to Montreal after a holiday in Tunisia. Arar was detained in New York for eleven days prior to the use of the 'questionable practice of extraordinary rendition' (defined as the taking of someone across international borders beyond the bounds of international law or due process that involves 'multiple violations of international law') to transfer him to Syria via Jordan.[1] In Syria, Arar was subject to physical abuse and torture, and held until October 2003. Following his release a commission of inquiry was held. Among other things this commission documented issues with the Canadian state's sharing and receiving of material about Arar and his mistreatment and torture in Syria. Via engagement with material from the 'Inquiry into the Actions of Canadian Officials in Relation to Maher Arar' (hereafter the Arar Commission) this chapter highlights issues that can arise with the sharing of the Official Record between states – in particular, issues with information sharing with the US in the aftermath of 9/11 by a branch of the Canadian Royal Military Police (RCMP) and the uncritical distribution within the Canadian government of material received from the Syrian state that was likely the product of torture. The chapter draws extensively from a 2006 commission report, titled *Report of the Events Relating to Maher Arar: Analysis and Recommendations* (hereafter **Document 1**) and an October 2005 document *Appendix 7: Report of Professor Stephen J. Toope, Fact Finder* (hereafter **Document 2**) written by the academic Stephen J. Toope after he was tasked by the Arar Commission to document Arar's experience. Key portions of **Document 1** and **Document 2** can be found in the Document Appendix at the end of this chapter. As with other chapters, document extracts are chosen to reflect broader points or themes. While some of the references to these documents in this chapter refer to the material in the Document Appendix, some refer to material elsewhere in these documents. To gain a greater understanding of the documents, readers are encouraged to seek out the full documents.

The chapter evolves in three main sections. The first section documents
the circumstances that led to the capture of Arar in New York, his treatment
in custody in the US, his rendition to, and brief detention in, Jordan, and
his transfer to and almost year-long detention in Syria. As we shall see,
Arar was mistreated while in Jordan, and over a more prolonged period in
Syria was tortured. Next the chapter outlines the main documents placed
into the Public Record by the Arar Commission. Finally the chapter highlights
two key issues arising from the sharing of the official records between two
different states. In the first instance we shall discuss a failure to place caveats
or restrictions on material shared with the US, before looking at the uncritical
sharing of material received from the Syrian state that was likely the product
of torture. These discussions draw from the Official Record rubric introduced
in this volume's Preface and Introduction. All told, the evidence presented
in this chapter suggests that there is a need for further study of how the
Official Record of one state passes to other states, and how it is managed
after it has been received. In so doing the chapter explores the potentially
horrendous individual consequences from poorly managed 'information
flow' and illustrates that 'what gets left out can be just as important to [...]
accountability' and we would add, to the experience of individuals caught
in the crosshairs of national security investigations, 'as what gets passed
around'.[2]

The treatment of Maher Arar

Beginning with the broader context to Arar's capture, and ending with
his release, this section documents Arar's detention. The RCMP branch
investigating Arar was named Project A-O Canada. Opened in October 2001
to manage terrorism investigations transferred from the Canadian Security
Intelligence Service (CSIS) to the RCMP post-9/11, Project A-O Canada
operated in an 'environment' where those labelled as 'Islamic extremist' were
'automatically seen as a serious threat'.[3] Despite no evidence, a perception
of Arar as a threat evolved. This perception arose from his association with
Abdullah Almalki, a Canadian of Syrian origin detained and tortured in
Syria at a similar time to Arar. Almalki received a Canadian government
apology in 2017 'for any role Canadian officials may have played in' his
mistreatment.[4]

Arar initially became a 'peripheral' '"person of interest"'. However, in
documents shared with US authorities he was, among other similar labels,
described as an '"Islamic Extremist"' with suspected links to '"Al Qaeda"'.
Such descriptions were 'either completely inaccurate or, at a minimum',
'overstate[d] his importance'. Though some documents were accurate, 'the

written record provided to' US 'agencies contained many inaccuracies, some […] very serious'. Such inaccuracies, as per **Document 1**, 'can have grossly unfair consequences'.[5]

On 16 September 2002 'Arar arrived' at JFK 'on a flight from Zurich, Switzerland'. He began 'his trip in Tunisia, and was headed to Montreal via' JFK. At JFK 'he was detained upon arrival'. About an hour prior to his landing, the Federal Bureau of Investigation 'called Project A-O Canada to notify it of' Arar's 'pending arrival and' their 'intention to question him and deny him entry' to the US. They 'indicated' that Arar would be returned to Zurich. Initially Arar 'was held […] for four days without any access to a lawyer or his family' as no Canadian official 'knew where he was'. On 1 October the US Immigration and Naturalisation Service (INS) 'instituted removal proceedings', while Arar's brother told the Canadian Department of Foreign Affairs and International Trade (DFAIT)[6] that Arar 'had indicated that he would be deported to Syria'. On the same day, 'a senior [INS] officer' highlighted the seriousness of Arar's case, suggesting that 'the Canadian ambassador in Washington contact the [US] Department of Justice'.[7]

By 2 October Canadian consular officials had learnt 'Arar was being held' in a 'wing for terrorism suspects' at the Metropolitan Detention Centre, New York. On 3 October US 'authorities sent Project A-O Canada seven questions about' Arar and the Canadian consul learned that US 'authorities were alleging' Arar was an al-Qaeda member. On the same day Arar told 'the Canadian consul' that while 'held at the airport in New York, two immigration officers' told him 'he would be sent to Syria'. During early October, Canadian officials facilitated legal representation, with a lawyer visiting Arar on 5 October. On 6 October Arar was interviewed without his lawyer following a miscommunication.[8] The following day INS found Arar was 'a member of al-Qaeda', ordering 'his removal'. Two days later Arar 'was flown to Jordan' while 'still in American custody'. The Arar Commission 'found no evidence […] that RCMP officers participated or acquiesced in the American decision to' remove Arar. Yet, it also found it 'likely that the decision was based, at least in part, on evidence provided by the RCMP'.[9]

On 8 October 'Arar was awakened […] and told that he was' being 'removed to Syria'.[10] He was flown to Amman, Jordan, via Italy, whilst 'chained and shackled' on a plane with the tail number N829MG.[11] The 'shackles were removed only at the end of the trip'.[12] Once in Jordan, a sleep-deprived Arar 'was transported to a detention centre', 'suffered blows' from 'Jordanian guards and was blindfolded'. He was 'taken into a room, where the blindfold was removed'. He was questioned before being 'blindfolded again' and 'led to a cell'. The following day Arar was blindfolded and transported to a Syrian Military Intelligence (SMI) detention centre in Damascus called Far Falestin. He arrived 'exhausted, hungry, and terrified'.[13]

Initially, Arar was held incommunicado (unacknowledged). On 21 October 'the Syrian deputy foreign minister' erroneously informed the Canadian Ambassador Franco Pillarella that Arar 'had arrived in Syria' that day. This false statement followed a ten-day period when numerous Canadian representatives had tried to gain information from Syrian counterparts. The first Canadian consular visit occurred on 23 October. Following this visit Pillarella was given 'a *bout de papier* setting out in very summary form the results of the Syrian interrogation of' Arar.[14] Yet, though this '*bout de papier* was circulated' to Canadian Department of Foreign Affairs and International Trade Foreign Intelligence Division, the RCMP, and the Canadian Security Intelligence Agency in relatively short order,

> no one attached a reliability assessment or cautionary note to it to point out that Mr Arar had made the statement while held incommunicado and that at least some DFAIT [Canadian Department of Foreign Affairs and International Trade] officials had developed the 'working or operating assumption' that physical abuse or torture had been used to obtain it. Recipients were left to make of it what they would.[15]

On arrival in Syria, Arar 'was interrogated for approximately four hours by a man called 'George', subsequently identified as George Salloum, the head interrogator at Far Falestin. During this interrogation 'no physical violence was used' though 'ominous threats were made'. Arar decided 'to "say anything" necessary to avoid torture'. The following day Arar was 'exhausted' as he was unable 'to sleep' in his cell, while in an interrogation Salloum 'immediately started hitting' Arar and 'brought a black cable [...] into the room with him'. Salloum told 'Arar to open his right hand, then raised the cable high and brought it down hard'. The 'process was repeated with his left hand'. During 'breaks' in another room, Arar 'could hear other people screaming'. When 'brought back into the interrogation room', Arar 'was beaten' and questioned. This lasted 'approximately 10 hours'. His third day in custody was the most '"intensive"', with '16 to 18 hours' of questioning involving 'great physical and psychological abuse'. Interrogations then 'became less intense physically', with 'less use of the cables, and more punching and hitting'. By 17 October 'beatings diminished', though 'threats intensified', and 'psychological pressure remained extreme'. Arar's general 'conditions of detention were atrocious'. His 'basement cell [...] was seven feet high, six feet long, and three feet wide' and 'contained only two thin blankets, a "humidity isolator," and two bottles — one for water and one for urine'. Arar's 'only source of light in the cell was a small [ceiling] opening'. He was not allowed to visit an outside courtyard until April 2003.[16]

While at Far Falestin, Arar had nine consular visits from Léo Martel, the Canadian Consul, between October 2002 and August 2003, including an April 2003 visit attended by two Canadian MPs. These visits 'provided' some 'hope' and 'connection' to 'family', but were also '"frustrating"'. Shortly after a final consular visit on 14 August 2003, 'Arar was moved [...] to [another prison named] Sednaya', where 'conditions of imprisonment were much less severe'. That said, at Sednaya 'he experienced some further beatings' designed to 'punish or intimidate' rather than 'gain information', but there were 'not of quite the intensity of those in Far Falestin'. He 'remained at Sednaya until his release on October 5, 2003'. After his release 'Martel accompanied him back to Canada'.[17]

Having mapped the experience of Arar through to his release, or at least a version of it found in the Canadian Official Record collated by the Arar Commission, this chapter now turns to his experience after release, and the operation of the Arar Commission up to December 2006.

Post-release and the Arar Commission

This section begins by documenting elements of Arar's experience after his release in October 2003. It also details the outputs of the Arar Commission, which have been key in documenting the experience of Arar within the Canadian Official Record.

Following his release Arar was subject to a series of leaks that portrayed him negatively, often repeating similar tropes to those in the initial material shared without caveats with the US prior to his initial capture. He spoke 'publicly for the first time at a press conference on November 4, 2003'. Following 'the press conference, Canadian officials took a number of steps to register Canada's objections with the Syrian government concerning the abuse Mr. Arar had suffered'. The Arar Commission was set up in February 2004 when Justice Dennis O'Connor was appointed Commissioner. O'Connor was mandated to carry out a 'Factual Inquiry' and a 'Policy Review'. His work led to the publication of two reports in September and December 2006. The September report, **Document 1**, stretched to 373 pages. With a particular focus on the RCMP, **Document 1** details the circumstances leading to Arar's detention at JFK in September 2002, his experience in detention in New York, rendition to Syria via Jordan, detention in Syria for almost a year, release to Canada in October 2003 and a sustained series of leaks that unfairly continually cast doubt on Arar. It contains 23 recommendations designed to 'provide standards against which the RCMP's national security activities may be measured by' an 'independent review body'.[18] The bulk of the report was released, with some portions unredacted in August 2007 following a Federal Court order.[19] Some parts remain redacted.[20]

The *Analysis and Recommendations Report* was accompanied by two further volumes of factual background information that together run to more than eight hundred pages. They contain an extended narrative of Arar's experience, the engagement of various parts of the Canadian state with his case, and annexes and appendices.[21] One appendix of particular note is *Appendix 7: Report of Professor Stephen J. Toope, Fact Finder, October 14, 2005* (**Document 2**). **Document 2** was written by academic Stephen J Toope after he was tasked by O'Connor to 'investigate and report to the Commission on Mr. Maher Arar's treatment during his detention in Jordan and Syria and its effects upon him and his family'. Drawing on interviews with Arar, and other Canadians held in Syria at a time that overlapped with Arah's detention such as Abdullah Almalki, Toope concluded that 'the treatment of Mr. Arar in Far Falestin constituted torture as understood in international law.' Expanding further, Toope said that the techniques applied to Arah 'were meant to inflict severe pain and suffering. The pain was clearly physical. But in addition, the techniques of humiliation and the creation of intense fear were forms of psychological torture.'[22] **Document 2** was a key source for **Document 1**.[23]

The 630-page December 2006 report, titled *A New Review Mechanism for the RCMP's National Security Activities*, focused mainly on the RCMP, explored aspects of the history of Canadian national security operations, the post-9/11 environment, various policy questions related to the actions of the Canadian state with relation to Arar in particular and national security operations in general, as well as exploring models for national security oversight adopted in states such as Australia, Germany, the UK and the US.[24] It closes with recommendations designed to 'complement' those in the *Analysis and Recommendations Report* and provide 'robust independent, arm's-length mechanism for the review of the RCMP's national security activities'.[25] The Arar Commission also has a website, itself archived in seven different versions, containing a wealth of material related to the treatment of Arar and the actions of various parts of the Canadian state, much of which fed into the reports and factual backgrounds outlined above.[26]

In 2007 the then Canadian Prime Minister Stephen Harper formally apologised to Arar, saying, 'I wish to apologize to you, Monia Mazigh [Arar's wife] and your family for any role Canadian officials may have played in the terrible ordeal that all of you experienced in 2002 and 2003'.[27] Arar received CA$10 million in compensation from the Canadian government. Reflecting on his experience, Arar said, 'I've learned a hard lesson. I don't feel safe as I used to feel before this happened to me, and I don't take anything for granted anymore', expanding that 'I don't think the average Canadian citizen should take anything for granted'.[28]

All told, the Arar Commission contributed significantly to the official, public and historical records of the Canadian state. Though, as we shall see, which material related to it should enter the public domain was subject to contestations. Now the operation of the Arar Commission has been explored, the final section of the chapter will highlight troubling aspects of the Arar case documented by the commission related to the sharing of the Official Record between states.

Sharing and receiving the Official Record

One important theme to arise from the Arar Commission in light of the Official Record is the relationship between official records of different states, and the need to ensure that care is taken when material passes between states. This section highlights troubling matters arising from the sharing of the Canadian Official Record with the US and Syrian Official Record with Canada. First, it illuminates issues related to Canada's sharing of materials with the US. Next, the flawed treatment of information received by Canada from Syria is highlighted. These discussions build on the Official Record rubric introduced in the Preface and the Introduction of this volume.

One way the transfer of portions of the Official Record from one state to another is managed is via the use of caveats, which are 'written restrictions on the use and further dissemination of shared information'. Such caveats, it must be noted, 'are not a panacea' against the misuse or misinterpretation of information, and their use 'does not guarantee that information will not be shared in breach of those caveats'.[29] Yet they do at least provide guidance for receiving states, and thus create a standard by which they can be held over the use of information.

In the case of Arar specifically, caveats could, for instance, have thrown shade on the erroneous mischaracterisations of Arar as an '"Islamic Extremist"' with suspected links to '"Al Qaeda"' in material passed between Project A-O Canada and the US. Yet, in the period prior to his detention at JFK, caveats, according to Project A-O Canada project managers, 'were down', meaning that 'it was not necessary to attach caveats to documents being shared with the other [US partner] agencies, and that RCMP policies requiring this to be done did not apply'. They further believed 'there was an implicit understanding that the information would be used for intelligence purposes only', but, somewhat contradictorily, that they were engaging in an '"open-book investigation"' with the US designed to facilitate the '"free-flow-of-information"' where both states, or 'parties', could 'share information received from one party to the agreement with the other parties without the consent of the originator, even if caveats had been attached by the originator'. It should be noted that senior RCMP intelligence officials refute the assertion that caveats were down, and that 'the RCMP, as an institution, had not intended that RCMP officers, including members of Project A-O Canada, deviate from RCMP policies' related to the use of caveats.[30]

Contestations about official policy notwithstanding, the outcome of the belief by Project A-O Canada project managers that caveats were down was that material was shared without caveats being attached. In April 2002, for instance, Canadian officials shared an 'entire [...] [RCMP] database containing the relevant investigation file to the U.S. agencies, and that it had done so without screening the information for relevance or accuracy and without attaching caveats, as required by policy'. Moreover, 'each time the RCMP had supplied information related to the pertinent investigation to American agencies prior to Mr. Arar's detention in New York, it had done so without attaching caveats as required by RCMP policy'. There were also Canadian and US 'border lookout' requests placed for both Arar and his wife Dr Monia Mazigh, designed to ensure they 'would undergo both primary and secondary examinations when entering Canada'. Anyone 'entering Canada may be subjected to a secondary examination; however, when there is a lookout, the front-line Customs officers must refer the person for a secondary examination'. However, the Arar Commission found 'no basis or justification' for the 'description' of 'Arar and Dr. Mazigh as Islamic extremist individuals suspected of being linked to the al-Qaeda terrorist movement' in 'letters requesting the Canadian and American lookouts'.[31]

As well as highlighting issues with how Canada shared elements of the Canadian Official Record with the US, the Arar Commission also documents problems with the uncritical distribution of elements of the Syrian Official Record within the Canadian state. As per **Document 1**, on 'November 3, 2002, the SMI provided Ambassador Pillarella with a *bout de papier*, or informal written communication, setting out certain information that the SMI had obtained from Mr. Arar, including the fact that he had taken mujahedeen training in Afghanistan in 1993'. Pillarella then 'passed the *bout de papier* on to DFAIT Headquarters, which distributed it to the RCMP and CSIS'. Yet, as **Document 1** notes, at 'this point, DFAIT should have been aware that Mr. Arar's statements to the SMI were likely the product of torture', and thus of dubious reliability and raising troubling (to say the least) ethical and legal questions.[32]

Discussing whether Pillarella should have accepted the bout de papier, the Arar Commission argues that, as Syria was by then 'permitting Canada access' to Arar, it was 'unlikely' that Arar 'would be subjected to any physical abuse in the future', thus meaning it was not 'improper or inappropriate' for Pillarella to do so. Moreover, according to the Arar Commission 'there was potentially a benefit to Canadian officials' knowing what Syrian authorities considered to be "the case" against Mr. Arar'.[33] Yet **Document 1** further notes:

> when they received the information, DFAIT officials should have conducted a proper assessment of its reliability. Had they done so, they would have concluded that it was likely the product of torture and therefore of doubtful reliability. That assessment should then have accompanied the *bout de papier* when DFAIT distributed it to the RCMP and CSIS.[34]

The danger in not doing so is demonstrated by the fact that 'some RCMP officers did not consider the likelihood of torture when assessing Mr. Arar's possible involvement in terrorism-related activities'.[35]

In short the Arar Commission found that there was no issue with Pillarella having accepted the *bout de papier*, but that it had not been dealt with appropriately once it became part of the Canadian Official Record. As the Arar Commission notes with some understatement, '[t]his was unfortunate and unfair to Mr. Arar'. This chain of events led the commission to 'recommend that, when Canadian officials receive information from a country with a questionable human rights record, such as Syria, they conduct a reliability assessment and ensure that their conclusions accompany the information if they disseminate it'.[36]

Together the sharing of flawed material about Arar with the US without caveats, as well as the uncritical distribution of evidence obtained by the Syrian state via the torture of Arar illustrates troubling issues that can arise through the distribution of elements of the Official Record of a state with other states. They further illustrate that these issues can arise for both the states providing information and those receiving it. Indeed, **Document 1** illuminates the perils that can arise if care is not taken around the receiving and sharing of the Official Record and the very real-world consequences it can have for individuals involved, with **Document 2** providing painstaking details of what can arise if such care is not taken.[37]

Conclusion

As highlighted in the Introduction of this volume, and illustrated by this chapter, the sharing and receiving of material from the official record of another state is common. Material discussed in this chapter was shared by states; however, as illustrated in the Introduction, this is not always the case and often states seek out to obtain information from the Official Record of other states surreptitiously. It should be noted here that the sharing and receiving of information between states is not necessarily illegitimate and, if due care and attention are taken via practices such as the use of caveats, then they can be useful. Indeed, evidence from the Covid-19 pandemic suggests that greater sharing of information about the virus, especially in the early stages of the pandemic, might have helped curtail the pandemic as it was taking hold. Yet material from the Arar Commission, which in and of itself contributed significantly to the Canadian official record, illustrates that, rather than being a dry and uncontested ledger of events, the Official Record is a dynamic social artefact that needs to be read with the same critical eye as other primary material.

Other chapters in this volume illuminate the need for states to do this within their own operation and dealing with their own official record. However, **Document 1** and **Document 2** illustrate the need for this same critical eye to be maintained when states are sharing and receiving information amongst themselves. The misrepresentation, capture, rendition, detention and torture of Arar are real-world manifestations of what can occur if this is not maintained. Troublingly, rather than a single aberration, elements of the experience of Arar reflects that of other Canadians such as Almalki.[38] This provides greater understanding of the experience of Arar, and how it is documented in the Canadian Official Record, and the Official Record of other states (and how portions of different official records move between states).

Document appendix

1) Extract from: Commission of Inquiry into the Actions of Canadian Officials in Relation to Maher Arar, *Report of the Events Relating to Maher Arar: Analysis and Recommendations* (2006)
2) Extract from: S. J. Toope, *Report of Professor Stephen J. Toope, Fact Finder, October 14, 2005* (2005), Appendix 7 in Commission of Inquiry into the Actions of Canadian Officials in Relation to Maher Arar, *Report of the Events Relating to Maher Arar: Factual Background*, Vol. II (2006), 789–819

1) **Extract from: Commission of Inquiry into the Actions of Canadian Officials in Relation to Maher Arar, *Report of the Events Relating to Maher Arar: Analysis and Recommendations* (2006)**

4. Summary of main conclusions

The following are my main conclusions, presented under four headings that reflect the different stages examined: information sharing prior to Mr. Arar's detention, Mr. Arar's detention in New York and removal to Syria, his imprisonment and mistreatment in Syria, and the period after his return to Canada.

4.1. Information sharing prior to Mr. Arar's detention

- The RCMP provided American authorities with information, including the entire database from the aforementioned terrorism investigation, in ways that did not comply with RCMP policies requiring screening for relevance, reliability and personal information. Some of the information related to Mr. Arar.
- The RCMP provided American authorities with information about Mr. Arar that was inaccurate, portrayed him in an unfairly negative fashion and overstated his importance in the RCMP investigation.
- The RCMP provided American authorities with information about Mr. Arar without attaching written caveats,* as required by RCMP policy, thereby increasing the risk that the information would be used for purposes of which the RCMP would not approve, such as sending Mr. Arar to Syria.
- The RCMP requested that American authorities place lookouts for Mr. Arar and his wife, Monia Mazigh, in U.S. Customs' Treasury Enforcement Communications System (TECS). In the request, to which no caveats were attached, the RCMP described Mr. Arar and Dr, Mazigh as 'Islamic Extremist individuals suspected of being linked to the Al Qaeda terrorist movement.'* The RCMP had no basis for this description, which had the potential to create serious consequences for Mr. Arar in light of American attitudes and practices at the time.
- Project A-O Canada was the front-line investigative unit in the RCMP that conducted the investigation in which Mr. Arar was a person of interest, and it was that unit that provided information about Mr. Arar to American agencies. The RCMP, as an institution, gave Project A-O Canada unclear and, in some instances, misleading direction concerning the manner in which information should be shared, and failed to properly oversee the Project's investigation, including its information-sharing practices.
- CSIS did not share any information about Mr. Arar with the American authorities prior to his detention in New York and removal to Syria.

4.2. Detention in New York and removal to Syria

- There is no evidence that Canadian officials participated or acquiesced in the American authorities' decisions to detain Mr. Arar and remove him to Syria.
- It is very likely that, in making the decisions to detain and remove Mr. Arar, American authorities relied on information about Mr. Arar provided by the RCMP.

- While Mr. Arar was being detained in New York on September 26, 2002, the RCMP provided the U.S. Federal Bureau of Investigation (FBI) with information about him, some of which portrayed him in an inaccurate and unfair way.
- Without the evidence of the American authorities, I am unable to conclude what role, if any, the TECS lookout requested by the RCMP played in the American decisions to detain Mr. Arar and remove him to Syria.
- During Mr. Arar's detention in New York, consular officials with the Canadian Department of Foreign Affairs and International Trade (DFAIT)* took reasonable steps to provide Mr. Arar with consular services, including addressing the possibility that he might be sent to Syria.

4.3. Imprisonment and mistreatment in Syria

- Mr. Arar arrived in Syria on October 9, 2002 and was held incommunicado until October 22, 2002. In the intervening period, he was interrogated and tortured.

I am unable to conclude whether or not Canadian officials could have obtained Mr. Arar's release from Syrian imprisonment at an earlier point in time. However, there is cause for serious concern in regard to a number of actions taken by Canadian officials during Mr. Arar's imprisonment, including some that could have had an effect on the time taken to release Mr. Arar:

- On receiving a summary of a statement made by Mr. Arar while in Syrian custody in early November 2002, DFAIT distributed it to the RCMP and CSIS without informing them that the statement was likely a product of torture. That statement became the basis for heightened suspicion in some minds about Mr. Arar's involvement in terrorism. That was unfair to him.
- In November 2002, CSIS received information about Mr. Arar from the Syrian Military Intelligence (SMI) and did not do an adequate reliability assessment as to whether the information was likely the product of torture. Indeed, its assessment was that it probably was not.
- In January 2003, the RCMP, acting through the Canadian Ambassador, sent the SMI questions for Abdullah Almalki, the subject of the relevant investigation and also in Syrian custody. This action very likely sent a signal to Syrian authorities that the RCMP approved of the imprisonment and interrogation of Mr. Almalki and created a risk that the SMI would conclude that Mr. Arar, a person who had some association with Mr. Almalki, was considered a serious terrorist threat by the RCMP.
- In March and April 2003, DFAIT failed to take steps to address the statement by Syrian officials that CSIS did not want Mr. Arar returned to Canada.

- In May and June 2003, the RCMP and CSIS were not supportive of a DFAIT initiative to send the Syrians a letter conveying that Canada spoke with one voice in seeking Mr. Arar's release.
- From time to time, DFAIT distributed reports of consular visits with Mr. Arar to the RCMP and CSIS. Ostensibly, this was done to seek assistance for Mr. Arar. However, DFAIT failed to make that purpose clear or to ensure that the reports were used only for that purpose.
- On several occasions, there was a lack of communication among the Canadian agencies involved in Mr. Arar's case. There was also a lack of a single, coherent approach to efforts to obtain his release.
- DFAIT consular officials took reasonable steps to obtain consular access to Mr. Arar throughout his imprisonment in Syria.

4.4. After Mr. Arar's return to Canada

- Following Mr. Arar's return, reports were prepared within government that had the effect of downplaying the mistreatment or torture to which Mr. Arar had been subjected.
- Both before and after Mr. Arar's return to Canada, Canadian officials leaked confidential and sometimes inaccurate information about the case to the media for the purpose of damaging Mr. Arar's reputation or protecting their self-interests or government interests.
- When briefing the Privy Council Office and senior government officials about the investigation regarding Mr. Arar, the RCMP omitted certain key facts that could have reflected adversely on the Force.

2) Extract from: S. J. Toope, *Report of Professor Stephen J. Toope, Fact Finder, October 14, 2005* (2005), Appendix 7 in Commission of Inquiry into the Actions of Canadian Officials in Relation to Maher Arar, *Report of the Events Relating to Maher Arar: Factual Background*, Vol. II (2006), 789–819

I conclude that the treatment of Mr. Arar in Far Falestin constituted torture as understood in international law. The interrogation techniques used on Mr. Arar, especially in the first three days but also sporadically in the first two weeks of his detention amounted to torture. The use of the black cable in particular, and the generalized beatings he endured, could only have been 'intentional'. They were meant to inflict severe pain and suffering. The pain was clearly physical. But in addition, the techniques of humiliation and the creation of intense fear were forms of psychological torture. This is particularly true of the strategy of blindfolding Mr. Arar and making him wait for the next interrogation session in a corridor or room where he could hear the screams of other victims. The threats to use other forms of physical torture, such as the tire and the chair, also amounted to psychological torture. This was particularly the case for a man like Mr. Arar who so clearly feared physical violence. The infliction of pain and suffering was for a purpose considered relevant by international law: the extraction of a confession. As it happens, Mr. Arar did succumb to the pain and suffering he experienced, and he did "confess". But even if he had not done so, the purpose of the interrogation techniques would have been the same. For the purposes of determining if torture occurred, it does not matter whether or not the confession was 'true'. Finally, there is no doubt that the perpetrators of the torture were Syrian public officials. Far Falestin is known to be run by Syrian military intelligence.

Notes

1 Commission of Inquiry into the Actions of Canadian Officials in Relation to Maher Arar, *Report of the Events Relating to Maher Arar: Analysis and Recommendations* (2006), 42. Available at: https://epe.lac-bac.gc.ca/100/206/301/pco-bcp/commissions/maher_arar/07-09-13/www.ararcommission.ca/eng/AR_English.pdf (Accessed 29 October 2023). C. Black, R. Blakeley and S. Raphael, *CIA Torture Unredacted* (2019), 18, 77, 308. Available at: https://www.therenditionproject.org.uk/unredacted/the-report.html (Accessed 29 October 2023).
2 R. Bahdi and W. De Lint, 'Access to Information in an Age of Intelligentized Governmentality', in M. Larsen and K. Walby (eds), *Brokering Access: Power, Politics, and Freedom of Information Process in Canada* (Vancouver, BC: UBC Press, 2012). 115–41, 117.
3 Arar Commission, *Analysis and Recommendations Report*, 115.
4 Arar Commission, *Analysis and Recommendations Report*. 113; C. Freeland and R. Goodale, *Statement of Apology to Mr. Almalki, Mr. Abou-Elmaati, Mr. Nureddin* (2017). Available at: https://www.canada.ca/en/public-safety-canada/news/2017/03/statement_of_apologytomralmalkimrabou-elmaatimrnureddin.html (Accessed 30 June 2022). Abdullah Almalki is a Canadian of Syrian origin who was detained in Syria from May 2002 to July 2004, thus overlapping with Arar. Unlike Arar, Almalki was captured in Syria after travelling there of his own accord. A Canadian Commission of Inquiry examining the treatment of Almalki, and two other detainees, found that he had been called an 'Islamic extremist' in documents shared with US authorities without 'adequate measures to ensure that it was accurate, reliable or properly qualified', with similar issues arising in Canadian correspondence with Syrian authorities. In Syria he 'was held in degrading and inhumane conditions, interrogated and mistreated' and 'suffered mistreatment amounting to torture as defined in the UN *Convention Against Torture*'. The commission did not 'conclude that any mistreatment resulted directly from any action of Canadian officials', but did 'find that mistreatment suffered by Mr. Almalki in Syria resulted indirectly from two actions of Canadian officials: (1) in April 2002, the RCMP shared its Supertext database, which

contained a considerable amount of information regarding Mr. Almalki, with U.S. agencies; and (2) in January 2003, the RCMP sent Syrian officials questions to be posed to Mr. Almalki while in Syrian detention'. The commission found these 'actions [...] deficient in the circumstances'. It further found that 'consular services to Mr. Almalki in Syria were deficient'. Internal Inquiry into the Actions of Canadian Officials in Relation to Abdullah Almalki, Ahmad Abou-Elmaati and Muayyed Nureddin, *Report of Internal Inquiry into the Actions of Canadian Officials in Relation to Abdullah Almalki, Ahmad Abou-Elmaati and Muayyed Nureddin* (2008), 37–8, 400–3. Available at: https://publications.gc.ca/collections/collection_2014/bcp-pco/CP32-90-2008-1-eng.pdf (Accessed 29 October 2023).

5 Arar Commission, *Analysis and Recommendations Report*, 61, 113–14.
6 This body is now called Global Affairs Canada
7 Arar Commission, *Analysis and Recommendations Report*, 140, 155, 156, 172.
8 A more troubling version of this is that Arar's lawyer was informed about the interview only via her work voicemail on a Sunday. On hearing this voicemail on Monday, the lawyer contacted INS, and was informed that 'Arar had been taken to Manhattan and would then be transferred to New Jersey, and later that Arar had been taken to a New Jersey detention facility'. In fact INS Regional Director J. Scott Blackman issued the Final Notice of Inadmissibility. In the notice, relying on classified and unclassified information never divulged to Arar, Blackman determined that Arar was an al-Qaeda member and 'that his removal [to Syria] was consistent with Article 3 of the United Nations Convention Against Torture and other Cruel, Inhuman, or Degrading Treatment or Punishment'. J. Lobel, 'Extraordinary Rendition and the Constitution: The Case of Maher Arar', *Review of Litigation* 28:2 (2008), 479–500, 483.
9 Arar Commission, *Analysis and Recommendations Report*, 30, 159, 164–9, 203.
10 Arar Commission, *Analysis and Recommendations Report*, 54.
11 Arar Commission, *Analysis and Recommendations Report*, 54; Black, Blakeley and Raphael, *CIA Torture Unredacted*, 308.
12 Arar Commission, *Analysis and Recommendations Report*, 54.
13 Arar Commission, *Analysis and Recommendations Report*, 54–5; S. J. Toope, Report of Professor Stephen J. Toope, *Fact Finder*, 14 October 2005 (2005), Appendix 7 in Commission of Inquiry into the Actions of Canadian Officials in Relation to Maher Arar, *Report of the Events Relating to Maher Arar: Factual Background*, Vol. II (2006), 805–6.
14 Arar Commission, *Analysis and Recommendations Report*, 183–5, 192–3.
15 Arar Commission, *Analysis and Recommendations Report*, 192–3.
16 Arar Commission, *Analysis and Recommendations Report*, 55–7; Toope, *Report of Professor Stephen J. Toope*, 806–9.
17 Arar Commission, *Analysis and Recommendations Report*, 55–7, 230, 237, 251; Toope, *Report of Professor Stephen J. Toope*, 792, 803, 809–10.
18 Arar Commission, *Analysis and Recommendations Report*, 46–7, 253–4, 311.
19 CBS News, News In Depth: The Arar inquiry (2007), CBS News. Available at: https://www.cbc.ca/news2/background/arar/arar_inquiry.html (Accessed 2 September 2022).

20 Arar Commission, *Analysis and Recommendations Report*, 28, 66, 75, 99, 126, 129, 148–9, 160, 165, 173.

21 Commission of Inquiry into the Actions of Canadian Officials in Relation to Maher Arar, *Report of the Events Relating to Maher Arar: Factual Background*, Vol. I (2006); Commission of Inquiry into the Actions of Canadian Officials in Relation to Maher Arar, *Report of the Events Relating to Maher Arar: Factual Background*, Vol. II (2006).

22 Toope, *Report of Professor Stephen J. Toope*, 350.

23 Arar Commission, *Analysis and Recommendations Report*, 58–64, 187–8, 252, 262, 297.

24 Commission of Inquiry into the Actions of Canadian Officials in Relation to Maher Arar, *A New Review Mechanism for the RCMP's National Security Activities* (2006).

25 Arar Commission, *Analysis and Recommendations Report*, 311.

26 Commission of Inquiry into the Actions of Canadian Officials in Relation to Maher Arar, *Archived Website Versions* (2022). Available at: https://www.canada.ca/en/privy-council/services/commissions-inquiry/arar.html (Accessed 29 June 2022).

27 Harper, *Letter of Apology to Maher Arar* (2007). Available at: https://www.canada.ca/en/news/archive/2007/01/prime-minister-releases-letter-apology-maher-arar-his-family-announces-completion-mediation-process.html (Accessed 8 November 2023).

28 CBC News, '9/11 Saw Maher Arar Learn "hard lesson"' (2011), CBC News. Available at: https://www.cbc.ca/news/canada/ottawa/9-11-saw-maher-arar-learn-hard-lesson-1.1016629 (Accessed 8 September 2022).

29 Abdullah Almalki, Ahmad Abou-Elmaati and Muayyed Nureddin Inquiry, *Report of Internal Inquiry into the Actions of Canadian Officials*, 401.

30 Arar Commission, *Analysis and Recommendations Report*, 23, 108–10, 113.

31 Arar Commission, *Analysis and Recommendations Report*, 48, 115, 263–4.

32 Arar Commission, *Analysis and Recommendations Report*, 34.

33 Arar Commission, *Analysis and Recommendations Report*, 34.

34 Arar Commission, *Analysis and Recommendations Report*, 34.

35 Arar Commission, *Analysis and Recommendations Report*, 34.

36 Arar Commission, *Analysis and Recommendations Report*, 34.

37 Toope, *Report of Professor Stephen J. Toope*.

38 Abdullah Almalki, Ahmad Abou-Elmaati and Muayyed Nureddin Inquiry, *Report of Internal Inquiry*; Bahdi and De Lint, 'Access to Information', 118–19; Toope, *Report of Professor Stephen J. Toope*.

5

Targeted killing: The constitutionality of killing US citizens

Christine Sixta Rinehart

Between November 2002 and January 2015 the United States' drone (Remotely Piloted Aircraft, RPA)[1] war killed approximately twelve United States (US) citizens with armed Predator or Reaper RPA. Targeted killing or the assassination of foreign citizens is not new for the US.[2] However, the targeted killing of US citizens by their own government abroad, let alone killing with RPA, is a relatively new concept. The first US citizen killed was Kemal Darwish, who was killed in a strike authorised by President George W. Bush[3] on 3 November 2002, in Yemen. Darwish, a US-born citizen with Yemeni ancestry, was a recruiter for an al-Qaeda terrorist cell based in Buffalo, New York. He was accompanied by Abu Ali al-Harithi, an al-Qaeda leader suspected of involvement in the October 2000 USS *Cole* attack.[4] Other controversial targeted killings occurred in Yemen when Anwar al-Awlaki was killed by an RPA strike on 30 September 2011. His sixteen-year-old son, Abdulrahman al-Awlaki, and two friends were targeted on 14 October 2011, at a restaurant in Yemen. The CIA targeted both individuals. While Anwar was an al-Qaeda propagandist, and potentially a top al-Qaeda member responsible for planning several attacks (although there is some debate on this),[5] his son was not.

Bush signed the Authorization for Use of Military Force (AUMF) Act to retaliate against those involved in the 11 September 2001 terrorist attacks. Four US citizens, including Darwish and three whose names are unknown, were killed during the Bush administration.[6] Under President Barack Obama's Administration eight US citizens are known to have died in US RPA strikes, while a ninth US citizen claims he was targeted but survived five strikes. Details of US citizens known to have been killed and/or targeted by RPA strikes are listed in Table 5.1, while the number of RPA strikes carried out by US presidential administrations up to June 2020 are in Table 5.2. This chapter engages with the US official and public records, as defined in the Preface of this volume, to explore the killing and targeting of US citizens by RPA strikes. In particular, under Obama, Department of Justice White

Table 5.1 US citizens killed and/or targeted, or who claim to have been targeted, by RPA strikes

Name	Acknowledged as targeted in Official and Public Record?	Date killed, location of death	Terrorist group
1. Kemal Darwish (Abu Ahmad al-Hijazi)[1]	No, but presence likely known. Deputy Secretary of Defense Paul Wolfowitz acknowledged this RPA strike, though Darwish is not mentioned in a related CNN article.	3 November 2002, Yemen	Al-Qaeda
2.[2]		June 2007, Somalia	
3.[3]	No. Bush administration official told Chris Woods they knew of no US citizens 'intentionally targeted'. According to Bob Woodward, CIA Director Michael Hayden told Pakistan's President Asif Ali Zardari 'many Westerners, including some US passport holders, had been killed'. He claimed he could not say more because of 'implications under American law'.	7 November 2008, '[M]ilitant training camp' in North Waziristan, Pakistan	
4.[4]	As per No.3	7 November 2008, '[M]ilitant training camp' in North Waziristan, Pakistan	
5. Inaam[5]		November 2010?, Pakistan	
6. Anwar al-Awlaqi[6]	Yes	30 September 2011, Yemen	Al-Qaeda

Table 5.1 US citizens killed and/or targeted, or who claim to have been targeted, by RPA strikes (Continued)

Name	Acknowledged as targeted in Official and Public Record?	Date killed, location of death	Terrorist group
7. Samir Khan[7]	According to Eric Holder 'not specifically targeted', but many question this claim.	30 September 2011, Yemen	Al-Qaeda
8. Abdulrahman al-Aulaqi[8]	As per Samir Khan	14 October 2011, Yemen	Al-Qaeda
9. Jude Kenan Mohammed[9]	As per Samir Khan	16 November 2011, Pakistan	Al-Qaeda and TTP
10. Warren Weinstein[10]	No. Contractor held as hostage.	14 January 2015, Pakistan	Al-Qaeda hostage
11. Ahmed Farouq[11]	According to White House statement not 'specifically targeted'	14 January 2015, Pakistan	Al-Qaeda
12. Adam (Pearlman) Gadahn[12]	As per Ahmed Farouq	14 January 2015, Pakistan	Al-Qaeda
13. Targeted (?): (Darrell Lamont Phelps) Bilal Abdul Kareem[13]		Still alive, claims to have escaped five strikes	

Notes

[1] P. Bergen, *'Testimony to Senate Committee on the Judiciary Subcommittee on the Constitution, Civil Rights and Human Rights "Drone Wars: The Constitutional and Counterterrorism' Implications of Targeted Killing"'* (2013). 11; CNN, 'U.S. Missile Strike Kills al Qaeda Chief', CNN (2002). Available at: https://edition.cnn.com/2002/WORLD/meast/11/05/yemen.blast/ (Accessed 20 November 2022); D. Gettinger, 'AQAP Outline', *Center for the Study of the Drone at Bard College* (n.d.). Available at: https://dronecenter.bard.edu/files/2015/04/AQAP-Outline-1.pdf (Accessed 4 May 2020); C. Woods and J. Serle, 'Hostage Deaths Mean 38 Westerners Killed by US Drone Strikes, Bureau Investigation Reveals' (2015), *The Bureau of Investigative Journalism*. Available at: https://www.thebureauinvestigates.com/stories/2015-04-23/hostage-deaths-mean-38-westerners-killed-by-us-drone-strikes-bureau-investigation-reveals (Accessed 20 November 2022).
[2] C. Woods, *Sudden Justice* (Oxford: Oxford University Press, 2015), 289–90. Airstrike with 'other asset'.
[3] N. Shachtman, '10 More Dead as Drone War over Pakistan Continues', *Wired* (2008) Available at: https://www.wired.com/2008/11/us-drone-war-ov/ (Accessed 20 November 2022); Woods, *Sudden Justice*, 142, 289–90; Woods and Serle, 'Hostage Deaths'.

Table 5.1 US citizens killed and/or targeted, or who claim to have been targeted, by RPA strikes (Continued)

[4]Shachtman, '10 More Dead'; Woods, *Sudden Justice*, 142, 289–90; Woods and Serle, 'Hostage Deaths'.

[5]Woods, *Sudden Justice*, 289–90. Not a confirmed US citizen.

[6]Eric Holder, *May 22 2013 Letter to Patrick Leahy* (2013). Available at: https://www. justice.gov/slideshow/AG-letter-5-22-13.pdf (Accessed 8 November 2023). Scott Shane, *Objective Troy* (New York: Random House, 2015).

[7]Holder, *Letter*; Shane, *Objective Troy*.

[8]Holder, *Letter*; Scott Shane, *Objective Troy*.

[9]Bureau of Investigative Journalism, *Naming the Dead* (2020). Available at: https:// v1.thebureauinvestigates.com/namingthedead/people/nd477/?lang=en (Accessed 4 May 2020); Holder, *Letter*; E. Schmitt, 'One Drone Victim's Trail from Raleigh to Pakistan' (2013), *New York Times*. Available at: https://www.nytimes.com/2013/05/23/us/one-drone-victims-trail-from-raleigh-to-pakistan.html (Accessed 4 May 2020).

[10]D. Bergner, 'The Killing of Warren Weinstein' (2016), *The New York Times*. Available at: https://www.nytimes.com/2016/02/14/magazine/the-killing-of-warren-weinstein.html (Accessed 4 May 2020); White House, *April 23 Statement by the Press Secretary* (2015). Available at: https://obamawhitehouse.archives.gov/the-press-office/2015/04/23/statement-press-secretary (Accessed 8 November 2023).

[11]G. Botelho and J. Sciutto, 'Ahmed Farouq: Leader of al Qaeda's Indian Branch Killed by U.S' (2015), CNN. Available at: https://edition.cnn.com/2015/04/23/world/ahmed-farouq-al-qaeda/index.html (Accessed 8 November 2023). White House, *April 23 Statement*.

[12]White House, *April 23 Statement*.

[13]S. Hsu, Judge Allows Journalist to Challenge Claimed Inclusion on U.S. Drone "kill list"' (2018), *Washington Post*. Available at: https://www.washingtonpost.com/local/public-safety/judge-allows-journalist-to-challenge-claimed-inclusion-on-us-drone-kill-list/2018/06/13/956fe70c-6f5d-11e8-afd5-778aca903bbe_story.html (Accessed 8 December 2022).

Table 5.2 Estimated RPA strikes by presidents in Afghanistan, Iraq, Libya, Pakistan, Somalia, Syria and Yemen

President	Term	Estimated RPA strikes[1]
George Walker Bush	20 January 2001 to 20 January 2009	115
Barack Hussein Obama	20 January 2009 to 20 January 2017	30,302
Donald John Trump	20 January 2017 to 6 January 2020	12,297

[1]C. Sixta Rinehart, *Drones and Targeted Killing in the Middle East and Africa: An Appraisal of American Counterterrorism Policies* (Lanham, MD: Lexington Books, 2016); Bureau of Investigative Journalism, 'Bureau of Investigative Journalism: The Covert Drone Wars Archive' (2001–20), *Air Wars*. Available at: https://airwars.org/archives/bij-drone-war (Accessed 30 October 2023); Bureau of Investigative Journalism, 'Drone Wars: The Full Data' (2010–20), Bureau of Investigative Journalism. Available at: https://www.thebureauinvestigates.com/stories/2017-01-01/drone-wars-the-full-data (Accessed 30 October 2023).

Paper 020413 (hereafter **Document 1**) delineated a legal framework, discussed later, under which the US could use lethal force abroad against a US citizen considered an imminent threat. Yet, via Article V of the Bill of Rights (hereafter **Document 2**), the US Constitution provides citizens due process, stipulating the right to a trial within the US legal system. As with other chapters, document extracts are chosen to reflect broader points or themes. While some of the references to these documents in this chapter refer to the material in the Document Appendix, some refer to material elsewhere in these documents. To gain a greater understanding of the documents, readers are encouraged to seek out the full documents.

It is, in part, the tension between the legal justification laid out in **Document 1** and the due process provided for in **Document 2** that this chapter explores. Discussions of the intelligence cycle and its critics, as well as the process of RPA strikes as they relate to the intelligence cycle, are also present. These discussions, based in large part on the work of the author with the US Air Force, occur first, providing contextual and empirical grounding on the US RPA strike process. Next, the data on US citizens killed and/or targeted, or who claim to have been targeted, by RPA strikes are presented. A legal case brought by the US citizen Bilal Abdul Kareem, who claims he was targeted, is explored to illuminate the restrictions of judicial oversight arising from the secrecy surrounding US RPA strikes. Key aspects of the evolution of targeted killing from Bush to the administration of President Joe Biden are then highlighted, before the concepts of due process, imminence and feasibility are discussed in the final section. These discussions take place with relation to **Document 1** and **Document 2**, providing troubling evidence of linguistic gymnastics present in the Official Record of the Obama administration related to the targeting of US citizens.

Targeted killing and the intelligence cycle

As defined by the international law expert Nils Melzer, targeted killing is 'the use of lethal force attributable to a subject of international law with the intent, premeditation, and deliberation to kill individually selected persons who are not in the physical custody of those targeting them'.[7] RPAs are most frequently used for reconnaissance and surveillance, while targeted killing by RPA occurs rarely in comparison. That said, an absolute comparison is not quantifiable as the data are not available. Targets are found and/or tracked by pilots and sensor operators located primarily at Creech Air Force Base outside Las Vegas, Nevada, or the Air Operations Center (AOC) at al-Udeid Air Base in Qatar. Holloman Air Force Base is primarily responsible for the training of pilots and sensor operators in Alamogordo, New Mexico, due to its huge expanse of uninhibited air space, although there are other bases used for specific training or certification purposes by the Air Force. Central Command (CENTCOM) in Doha, Qatar, maintains the communication, intelligence and collaboration.[8]

Differences between the pilots and the sensor operators are especially important, and it is not appropriate to describe a sensor operator as a co-pilot. Pilots are commissioned officers, while sensor operators may come straight from high school with a diploma or General Educational Development test equivalent. Sensor operators help determine wind speeds and weather conditions to assist pilots, as well as guiding Hellfire missiles to the target once fired. Sensor operators execute a targeted killing, though, as this chapter explores, decisions are taken higher in the chain of command. Pilots are responsible for remotely flying RPAs, and pilots and sensor operators sit next to one another communicating constantly, as they fly RPAs located on bases across the Middle East and Africa. RPA care and maintenance occurs at bases in the Middle East and Africa while RPAs are tracked and monitored by Distributed Common Ground System (DCGS) teams, which are located globally.[9]

The elementary model of the intelligence cycle on the CIA's website is shared in Figure 5.1. The first stage is Planning and Direction, when users

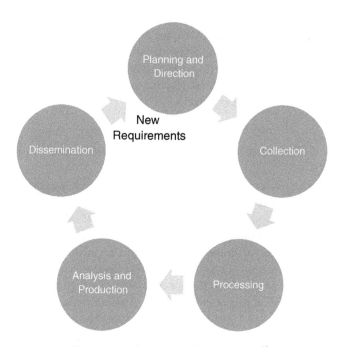

Figure 5.1 The CIA intelligence cycle[10]

ask for the intelligence they need. The user may be anyone from a military colonel to the Department of Homeland Security. In the second step, entitled Collection, information is gathered covertly and overtly from numerous sources by various intelligence entities. In the third stage data are analysed and put into an intelligence report. The fourth stage includes analysis and production, where the effects of information are synthesised. Finally information is disseminated to the original user and other parties that may need to know the intelligence.[11]

The targeted-killing intelligence cycle does not exactly follow the above model, yet this overview provides a sound starting point. Highlighting, however, the need to keep distinctions between theory and reality in mind, the veteran Air Force Officer Arthur S. Hulnick states: 'The intelligence cycle is a flawed vision, and thus poor theory. One need only ask those who have toiled in the fields of intelligence.'[12] The academics Peter Gill and Mark Phythian, meanwhile, maintain that the intelligence-cycle model has multiple flaws; agencies often use bulk data they can refine to get around surgical data collection: intelligence agencies do not wait for policy-makers to identify targets, the agencies often find targets themselves; policy-makers such as US presidents do not wait on analysis before they make a decision, although they may scapegoat the agency if they receive bad intelligence; lastly covert action is not included in the intelligence cycle and the ethical improprieties that can occur with covert intelligence gathering have no place in the previous model.[13]

Returning to the intelligence-cycle model, and the aforementioned critiques notwithstanding, the planning and direction stage in the targeted killing intelligence process can be initiated by numerous actors including the president and administration officials, the CIA, military leaders or on-the-ground Air Force personnel. There are two kinds of targeted killing strikes: personality and signature strikes. Personality strikes are strikes on a person identified as a terrorist leader. These strikes are usually ordered by the president or top officials, depending on the administration in power. Signature strikes, meanwhile, target potential militants who might be unknown, but have been determined through patterns of life and surveillance to be a part of a terrorist organisation. For signature strikes Air Force personnel are often gathering information, analysing it and then making decisions, therefore deciding, and conducting stages two to five of the intelligence cycle. Bush initiated personality strikes in Afghanistan, while the 'Terror Tuesday' meetings that Obama controlled were predominately organised for personality strikes.[14]

Conceptualising the intelligence cycle as it relates to targeted killing, Figure 5.2 visualises the US Air Force intelligence cycle of targeted killing in the US Air Force that the author created through her work with the US Air Force. One point of note is that there is more detail at the lower end

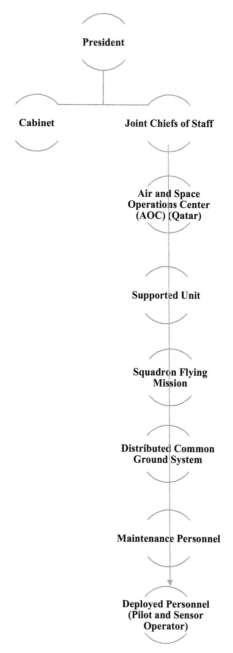

Figure 5.2 The intelligence cycle of targeted killing

of the cycle than the administrative side above AOC, meaning more research is needed on the AOC and above. Suffice to say, it is evident that the order for the target comes from higher up the chain than the AOC.

Reflecting the planning and direction stage, and depending on the presidential administration, orders related to any particular target being dealt with via the process mapped in Figure 5.2 may come from the president, his staff, the Joint Chiefs of Staff, the CIA, the FBI, the Department of Homeland Security or military intelligence. A Judge Advocate General (JAG) next approves all strikes at the AOC in Qatar. The order is then given to the AOC. The AOC finds the proper supported unit, which may be RPA or a jet such as an F-16. The proper squadron is located and the DCGS, which controls communication between the various components throughout the world, is contacted. Most likely the RPA maintenance on the ground in Qatar is the primary contact in this step of the DCGS. Lastly maintenance personnel and the deployed personnel are notified before the mission occurs. The RPA takes off from the base, flown by pilots and sensor operators at AOC, and is then taken over mid-air by pilots at Creech. It takes approximately seventy-two hours from the time that AOC is alerted to the assassination of the target.[15] Having detailed the intelligence cycle and its critics, and mapped how it can occur in the case of RPA strikes, this chapter now moves on to document US citizens killed or targeted by RPA strikes 2002–15.

US citizens killed and targeted by RPA

As detailed above in Table 5.1, since the US RPA targeted killing programme began, approximately twelve US citizens have been killed. Despite official protestations to the contrary documented in Table 5.1, there is evidence to suggest that most were purposefully targeted by President Obama, although Warren Weinstein (a US contractor with no terrorist affiliations who was kidnapped by al-Qaeda) was supposedly an accident. So far as is known, neither President Donald Trump nor President Joe Biden has targeted any US citizens. Where affiliation is known, all US citizens targeted had some type of affiliation with al-Qaeda and were targeted because of their affiliation. This is interesting as the US also targets al-Shabaab in Somalia, the Taliban in Afghanistan and Pakistan, Boko Haram in Nigeria and ISIS in Syria and Iraq, yet there have not been any US citizens assassinated who were affiliated with those groups. ISIS alone contained numerous US citizens, with some who have been captured repatriated to the US.[16] In Table 5.1 the known US citizens targeted by the United States government are listed along with their occupations, affiliations, place of birth and location of death.

An interesting point of note is the final US citizen listed in the table, and the only one still alive, Bilal Abdul Kareem, originally known as Darell Lamont Phelps prior to his conversion to Islam. Kareem is a journalist who says he has been purposefully targeted by the US government several times, eventually coming to believe he had been placed on its 'Kill List'. This list is based on metadata and flags a person for having too many data points in common with a specified list of terrorist characteristics. Phelps changed his name to Bilal Abdul Kareem after converting to Islam, while a perceived pro-jihadist stance and a residency move to Syria may have been red flags to the US government in terms of metadata.[17] According to a brief filed on his behalf with the US Supreme Court, 'Kareem reasonably believed, based on publicly available information about how the U.S. identifies targets for lethal action, that the locations of his cell phone and other signal-emitting devices he used while interviewing rebels had led U.S. agencies to conclude wrongly that he was a part of a terrorist organization and should be placed on the U.S. government's so-called Kill List'.[18]

Kareem originally filed a complaint in District Court in Washington, DC, on 30 March 2017, appealing to the US government to take him off the list of assassination targets. In June 2018 Judge Rosemary Collyer ruled that Kareem could not be targeted without a trial.[19] Whether he has been targeted several times is at least debatable, as the RPA pilots rarely miss or abort a missile. Indeed, according to *New York Times* reporting, RPAs operate with 'near-unerring accuracy'.[20] The case was, however, dismissed by Collyer in September 2019 as the US government invoked the 'state secret' privilege to avoid disclosing intelligence information.[21] The US Supreme Court rejected a petition to hear Kareem's case because he could not 'explicitly link the United States' to the attacks against him.[22]

The truth about whether Kareem was targeted by drones notwithstanding, his case has seen debates about due process play out within the US judicial system, and thus in the official and public records. As Judge Collyer noted in her 2018 ruling, '[d]ue process is not merely an old and dusty procedural obligation [...]. Instead, it is a living, breathing concept that protects U.S. persons from overreaching government action even, perhaps, on an occasion of war.'[23] As per *Washington Post* reporting, at the hearings that fed into Collyer's ruling, US government lawyers requested Judge Collyer to 'toss out the lawsuit', arguing that Kareem 'could not substantiate his claims given the secrecy surrounding targeting decisions and asserting the executive branch's unfettered authority to conduct military operations abroad', essentially saying that due to the secrecy around the RPA campaign, it was impossible for him to prove he had been targeted.[24] Having highlighted US citizens killed or targeted by RPA, and explored issues raised by the case of Kareem, this chapter now moves on to document the evolution of targeted killing via US RPA strikes since the Bush Administration.

The Evolution of Targeted Killing

Table 5.2 lists the number of strikes under each US president up to June 2020. It should be noted that the twelve US citizens discussed above are a tiny fraction of the total killed in these strikes. Yet, given the due process protections afforded to US citizens by Article V of the US Constitution, studying them offers an important window on to both presidential power and the US Official Record, of which the US Constitution is a cornerstone.

Targeted killing with RPA began under Bush in response to the al-Qaeda terrorist attacks of 11 September 2001. On 14 September 2001 Congress passed the AUMF, which was signed into law by Bush on 18 September 2001. The AUMF 'authorized' the use of 'all necessary and appropriate force against those nations, organizations, or persons he [the President] determines planned, authorized committed, or aided the terrorist attacks that occurred on 11 September 2001, or harbored such organizations or persons, in order to prevent any future acts of international terrorism against the United States by such nations, organizations or persons'.[25] Bush used the AUMF to conduct RPA strikes to target terrorists in Yemen in 2002, shortly thereafter adding Pakistan and Afghanistan to the list. Around 115 RPA strikes occurred under Bush, with four US citizens killed.[26] Except for the strike that killed Darwish, explored above, little is known about the deaths of these US citizens, and it remains possible the remainder were killed by mistake. Obama added Libya, Nigeria, Iraq, Syria and Somalia to the list of countries attacked, with an estimated 30,302 RPA strikes carried out during his administration.[27] Regardless of the reasons, this is a huge increase from Bush to Obama.

After the strikes against Anwar al-Awlaki, and his sixteen-year-old-son Abdulrahman Anwar al-Awlaki, in September and October 2011, it was clear that more justification to target US citizens was needed. With the Attorney General Eric Holder leading, the Obama Administration drafted **Document 1**, justifying the targeting of US citizens under certain criteria:

> Here the Department of Justice concludes only that where the following three conditions are met, a U.S. operation using lethal force in a foreign country against a U.S. citizen who is a senior operational leader of al-Qaeda or an associated force would be lawful:
>
> (1) an informed, high-level official of the U.S. government has determined that the targeted individual poses an imminent threat of violent attack against the United States;
> (2) capture is infeasible, and the United States continues to monitor whether capture becomes feasible; and
> (3) the operation would be conducted in a manner consistent with applicable law of war principles.[28]

Following high civilian casualties, Obama published Executive Order 13732 on 1 July 2016, which created new pre- and post-strike measures to address civilian casualties. The Director of National Intelligence would from 1 January 2016 to 31 December 2016 publish the number of RPA strikes, combatant and non-combatant deaths resulting from those strikes, and publicly release an unclassified summary of such information no later than 1 May 2017. Executive Order 13732 also promised investigations and reparation payments for civilian families whose loved ones were killed in RPA strikes.[29] Although there are a few anecdotal stories where the US paid for reparations, there is not enough data to verify these payments.[30] Strike numbers and deaths were not released either, and, though the Air Force published some data, it appeared inaccurate.[31]

Preferring to leave targeted killing to the military and intelligence community, Trump rescinded Executive Order 13732 with Executive Order 13862, no longer requiring the release of data on RPA strike numbers and civilian deaths.[32] Unlike Obama's micromanagement of the 'Kill List', Trump delegated strikes to the CIA and the US military, thus potentially providing more oversight by placing multiple decision-makers in the process – though given the opacity of the RPA strive process it is hard to fully judge. Under President Trump's Administration, there were 12,297 strikes as of 1 June 2020.[33] The Trump Administration's Principles, Standards and Procedures plan[34] was approved on 14 September 2017. Under this plan Trump continued Obama's policies of targeting high-value targets considered a 'continuing and imminent threat' to US citizens. Trump also extended the policy to include 'foot-soldier jihadists with no special skills or leadership roles', although Obama had already been targeting these individuals. Trump also stopped RPA attacks and raids being subject to high-level screening by the Oval Office. Reflecting Obama, there was no targeting of civilians, though neither Obama nor Trump was concerned about killing family members of targets. In short Trump extended the 'pattern of giving broader day-to-day authority to the Pentagon and the CIA – authorizing the agencies to decide when and how to conduct high risk counterterrorism operations'.[35] Presidential approval was still needed to conduct strikes in new countries. With 'country plans' to be reviewed annually with concern to international law, the US still needed to obtain consent from a country's leaders to commit strikes abroad.[36]

Although one cannot know if Biden has targeted any US citizens, it appears that this is not the case, with his use of RPA strikes limited in general. In his first six months in office, for instance, Biden did not authorise a single RPA strike. That said, some Biden-era strikes have incurred high civilian death rates, with a 29 August 2021 strike in Kabul, Afghanistan, that killed ten civilians being particularly troubling.[37] In August 2022, meanwhile, al-Qaeda spokesman Ayman al-Zawahiri, was killed in another Kabul drone strike.[38] Speaking to the approach adopted under Biden, Chris Woods, director of the British non-governmental organisation Airwars stated, '[p]rivately, we're hearing of the emergence of a hybrid Trump-Obama approach, which, if true, could mean less protections in place for civilians than during the latter part of Obama. That's a worry.'[39] Having tracked the overarching evolution of RPA strikes from Bush to Biden, the final section explores due process, and linguistic gymnastics related to the concepts of imminence and feasibility.

Due process, imminence and infeasibility

On 8 June 1789 James Madison introduced the Bill of Rights (**Document 2**), which contained the first ten amendments to the US Constitution. **Document 2** provides important constraints on government power, the most relevant here being found in Article V, containing as it does a due process clause that states that 'No person [...] shall be compelled in any criminal case to be a witness against himself, nor be deprived of life, liberty, or property, without due process of law'.[40] The nuances of the exact meaning of Article V are, as one would expect, contested. Yet it would be fair to say that, as a result, any US citizens targeted by their own government deserve access to due process: to a trial, to refute their accusers and see the evidence presented against them. In *Al-Aulaqi* [Awlaki] *v. Panetta (Al-Awlaki v. Panetta)* 2012, a case dismissed by the United States District Court for the District of Columbia, for example, the plaintiffs state that the US government's killings of US citizens Anwar al-Awlaki, Samir Khan and Abdulrahman al-Awlaki documented in Table 5.1 violated the Constitution's fundamental guarantee against the deprivation of life without due process of law.[41] Yet, as a 2016 RAND paper notes, '[i]ssues in such cases include the protections that' **Document 2** 'provides American citizens and criminal prohibitions against killing American nationals abroad'.[42]

Turning to the term 'imminence', which has been the basis for the claims of the need to be able to carry out RPA attacks against US citizens, it is worth highlighting the difference between the term as generally understood and the definition adopted by the US government within the Official Record. As commonly understood, it means 'coming or likely to happen very soon'.[43] Yet, in 2011, **Document 1** stated that 'the condition that an operational leader present an "imminent" threat of violent attack against the United States does not require the United States to have clear evidence that a specific attack on U.S. persons will take place in the immediate future'.[44] Thus there is a clear contradiction, or one might say the need for linguistic gymnastics, between the term 'imminent threat of violence' as generally understood, and as defined in **Document 1**. As Luca Trenta has noted, the adoption of this definition was part of an attempt to 'change the criteria' for RPA strikes to 'a more permissive imminence' whilst simultaneously attempting 'to maintain its normative colour'.[45]

A second pillar used to justify RPA strikes on US citizens is the supposed infeasibility of capturing those targeted. Clearly in some cases infeasibility of capture will be the case. Yet, once again we see a disconnect between the term as generally understood and as defined by the Obama-era Justice Department. As generally understood, 'feasible' means 'the possibility that can be made, done, or achieved, or is reasonable'.[46] However, **Document 1** provided the following multi-caveated discussion of feasibility, thus lowering the bar for infeasibility:

> [C]apture would not be feasible if it could not be physically effectuated during the relevant window of opportunity or if the relevant country were to decline to consent to a capture operation. Other factors such as undue risk to U.S. personnel conducting a potential capture operation also could be relevant. Feasibility would be a highly fact-specific and potentially time-sensitive inquiry.[47]

Speaking to both feasibility and imminence as defined in **Document 1**, Conor Friedersdorf notes that 'the Obama Administration took a process that is supposed to constrain the president within the law's confines; nodded toward the notion that they can kill only if capture is infeasible and the threat of attack imminent; and then qualified those constraints so drastically that it would be more honest to acknowledge that neither imminence nor infeasible capture are really required'.[48] In this way Friedersdorf captured the linguistic gymnastics underpinning **Document 1**.

Conclusion

The use of the Executive Branch to target US citizens is not prescribed by the US Constitution. President Obama, in particular, made unilateral decisions on which terrorists to kill and who should be on the terrorist 'Kill List' of the US government. With *The Guardian* explaining that

> The president's underlings compile their proposed lists of who should be executed, and the president – at a charming weekly event dubbed by White House aides as 'Terror Tuesday' – then chooses from 'baseball cards' and decrees in total secrecy who should die. The power of accuser, prosecutor, judge, jury, and executioner are all consolidated in this one man, and those powers are exercised in the dark.[49]

The killing selection became so routine that William Daley, Obama's Chief of Staff in 2011, summarised the situation as follows, '[o]ne guy gets knocked off, and the guy's driver, who's No. 21, becomes 20? At what point are you just filling the bucket with numbers?'[50] As per **Document 2**, neither the US president nor any one person should be judge, jury and executioner.

To close, the targeted killing of US citizens abroad is, bar the small possibility of instances when high standards of imminence and infeasibility of capture are present, unconstitutional. In particular it violates the due process clause of Article V of **Document 2**. Such violations, especially when based on the linguistic gymnastics present in the Official Record of the Obama administration and visible in **Document 1**, call into question the longer-term value of the US Constitution and the Bill of Rights as guardrails against executive power.

Document appendix

1) Extract from: Department of Justice, *White Paper 020413* (2011)
2) Extract from: US Government, *Bill of Rights* (Ratified 15 December 1791)

1) Extract from: Department of Justice, *White Paper 020413* (2011)

Lawfulness of a Lethal Operation Directed against a U.S. Citizen Who Is a Senior Operational Leader of Al-Qaʻida or an Associated Force

This white paper sets forth a legal framework for considering the circumstances in which the U.S. government could use lethal force in a foreign country outside the area of active hostilities against a U.S. citizen who is a senior operational leader of al-Qaʻida or an associated force of al-Qaʻida-that is, an al-Qaʻida leader actively engaged in planning operations to kill Americans. The paper does not attempt to determine the minimum requirements necessary to render such an operation lawful; nor does it assess what might be required to render a lethal operation against a U.S. citizen lawful in other circumstances, including an operation against enemy forces on a traditional battlefield or an operation against a U.S. citizen who is not a senior operational leader of such forces. Here the Department of Justice concludes only that where the following three conditions are met, a U.S. operation using lethal force in a foreign country against a U.S. citizen who is a senior operational leader of al-Qaʻida or an associated force would be lawful: (1) an informed, high-level official of the U.S. government has determined that the targeted individual poses an imminent threat of violent attack against the United States; (2) capture is infeasible, and the United States continues to monitor whether capture becomes feasible; and (3) the operation would be conducted in a manner consistent with applicable law of war principles. This conclusion is reached with recognition of the extraordinary seriousness of a lethal operation by the United States against a U.S. citizen, and also of the extraordinary seriousness of the threat posed by senior operational al-Qa'ida members and the loss of life that would result were their operations successful.

[...]

Certain aspects of this legal framework require additional explication. *First*, the condition that an operational leader present an 'imminent' threat of violent attack against the United States does not require the United States to have clear evidence that a specific attack on U.S. persons and interests will take place in the immediate future. Given the nature of, for example, the terrorist attacks on September 11, in which civilian airliners were hijacked to strike the World Trade Center and the Pentagon, this definition of imminence, which would require the United States to refrain from action until preparations for an attack are concluded, would not allow the United States sufficient time to defend itself.

[...]

Second, regarding the feasibility of capture, capture would not be feasible if it could not be physically effectuated during the relevant window of opportunity or if the relevant country were to decline to consent to a capture operation. Other factors such as undue risk to U.S. personnel conducting a potential capture operation also could be relevant. Feasibility would be a highly fact-specific and potentially time-sensitive inquiry.

2) **Extract from: US Government, *Bill of Rights* (Ratified 15 December 1791)**

[...]

The Conventions of a number of the States, having at the time of their adopting the Constitution, expressed a desire, in order to prevent misconstruction or abuse of its powers, that further declaratory and restrictive clauses should be added: And as extending the ground of public confidence in the Government, will best ensure the beneficent ends of its institution.

[...]

Amendment V

No person shall be held to answer for a capital, or otherwise infamous crime, unless on a presentment or indictment of a Grand Jury, except in cases arising in the land or naval forces, or in the Militia, when in actual service in time of War or public danger; nor shall any person be subject for the same offence to be twice put in jeopardy of life or limb; nor shall be compelled in any criminal case to be a witness against himself, nor be deprived of life, liberty, or property, without due process of law; nor shall private property be taken for public use, without just compensation.

Notes

1 The rest of the chapter will use the term Remotely Piloted Aircraft (RPA) as this is the preferred term of the United States Air Force, which is the primary operator of these machines.
2 See, for instance, Chapter 1 above by Luca Trenta.
3 From here on in, Bush will refer to George W. Bush, rather than his father George H. W. Bush, who was also US president.
4 P. Smucker, 'The Intrigue Behind the Drone Strike' (2002), *The Christian Science Monitor*. Available at: https://www.csmonitor.com/2002/1112/p01s02-wome.html (Accessed 1 May 2020); C. Woods, *Sudden Justice* (Oxford: Oxford University Press, 2015), 58–60, 289.
5 Woods, *Sudden Justice*, 137–40.
6 Woods, *Sudden Justice*, 289–90.
7 N. Melzer, *Targeted Killing in International Law* (Oxford: Oxford University Press, 2008), 5.
8 C. Sixta Rinehart, 'The Intelligence Cycle of Targeted Killing in the United States', *Fletcher Security Review*, Special Issue on *Technology and Security* 6:1 (2019), 19–28, 20.
9 Sixta Rinehart, 'The Intelligence Cycle'.
10 Sixta Rinehart, 'The Intelligence Cycle', 22.
11 Central Intelligence Agency, *Kid's Zone: The Intelligence Cycle* (2013). Available at: https://www.cia.gov/kids-page/6–12th-grade/who-we-are-what-we-do/the-intelligence-cycle.html (Accessed 26 June 2020).
12 A. S. Hulnick, 'The Intelligence Cycle', in L. K. Johnson and J. J. Wirtz (eds), *Intelligence: The Secret World of Spies, An Anthology,* fourth edition (New York: Oxford University Press, 2015), 92.
13 P. Gill and M. Phythian, *Intelligence in an Insecure World*, third edition (Cambridge: Polity, 2012), 15–20.
14 Sixta Rinehart, 'The Intelligence Cycle'.
15 Captain OL, Interview by Author, Creech Air Force Base, 26 November 2018.
16 Department of Justice, *The United States Has Repatriated 27 Americans from Syria and Iraq Including Ten Charged with Terrorism-Related Offenses for Their Support to ISIS* (2020). Available at: https://www.justice.gov/opa/pr/united-states-has-repatriated-27-americans-syria-and-iraq-including-ten-charged-terrorism (Accessed 27 October 2023).
17 H. Parry, 'New York-born Muslim Journalist and US Citizen Living in Syria Sues the American Government Claiming He's Been Put on the Drone Strike

Kill List' (2018), *Daily Mail*. Available at: https://www.dailymail.co.uk/news/article-5972177/New-Yorker-Syria-sues-government-finding-hes-drone-kill-list.html (Accessed 4 May 2020).

18 Legal Counsel for Bilal Abdul Kareem, *Brief of Amicus Curiae Submitted to the US Supreme Court* (2021). Available at: https://www.supremecourt.gov/DocketPDF/20/20-827/188100/20210820140351793_20-827%20BRIEF%20OF%20AMICUS%20CURIAE%20BILAL%20ABDUL%20KAREEM%20IN%20SUPPORT%20OF%20THE%20RESPONDENTS.pdf (Accessed 4 May 2020).

19 S. Hsu, 'Judge Allows Journalist to Challenge Claimed Inclusion on U.S. Drone "kill list"' (2018), *The Washington Post*. Available at: https://www.washingtonpost.com/local/public-safety/judge-allows-journalist-to-challenge-claimed-inclusion-on-us-drone-kill-list/2018/06/13/956fe70c-6f5d-11e8-afd5-778aca903bbe_story.html (Accessed 8th December 2022).

20 A. Khan, 'Hidden Pentagon Records Reveal Patterns of Failure in Deadly Strikes' (2021), *New York Times*. Available at: https://www.nytimes.com/interactive/2021/12/18/us/airstrikes-pentagon-records-civilian-deaths.html (Accessed 29 November 2022); C. Sixta Rinehart, *Drones and Targeted Killing in the Middle East and Africa: An Appraisal of American Counterterrorism Policies* (Lanham, MD: Lexington Books, 2016). A point to note here is the potential difference between the accuracy of RPA strikes themselves as judged by what missiles are fired at, which is very accurate, and the accuracy of the overall RPA system. Any RPA strike is only as accurate as the information on which it is based. So one could strike exactly where intended, but, if the target was identified with poor intelligence, the strike could be problematic if judged in a broader context.

21 A. Ullah, 'US Court Dismisses Journalist Bilal Abdul Kareem's Lawsuit over "drone kill list"' (2019), *Middle East Eye*. Available at: https://www.middleeasteye.net/news/us-court-dismisses-journalist-bilal-abdul-kareems-lawsuit-drone-kill-list (Accessed 27 November 2022).

22 U. A. Farooq and S. Hooper, 'US Supreme Court Rejects Journalist Bilal Abdul Kareem's "kill list" Lawsuit' (2021), *Middle East Eye*. Available at: https://www.middleeasteye.net/news/us-supreme-court-rejects-bilal-abdul-kareem-journalist-kill-list-lawsuit (Accessed 27 November 2022).

23 Judge Collyer, *June 13, 2018 Opinion in Ahmad Muaffaq Zaidan et al v Donald J Trump* (2018) Available at: https://ecf.dcd.uscourts.gov/cgi-bin/show_public_doc?2017cv0581–13 (Accessed 27 November 2022).

24 Hsu, 'Judge Allows Journalist'.

25 President Bush, *President Signs Authorization for Use of Military Force Bill* (2001). Available at: https://www.congress.gov/107/plaws/publ40/PLAW-107publ40.pdf (Accessed 27 October 2023).

26 Sixta Rinehart, 'The Intelligence Cycle'.

27 Sixta Rinehart, *Drones and Targeted Killing*; Bureau of Investigative Journalism, 'Bureau of Investigative Journalism: The Covert Drone Wars Archive' (2001-2020), *Air Wars*. Available at: https://airwars.org/archives/bij-drone-war (Accessed:

30 October 2023). Bureau of Investigative Journalism, 'Drone Wars: The Full Data' (2010–20), *Bureau of Investigative Journalism*. Available at: https://www.thebureauinvestigates.com/stories/2017-01-01/drone-wars-the-full-data (Accessed 30 October 2023).

28 Department of Justice, *White Paper 020413* (2011). Available at: https://www.documentcloud.org/documents/566483-020413-doj-white-paper (Accessed 30 October 2023).

29 President Obama, *Executive Order 13732* (2016). Available at: https://www.govinfo.gov/app/details/DCPD-201600443 (Accessed 27 October 2023).

30 Khan, 'Hidden Pentagon Records'.

31 S. Ackerman, 'Obama Claims US Drones Strikes Have Killed up to 116 Civilians' (2016), *Guardian*, Available at: https://www.theguardian.com/us-news/2016/jul/01/obama-drones-strikes-civilian-deaths (Accessed 27 September 2022).

32 President Trump, *Executive Order 13862* (2019). Available at: https://www.govinfo.gov/app/details/DCPD-201900131 (Accessed 27 October 2023).

33 Bureau of Investigative Journalism, 'The Covert'; Bureau of Investigative Journalism, 'Drone Wars'.

34 L. Hartig, 'Trump's New Drone Strike Policy: What's Any Different? Why It Matters' (2017), *Just Security*. Available at: https://www.justsecurity.org/45227/trumps-drone-strike-policy-different-matters/ (Accessed 19 May 2020).

35 Sixta Rinehart, 'The Intelligence Cycle'.

36 C. Savage and E. Schmitt, 'Trump Poised to Drop Some Limits on Drone Strikes and Commando Raids' (2017), *The New York Times*. Available at: https://www.nytimes.com/2017/09/21/us/politics/trump-drone-strikes-commando-raids-rules.html (Accessed 19 May 2020).

37 J. Marcus, 'Declassified Footage Shows Disastrous US Drone Strike in Kabul that Killed 10 Civilians' (2022), *The Independent*. Available at: https://www.independent.co.uk/news/world/americas/afghanistan-drone-strike-new-video-b1996621.html (Accessed 9 December 2022).

38 R. Plummer and M. Murphy, 'Ayman al-Zawahiri: Al-Qaeda Leader Killed in US Drone Strike' (2022), BBC. Available at: https://www.bbc.co.uk/news/world-asia-62387167 (Accessed 9 December 2022).

39 J. Scahill, 'The Mysterious Case of Joe Biden and the Future of Drone Wars' (2021), *The Intercept*. Available at: https://theintercept.com/2021/12/15/drone-strikes-joe-biden-pentagon-kabul/ (Accessed 27 September 2022).

40 US Government, *Bill of Rights* (Ratified 1791).

41 American Civil Liberties Union, *Al-Aulaqi v. Panetta – Legal Documents* (2020). Available at: https://www.aclu.org/legal-document/al-aulaqi-v-panetta-legal-documents (Accessed 20 May 2020).

42 L. E. Davis, M. McNerney and M. D. Greenberg, *Clarifying the Rules for Targeted Killing*, RAND (2016), 10. Available at: https://www.rand.org/pubs/research_reports/RR1610.html (Accessed 27 October 2023).

43 *Cambridge Dictionary*, 'Imminent' (2022), Available at: https://dictionary.cambridge.org/dictionary/english/imminent (Accessed 9 December 2022).

44 Department of Justice, *White Paper 020413*.

45 L. Trenta, 'The Obama Administration's Conceptual Change: Imminence and the Legitimation of Targeted Killings', *European Journal of International Security* 3:1 (2017), 69–93, 92.

46 *Cambridge Dictionary*, 'Feasibility' (2022). Available at: https://dictionary. cambridge.org/dictionary/english/feasibility (Accessed 9 December 2022).

47 Department of Justice, *White Paper 020413*.

48 C. Friedersdorf, 'Obama's Memo on Killing Americans Twists "Imminent threat" Like Bush' (2013), *The Atlantic*. Available at: https://www.theatlantic.com/politics/ archive/2013/02/obamas-memo-on-killing-americans-twists-imminent-threat-like-bush/272862/ (Accessed 9 December 2022).

49 G. Greenwald, 'Chilling Legal Memo from Obama DOJ Justifies Assassination of US Citizens' (2013), *Guardian*. Available at: https://www.theguardian.com/ commentisfree/2013/feb/05/obama-kill-list-doj-memo (Accessed 29 May 2020).

50 J. Becker and S. Shane, 'Secret "Kill List" Proves a Test of Obama's Principles and Will' (2012), *The New York Times*. Available at: https://www.nytimes.com/ 2012/05/29/world/obamas-leadership-in-war-on-al-qaeda.html (Accessed 29 May 2020).

6

The Chilcot inquiry: political-legal tensions in going to war and the art of the possible for the Public Record

Louise Kettle

On 17 March 2003 the British government agreed to join a coalition of thirty-eight other countries in an invasion of Iraq. The coalition's mission, with the United States taking the lead, was to topple the Iraqi President, Saddam Hussein, destroy the threat of weapons of mass destruction and bring peace, security and democracy to the Iraqi people. It was one of Britain's biggest national security decisions of the twenty-first century.

In the early hours of 20 March 2003 the military operation (codenamed Operation Telic in the UK) began with air strikes, with the ground campaign following later that same evening. In total 46,000 UK personnel were deployed, making it the largest military operation since the 1990–91 Gulf War. Within three weeks the Iraqi government and military had collapsed; major combat operations were completed by 30 April 2003 and Saddam had been officially deposed,[1] leading the US President, George W, Bush, to pre-emptively declare 'mission accomplished'.[2] However, British forces would remain in Iraq for a further six years trying – and failing – to find weapons of mass destruction and to build peace and security. Eventually, a decision was made to withdraw, even though the mission had not been completed. UK combat troops left in July 2009 whilst US combat operations continued for another year. It was a humiliating failure. Across the course of Telic 148,990 individual UK Armed Forces personnel were deployed and 179 lost their lives.[3] By the beginning of 2010 the war had cost Britain £9.24 billion.[4]

From the very beginning the decision to go to war had been controversial. There was considerable media criticism, Cabinet resignations and large-scale street protests. In January 2003 a poll by *The Guardian* suggested that public opinion was 43 per cent against intervention in Iraq with only 30 per cent in favour, compounded by the failure to receive international backing in the form of a United Nations Security Council resolution.[5] Over time the public perception of the war deteriorated further; the failure to find any weapons of mass destruction, the growing violence and insurgency and the rising number of British casualties led to increasing dissatisfaction and calls for an official inquiry into how it went so wrong. Under significant political pressure, the Prime Minister, now Gordon Brown, announced the establishment of the Iraq inquiry, one month before British combat forces left Iraq.

This chapter will examine the events surrounding the Iraq Inquiry. It will discuss the rationale for its establishment, its challenges and significance for the Public Record and its impact on the subsequent historiography of the Iraq War. In addition this chapter will use the official and historical records gathered by the inquiry to demonstrate some of the competing political-legal tensions in planning a war. Finally it will warn of the current gaps and biases that exist in the Public Record on the war in Iraq and finish by offering conclusions about the ability to place more information, related to national security, into the Public Record. The Document Appendix features two documents that help tease out the political-legal tensions that are key to the narrative of the chapter. These documents are a 29 January 2003 note from the Foreign Secretary Jack Straw to the FCO Legal Adviser Michael Wood titled *Iraq: Legal Basis for Use of Force* (hereafter **Document 1**) and an untitled note from 3 February 2003 from the Attorney General Lord Goldsmith to Straw (hereafter **Document 2**).

The 'Chilcot' inquiry and the Public Record

During Operation Telic a number of inquiries took place into different aspects of the war. These occurred through the Intelligence and Security Committee, Parliamentary select committees, the National Audit Office, internal departmental reviews, external inquiries for issues related to torture and abuse, and two independent inquiries around issues of intelligence.[6] In each case a significant amount of material moved from the Official Record into the Public Record. However, calls for a further, much broader, inquiry into the Iraq War continued. Initially the government rejected these demands claiming them to be a 'huge diversion of effort' and inappropriate whilst Telic was ongoing.[7] The Labour government also argued that it was the responsibility of Parliament to scrutinise the war, not an external inquiry, but such a claim ignored the necessity to access the Official Record to be able to effectively offer such scrutiny. In fact, several of the early inquiries had complained about a lack of access to witnesses for interviews and requested materials from the Official Record. For example, the Chair of the House of Commons Foreign Affairs Committee wrote to the Chairman of the Joint Intelligence Committee, the Chief of Defence Intelligence, the Head of the Secret Intelligence Service and the Director of GCHQ without receiving a single reply. The committee declared, '[w]e regard the Government's refusal to grant us access to evidence essential to our inquiries as a failure of accountability to Parliament'.[8]

Eventually, on 15 June 2009, Brown announced the establishment of the Iraq Inquiry to identify lessons that could be learned from the conflict. Its terms of reference were extremely broad: to consider events from the summer of 2001 until withdrawal in July 2009, including how decisions and actions were taken, to determine what happened and what lessons could be learned from the experience for the future. It was established under the chairmanship of Sir John Chilcot – leading the inquiry to be unofficially titled 'The Chilcot Inquiry' with its subsequent report later given the moniker 'The Chilcot Report'. Chilcot was supported by a committee of four Privy Counsellors and, in contrast to previous inquiries, was promised unrivalled access to the Official Record. Brown wrote to Chilcot; 'As Privy Counsellors, you will have unhindered access to government documents. I have written to all relevant current and former Ministers to underline the importance of their full cooperation. And the Cabinet Secretary is writing to departments to underline the need for full transparency.'[9] Brown also urged the inquiry to consider asking witnesses to provide their evidence under oath. Chilcot went further and argued that it was 'essential to hold as much of the proceedings of the Inquiry as possible in public'.[10]

For Chilcot, the argument for transparency was focused upon ensuring public confidence in the integrity and independence of the inquiry, but it had the additional benefit of bringing much of the Official Record to the fore of the Public Record.[11] To achieve this endeavour, many witness hearings were open for the public to attend (via a free ticketing system) as well as journalists. They were also available to watch live on television and over the internet as well as recorded and transcribed, with both formats made publicly available on an independent website.[12]

The hearings were conducted in four tranches from November 2009 until February 2011 spanning a total of twenty weeks. In some cases witnesses were asked to more than one session, to offer further detail or to respond to subsequent evidence found by the committee. In total 125 public witness hearings were held. In addition, where confidentiality and national security issues were particularly pressing, sessions were held in private. Some forty-five such sessions took place with thirty-five witnesses. These were not recorded but redacted transcripts were also made available on the website. Overall 184 witnesses were heard, including the former Prime Minister Tony Blair, the former Chief of the Secret Intelligence Service Sir Richard Dearlove, several Secret Intelligence Service officers, Directors of Special Forces and the former Chief of the Defence Staff.[13] In addition seventy written witness statements were submitted, and published online, adding further records from the Historical Record into the Public Record fora.

To support the interviewing of witnesses the inquiry also published a number of documents on its website. The Chilcot report stated that the inquiry had no reason to believe that any documents were deliberately withheld from their view, but they did note the challenges involved in moving them into the Public Record. The process for agreeing the publication and disclosure of material was established in a protocol created especially for the inquiry based upon the balance of public interest.[14] In addition a significant number of 'gists' and quotations from documents were agreed for inclusion in the final report. In most cases this process worked well but there were specific challenges over the declassification of Cabinet papers and records of conversations between Blair and Bush. In January 2011 the Cabinet Secretary Sir Gus O'Donnell wrote to the inquiry to advise that he could not authorise the disclosure of exchanges between the Prime Minister and US President.[15] However, the inquiry persisted and three years later, the new Cabinet Secretary, Sir Jeremy Heywood, agreed to publication under the caveats that 'gists' were restricted to the UK side and would not allow the reader to infer any US views, and that direct quotations were kept to an absolute minimum.[16] In the end the report referred to 212 records of discussions between the British Prime Minister and the US President as well as referring to thirty notes between Blair and Bush, all but one of which were published on the inquiry website, thus placing them into the Public Record. This was unprecedented. Similarly, the report referred to ninety-two records of the meetings of Cabinet and 111 meetings of Cabinet committees, with the Cabinet Office granting permission for the text on Iraq from five particularly significant meetings to be published in their entirety.[17]

Over time, the inquiry sought permission to disclose further government documents, especially those that supported the conclusions that would be articulated in the final report. Eventually around 1,800 documents were published online.[18] As a result, Chilcot placed an unparalleled amount of material on the Iraq War and British national security into the Public Record, both through the creation of new materials (via witness statements) and the publication of documents, long before they would have been otherwise released through the official channels of the National Archives.[19] They were also digitalised, downloadable and searchable, therefore increasing accessibility and offering an extraordinary opportunity for media and researchers to peer behind the curtain of government, scrutinise and understand the drivers, challenges and complexities of decision-making for war. In addition the inquiry made public the existence of around seven thousand documents in the Official Record through references in its final report. This opened the possibility for future disclosure into the Public Record through Freedom of Information Act (2000) requests. The inquiry report noted that 'material agreed by the Government for disclosure by the Inquiry is highly unusual in its scale and sensitivity [...] This Report therefore contains, exceptionally, material of a kind which would normally be regarded as highly sensitive and confidential.'[20]

Releases were further supported by the final Iraq inquiry report itself. Published in 2016, it offered a rich, if unwieldy, twelve volumes and 2.6 million words of analysis of British policy and actions towards Iraq.[21] Covering British strategy, intelligence, legalities, military planning and equipment, security sector reform, reconstruction and the welfare of service personnel, the wide-ranging document offered a narrative of events that read like an official history. This was not surprising given the composition of the Iraq inquiry committee, which included two eminent historians: the Official Biographer of Sir Winston Churchill, Sir Martin Gilbert, and the Emeritus Professor of War Studies and Official Historian of the Falklands Campaign, Sir Lawrence Freedman. As a result the committee had significant historical awareness and its academic leanings and sensitivities were illustrated by the report's acknowledgement of the inquiry's source limitations and rigorous referencing.[22] Furthermore, whilst the report acts as a historical record of events, it is unlikely that the importance of the inquiry's role in facilitating the Public Record for researcher and historiographic reasons would have been lost on the committee as they conducted their business. Indeed the sheer volume of high-level materials that entered the Public Record because of the inquiry, and the synthesis of this work in the final report, will ensure that it has a significant impact on the historiography of the Iraq War for generations to come.

Revealing the political-legal tensions in going to war

The vast materials released as part of the Chilcot inquiry revealed the substantial political, legal, military, intelligence and constitutional tensions that present themselves in preparing for and managing a war. Upon the release of the report, Sir John Chilcot gave his public statement and highlighted one such significant tension: the political-legal dynamic. In his speech he stated that 'the circumstances in which it was decided that there was a legal basis for UK military action were far from satisfactory' and, while he clarified that it was not the role of the inquiry to determine whether the war was legal, the inquiry did explore the steps taken to find a legal justification for military action.[23] In fact the final Iraq Inquiry report dedicated 169 pages to examining this process. This was particularly unusual because legal advice given to the UK government is provided in confidence and is not disclosed without government authority. However, in spring 2005 the advice of the Attorney General, Lord Goldsmith, was leaked and the government eventually released its contents.[24] In addition, in 2009 the new Attorney General agreed to waive the confidentiality privilege in the exceptional circumstance of the inquiry. The Cabinet Secretary, Gus O'Donnell, also agreed to take the unusual step of declassifying documents around the legalities of the war. As a result the inquiry can be used to inform a broader understanding of the use and implementation of domestic and international law in relation to national security.

In the case of Iraq the changing legal advice of the Attorney General was of particular interest. Goldsmith appeared to adjust his emphasis in the crucial months leading up to the war, resulting in questions over the political pressure upon him to do so. As early as July 2002 Goldsmith had advised Blair that there were only three possible bases for the legal use of force: self-defence, exceptionally to avert an overwhelming humanitarian catastrophe and authorisation by the United Nations Security Council.[25] He warned that regime change did not justify military action and that no overwhelming catastrophe existed in the case of Iraq. Therefore the only legal justifications could be self-defence or a resolution. He clarified that self-defence could be used only if there was an imminent armed attack, the use of force was necessary to prevent such an attack and that the force applied was appropriate. However, he also concluded that the development of weapons of mass destruction (WMD) was not sufficient evidence of imminence. As a result, the focus turned to the final possible justification, a UN Security Council resolution.

The Attorney General referred to an example of the legal use of force against Iraq eleven years before, during the 1991 Gulf War. In that case Security Council resolution 678 (1990)[26] had included wording to authorise states 'to use all necessary means' to ensure Iraqi compliance with an earlier resolution (to withdraw forces from Kuwait)[27] if Iraq had not done so by 15 January 1991. As a result it provided a model for ensuring legality of any future war against Iraq. The advice was clear: 'A new Security Council resolution explicitly authorising the use of force under Chapter VII would plainly be the most secure, and preferred, legal basis for military action in the current situation [...] My view is that in the absence of a fresh resolution by the Security Council [...] military action would be unlawful.'[28] This advice was provided to Blair two days after he had already written to Bush stating, 'I will be with you, whatever' and outlining his own plans to achieve UN support.[29]

In line with the legal advice, on 8 November 2002 the Security Council adopted a new resolution against Iraq (1441).[30] It acknowledged Iraq's failure to comply with UN weapons inspectors and the International Atomic Energy Agency (IAEA), in violation of its ceasefire agreements established under resolution 687 (1991),[31] and determined that it would give Iraq 'a final opportunity to comply with its disarmament obligations'. An early draft of resolution 1441 had included the wording 'use all necessary means to restore international peace and security in the area', echoing the wording from resolution 678 thirteen years before, but this had been removed as part of the resolution negotiations. In addition the final wording did not determine a fixed deadline or outline a response for Iraqi non-compliance beyond reconvening the Security Council for further discussions. For these reasons, Goldsmith remained pessimistic about the legality of military action without a further resolution. In particular he advised that it was down to the Security Council to determine whether Iraq had been in 'material breach' of its obligations and to determine the subsequent recourse.[32]

However, the Foreign Secretary Jack Straw was already aware of the political and diplomatic challenges around achieving any further resolutions. In light of this Straw was keen for the Attorney General to examine other interpretations of the resolution and legal options should a second resolution not be possible.[33] This included the 'revival' argument that considered whether resolution 1441 could revive the authorisation to use force contained in resolution 678 in the absence of any further decision by the Security Council. The 'revival' argument had precedent as it had been used before to justify force against Iraq in 1993 and 1998 (although not without controversy). However, as late as mid-January 2003 Lord Goldsmith dismissed this argument and re-confirmed that there was no legal basis for war.[34] **Document 1** reveals how Straw refused to accept this interpretation, writing that during his experience as Home Secretary it had become clear to him that the law could be interpreted in different ways: 'even on apparently open and shut issues [...] there could be a different view, honestly and reasonably held'.[35] This led to a firm response from Goldsmith in **Document 2**: 'It is important for the Government that its lawyers give advice which they honestly consider to be correct [...] they should give the advice they believe in, not the advice which they think others want to hear. To do otherwise would undermine their function.'[36] But the Foreign Secretary refused to accept the advice being given and pushed again for alternative interpretations of the law. On 6 February 2003 he wrote, 'I have been very forcefully struck by a paradox in the culture of Government lawyers, which is that the less certain the law is, the more certain in their views they become'. Again, referring to his experience in a past Cabinet position, he stated, 'on the one hand, in well-rehearsed areas of domestic law the advice I'm offered has usually been acute, but also admitted to a range of possibilities. On the other hand, in issues of international law, my experiences of advice is more dogmatic, even though the range of reasonable interpretations is almost always greater than in respect of domestic law.'[37]

Throughout this time Blair continued to state publicly that he would not rule out military action without a second resolution. Instead he had requested that the UK's Permanent Representative to the United Nations, Sir Jeremy Greenstock, should discuss alternative options with Goldsmith.[38] The US administration also disagreed with Goldsmith's assessment. On 10 February the Attorney General was sent to Washington to meet with senior Bush Administration lawyers. Over the next two days he was persuaded to rethink his perspective and on 12 February he produced a revised draft of advice that reached a different conclusion: that a reasonable case could be made that resolution 1441 revived the authorisation to use force in resolution 678.[39] He advised Number Ten of this change of opinion on 27 February. This was significant and set the UK on a different course but, when pressed at the Iraq inquiry, Goldsmith said he did not know why he had changed his mind.[40]

This change also began the process of Goldsmith's role developing from adviser to advocate. Once the Attorney General's position reflected the political requirements, he was able to be used as part of the wider justification for war. Up to this point it had been requested that Goldsmith should not provide any formal legal advice, nor had he presented his view to Cabinet. Instead formal instructions to provide legal advice were sent on 9 December 2002 but with the express request that an immediate response should not be given. Similarly, when Blair went to meet Bush, Goldsmith was advised his legal advice was not required in advance of the trip. None the less, in a note to Blair on 7 March he concluded that, while the 'safest legal course' remained getting a second resolution, 'a reasonable case could be made that resolution 1441 was capable of reviving the authorization in resolution 678 without a further resolution'.[41] However, he advised that this could be achieved only by demonstrating hard evidence of Iraqi noncompliance and non-cooperation with weapons inspectors as a 'material breach'. The day before, Blair had similarly concluded that non-cooperation could be only determined by the Security Council[42] and a resolution had been drafted by the UK, US and Spain to secure this determination.

However, by 12 March it had become clear that the resolution was at risk of being vetoed. The next day Goldsmith changed his advice again and stated that he had 'come to the clear view that on balance the better view was that the conditions for the operation of the revival argument were met in this case'. Instead of arguing in preference for a second resolution, the weighting of his argument shifted, and he confirmed that 'in his minute of 7 March he had wanted to make sure that the Prime Minister was fully aware of the competing arguments. He was clear in his own mind, however, that the better view was that there was a legal basis without a second resolution.'[43] The timing was extraordinary.

The rest of the afternoon was spent preparing the legal argument for presentation to Cabinet and Parliament. A team was established by Goldsmith and Straw to help Goldsmith explain to the public the legal basis for war. It was determined that, since he had now reached a view, it was important that 'in public he needed to explain his case as strongly and unambiguously as possible'.[44] However, he suggested that Cabinet should be informed that the legal issues were finely balanced. Straw rejected this suggestion, advising that he should draft a letter to the Chairman of the Foreign Affairs Committee explaining the legal position and this should form the basis of his position in Cabinet due to 'the problem of leaks'.[45] In the end it was not until 17 March that official advice was presented. This included a written answer to a written question in Parliament and a briefing in the Cabinet based upon that answer. In both cases there was no debate or questioning of the Attorney General's position or discussion of the alternative view leading to the inevitable conclusion that the war was legal.[46]

Political-legal dynamics

Having explored the political-legal tensions, this section uses the Official Record, revealed by the Iraq Inquiry, to examine how the political-legal dynamics played out amidst the tensions. Firstly, **Document 1** demonstrated that there can be significant pressure for legal advisers to be malleable to suit political needs. Whilst Goldsmith, Blair and Straw claim that no pressure was placed on the Attorney General to reach a conclusion, the documents consigned into the Public Record reveal that it existed, whether Goldsmith felt it or not. In particular the exchanges between Straw and Goldsmith (see **Document 2**) expressed a political assumption that legal advisers existed to serve the government and to find a legal case for the government's decisions. This was particularly true for Iraq, where policy was determined quickly and the legal position struggled to keep up, but Straw revealed that similar policy-first examples had occurred during his previous role as Home Secretary. This leaves the broader question of whether policy or legalities come first in relation to national security.

Secondly, once a politically desirable legal position was reached, the next political pressure was for the legal team to move from malleability, and change role from adviser to advocate. In the case of Iraq, Goldsmith was held back from advising the broader government until he agreed that the legal case for war existed. Once this conclusion was reached, a team was built around him to present his case to the wider Cabinet, Parliament and public. Goldsmith's role shifted from impartiality to political player, as his position as Attorney General provided credence to the government's argument of legality and he became a useful ally for the purposes of persuasion. His failure to present conflicting legal arguments in various forums led to an undue impression that he was advocating for one position, and it is only through the declassification of the Official Record that this tension has been revealed.

Thirdly, the inquiry demonstrated the limitations of the Official Record. Whilst it must always be acknowledged by historians that certain conversations remain unrecorded, the inquiry showed that iterations of early legal advice – that did not align with government policy – were not shared with Cabinet and explicit requests were made for it not to be written or formalised. In fact, despite Goldsmith providing his thoughts from summer 2002, it was not until March 2003 that any official position was requested. Beyond this the report also noted that documentary records cannot, in themselves, reveal a full picture of events or negate the fact that each document was laden with its own ontological and epistemological biases. It was highlighted, for example, how meeting minutes are selective: primarily recording conclusions at the expense of debates and dissenting views.

Conclusion

To conclude, researchers must be reminded of the limitations of the Public Record in relation to the war in Iraq – no matter how expansive it may seem in comparison to other national security events: only documents that supported the report's arguments were published. In fact the inquiry viewed over 150,000 documents from 1997 to 2014 whereas only 1,800 made it into the Public Record for analysis. Of that 1,800 it is now quite challenging for researchers to read through the originals as the inquiry website has been archived by the National Archives as 'snapshots' therefore not retaining the capability of the evidence search function. When they can be found, it must be remembered that these documents were those that made it through the disclosure process, reaching the threshold of within 'the public interest' and with some redactions included. Similarly, while the gathering of oral history through the witness statements provides future researchers with a wealth of primary source materials for future analysis, there are always questions of witness bias and reliability, especially given the passing of time. In addition it is worth remembering who the witnesses were, the legacy they needed to protect and that the experiences of more junior staff were largely missing.[47] These limitations only serve to remind researchers of the importance of questioning how and why the official and public records are recorded, shaped, stored and accessed, as well as to query the biases and silences within these data.

None the less, despite these limitations, the inquiry revealed the extent of what *could* be placed into the Public Record. Whilst continuously emphasising the unique nature of the inquiry, and the subsequent decision to declassify certain documents, the Chilcot inquiry does provide further insight into the vast amount of Official Record that could enter into the Public Record – even on issues related to national security. This provides the opportunity for closer scrutiny and to identify lessons to be learnt for the future.[48] However, a fine balancing act remains. Scrutiny and research cannot trump the protection of national security and any increased tendency towards broader, earlier declassification is likely to result in less formal recording of communications across government, and more silences in the Official Record. Indeed, as O'Donnell originally advised Chilcot, '[a] UK Prime Minister may be less likely to have these exchanges (or allow them to be recorded) if he is concerned that this information would be disclosed at a later time against his wishes. Inhibiting this type of free and frank exchange would represent real prejudice.'[49] As a result, while the Chilcot inquiry provided a significant insight into the creation of national security – and some of the political-legal tensions in going to war – it is likely to remain a unique case for the official, public and historical records.

Document appendix

1) Note from Foreign Secretary Jack Straw to Michael Wood (FCO Legal Adviser), *Iraq: Legal Basis for Use of Force*, 29 January (2003)
2) Note from Attorney General Lord Goldsmith to Foreign Secretary Jack Straw, minute, no title, 3 February 2003

1) Note from Foreign Secretary Jack Straw to Michael Wood (FCO Legal Adviser), *Iraq: Legal Basis for Use of Force*, 29 January (2003)

I write in response to your minute to my Private Secretary of 24 January. I note your advice, but I do not accept it.

Let me first make a general point: in the Home Office the many legal issues in which I was involved were principally matters of domestic law. This is by its nature much more detailed and certain than almost any question of international law. We have courts sitting daily to determine outstanding questions. However, even on apparently open and shut issues the originators of the advice offered to me accepted that there could be a different view, honestly and reasonably held. And so it turned out to be time and again.

Such a tentative approach was even more pronounced when there was an issue involving both domestic and international law, most notably in the Pinochet cases. The received wisdom (on the basis of good authority) before these cases was that Heads of State had immunity from prosecution and other process for life, and not just whilst in post, in respect of official conduct whilst a Head of State. This 'wisdom' was affirmed by the initial Divisional Court judgement (by Lord Bingham). But the Law Lords had come to a very different range of views. They had to say 'yes' or 'no' to the lawfulness of my decision, but what was particularly interesting was that there was almost as many opinions as there were Law Lords. They accepted and acknowledged that this was not so certain territory and the received wisdom disappeared.

I am as committed as anyone to international law and its obligations, but it is an uncertain field. There is no international court for resolving such questions in the manner of a domestic court. Moreover, in this case, the issue is an arguable one, capable of honestly and reasonably held differences of view. I hope (for political reasons) we can get a second resolution. But there is a strong case to be made that UNSCR 687, and everything which has happened since (assuming that Iraq continues not to comply), provides a sufficient basis in international law to justify military action.

I have copied this to the Attorney and Sir David Manning as well as your copy recipients.

Jack Straw

2) Note from Attorney General Lord Goldsmith to Foreign Secretary Jack Straw, minute, no title, 3 February 2003

1. I refer to your note of 29 January to Michael Wood, which you copied to me. I would like to comment, not on the substance of the legal advice in relation to Iraq, which is a matter I will deal with separately, but on the points you make regarding the role of government legal advisers. We have already discussed this, but I thought it right to record my views on the point.
2. It is important for the Government that its lawyers give advice which they honestly considered to be correct: that is what they are there for. I regularly see Government lawyers at all levels and I make a practise of emphasising to them that they should give the advice which they believe in, not the advice which they think others want to hear. To do otherwise would undermine their function as a legal adviser in giving independent, objective and impartial advice. This is not to say, of course, that lawyers should not be positive and constructive in helping the Government achieve its policy objectives through lawful means and open minded in considering other points of view. But if a Government

legal adviser genuinely believes that a course of action would be unlawful, then it is his or her right and duty to say so. I support this right regardless of whether I agree with the substance of the advice which has been given.

3. Where a minister challenges the legal advice he or she has received, there are established mechanisms to deal with this. The principal such mechanism is to seek an opinion from the Law Officers.

4. I am copying this minute to Michael Wood, Sir David Manning and Sir Michael Jay.

The Rt Hon the Lord Goldsmith QC

Notes

1 Although he was not found by coalition forces until December 2003.

2 President Bush did not use this phrase but a banner with this phrase formed the backdrop of his speech on the USS *Abraham Lincoln*, 1 May 2003. Available at: https://georgewbush-whitehouse.archives.gov/news/releases/2003/05/20030501–15.html (Accessed 25 October 2022).

3 National Audit Office, *Ministry of Defence Operation TELIC – United Kingdom Military Operations in Iraq* (London: The Stationery Office, 2003), 1.

4 BBC 'Cost of Wars in Iraq and Afghanistan Tops £20bn' (2010), BBC. Available at: www.bbc.co.uk/news/10359548 (Accessed 24 October 2022).

5 A. Travis, 'Support for War Falls to New Low' (2003), *Guardian*. Available at: www.theguardian.com/politics/2003/jan/21/uk.iraq2 (Accessed 24 November 2022).

6 For a summary see: Louise Kettle, *Learning from the History of British Interventions in the Middle East* (Edinburgh: Edinburgh University Press, 2018), 194–25.

7 Margaret Beckett, Hansard HC Deb 31 Oct 2006, Vol. 451, col. 171.

8 House of Commons Foreign Affairs Committee, *The Decision to Go to War in Iraq*, HC 813–1 (London: The Stationery Office, 2003).

9 Gordon Brown, *Letter to Sir John Chilcot*, 17 June (2009). Available at: https://webarchive.nationalarchives.gov.uk/ukgwa/20090908174019mp_/http://www.iraqinquiry.org.uk/media/36038/pm-chilcot17jun.pdf (Accessed 24 October 2022).

10 Sir John Chilcot, *Letter to Gordon Brown*, 21 June (2009). Available at: https://webarchive.nationalarchives.gov.uk/ukgwa/20090908174022mp_/http://www.iraqinquiry.org.uk/media/36041/chilcot-pm21june.pdf (Accessed 25 October 2022).

11 Sir John Chilcot, *Opening Statement of the Iraq Inquiry, 30th July* (2009). Available at: https://webarchive.nationalarchives.gov.uk/ukgwa/20171123123427/http://www.iraqinquiry.org.uk/the-inquiry/news-archive/2009/2009-07-30-opening/statement-by-sir-john-chilcot-chairman-of-the-iraq-inquiry-at-a-news-conference-on-thursday-30-july-2009/ (Accessed 26 October 2023).

12 Initially available at: www.iraqinquiry.org but now available through The National Archives UK Government Web Archive: www.nationalarchives.gov.uk/webarchive.

13 The numbers do not add up because some witnesses were interviewed on more than one occasion and others were interviewed together in one session.

14 Cabinet Office, *Protocol: The Iraq Inquiry and Her Majesty's Government Regarding Documents and Other Written and Electronic Information* (2009). Available at: https://webarchive.nationalarchives.gov.uk/ukgwa/20171123123124/ http://www.iraqinquiry.org.uk/the-inquiry/protocols/regarding-documents-and-other-written-and-electronic-information/ (Accessed 22 November 2022).

15 Sir Gus O'Donnell, *Letter to Sir John Chilcot*, 11 January (2011). Available at: https://humanities-research.exeter.ac.uk/warningsfromthearchive/items/show/279#gallery (Accessed 22 November 2022).

16 Sir Jeremy Heywood, *Letter to Margaret Aldred, 'UK/US Records – Declassification Request'*, 22 May (2014). Available at: https://humanities-research.exeter.ac.uk/warningsfromthearchive/items/show/2403#gallery (Accessed 22 November 2022).

17 Sir Jeremy Heywood, *Letter to Margaret Aldred, 'Chilcot Inquiry – Cabinet Papers'*, 21 January (2014). Available at: https://humanities-research.exeter.ac.uk/warningsfromthearchive/items/show/2402#gallery (Accessed 22 November 2022).

18 The Iraq Inquiry, *The Report of the Iraq Inquiry*, Vol. I (HC 265-I) (London: HMSO, 2016), 10.

19 The Public Records Act (1958) required government departments to identify records of historical value and transfer them for permanent preservation and public release within thirty years. In 2013 the government began to transition this to twenty years (providing two years' worth of release for the next ten years). Therefore records for 2001 and 2002 were released in 2022.

20 The Iraq Inquiry, *Report*, Vol. I, 55–6.

21 Famously four times the length of Leo Tolstoy's epic *War and Peace* which is estimated at around 550,000 words.

22 The Iraq Inquiry, *Report*, Vol. I, 9–15.

23 Sir John Chilcot, *Public Statement*, 6 July (2016). Available at: https://webarchive.nationalarchives.gov.uk/ukgwa/20171123124608/http://www.iraqinquiry.org.uk/the-inquiry/sir-john-chilcots-public-statement/ (Accessed 26 October 2022).

24 J. Snow (2005), 'Complete Legal Documents' (27 April 2005), Channel 4 News. Available at: www.channel4.com/news/articles/politics/domestic_politics/complete%20legal%20documents/107545–2.html (Accessed 23 November 2022).

25 Lord Goldsmith, *Legal Advice to Tony Blair*, 30 July (2002). Available at: https://webarchive.nationalarchives.gov.uk/ukgwa/20171123123237/http://www.iraqinquiry.org.uk//media/46499/Goldsmith-note-to-PM-30July2002.pdf (Accessed 2 November 2022).

26 *UN Security Council Resolution S/RES/678* (1990). Available at: https://digitallibrary.un.org/ (Accessed 2 November 2022).

27 *UN Security Council Resolution S/RES/660* (1990). Available at: https://digitallibrary.un.org/ (Accessed 2 November 2022).

28 Goldsmith, *Legal Advice to Tony Blair*, 30 July.

29 Tony Blair, *Note on Iraq to George Bush*, 28 July (2002). Available at: https://webarchive.nationalarchives.gov.uk/ukgwa/20171123123237/http://www.iraqinquiry.org.uk//media/243761/2002–07–28-note-blair-to-bush-note-on-iraq.pdf (Accessed 10 November 2002).

30 *UN Security Council Resolution S/RES/1441* (2002). Available at: https://digitallibrary.un.org/ (Accessed 2 November 2022).

31 *UN Security Council Resolution S/RES/687* (1991). Available at: https://digitallibrary.un.org/ (Accessed 2 November 2022).

32 Lord Goldsmith, *Legal Advice to Tony Blair*, 14 January (2003). Available at: https://webarchive.nationalarchives.gov.uk/ukgwa/20171123123237/http://www.iraqinquiry.org.uk//media/46493/Goldsmith-draft-advice-14January2003.pdf (Accessed 10 November 2022).

33 The Iraq Inquiry, *Report*, Vol. V, 9–10.

34 Lord Goldsmith to Tony Blair, 14 January 2003.

35 Jack Straw, *Note to Michael Wood, 'Iraq: Legal Basis for Use of Force'*, 29 January, (2003). Available at: https://humanities-research.exeter.ac.uk/warningsfromthearchive/items/show/94 (Accessed 24 November 2022).

36 Lord Goldsmith, *Untitled Note to Jack to Straw, Minute*, 3 February (2003). Available at: https://webarchive.nationalarchives.gov.uk/ukgwa/20171123123237/http://www.iraqinquiry.org.uk//media/218284/2003–02–03-minute-goldsmith-to-foreign-secretary-untitled.pdf (Accessed 27 November 2022).

37 Jack Straw, *Letter to Lord Goldsmith, 'Iraq: Second Resolution'*, 6 February (2003). Available at: https://humanities-research.exeter.ac.uk/warningsfromthearchive/items/show/90 (Accessed 27 November 2022).

38 *Tony Blair to the House of Commons Liaison Committee*, 21 January (2003); *Blair Statement to Parliament*, 15 January (2003). Available at: https://publications.parliament.uk/pa/cm200203/cmselect/cmliaisn/334-i/3012108.htm (Accessed 26 October 2023). Tony Blair, Hansard, HC Deb 15 January 2003, Vol. 401, col 760.

39 The Iraq Inquiry, *Report*, Vol. V, 77–8.

40 The Iraq Inquiry, *Report*, Vol. V, 84.

41 Lord Goldsmith, *Legal Advice to Tony Blair*, 7 March (2003). Available at: www.channel4.com/news/articles/politics/domestic_politics/complete%20legal%20documents/107545–2.html (Accessed 27 November 2022).

42 *Cabinet Conclusions*, 6 March (2003). Previously available at: www.iraqinquiry.org. Now housed at: https://webarchive.nationalarchives.gov.uk/ukgwa/20171123123237/http://www.iraqinquiry.org.uk//.

43 Martin Hemming, *Letter to David Brummell, 'Iraq – Position of the CDS'*, 12 March (2003). Available at: https://humanities-research.exeter.ac.uk/warningsfromthearchive/items/show/191 (Accessed 27 November 2022).

44 Simon McDonald, *Minute, 'Iraq: Meeting with the Attorney General'*, 17 March (2003). Available at: https://humanities-research.exeter.ac.uk/warningsfromthearchive/items/show/81 (Accessed 27 November 2022).

45 McDonald, *Minute, 'Iraq: Meeting with the Attorney General'*.
46 The Iraq Inquiry, *Report*, Vol. V, 151.
47 There was some exemption to this. The Iraq Inquiry, *Report*, Vol. I, 9.
48 Kettle, *Learning from the History*, 13–21.
49 Sir Gus O'Donnell, *Letter to Chilcot*, 11 January (2011). Available at: https:// humanities-research.exeter.ac.uk/warningsfromthearchive/items/show/279#gallery (Accessed 22 November 2022).

7

'It's Mueller Time': The Mueller investigation, the Official Record and the rule of law

Peter Finn

Between December 2019 and February 2021 the US President Donald Trump became the first US President to be impeached, and acquitted, twice. In the first instance Trump was accused of unduly attempting to influence the Ukrainian President Volodymyr Zelenskyy, whilst the second impeachment arose from the incitement of Trump to those who participated in the 6 January 2021 invasion of the US Capitol building in Washington, DC. However, prior to these impeachments, a large chunk of Trump's presidency was dominated by an investigation into the actions of some involved in Trump's campaign for president and attempts by the Russian state, and related bodies, to influence the 2016 US presidential election. Indeed, from May 2017 until March 2019 the investigation into these matters by Special Counsel Robert Mueller dominated US political life. Ostensibly an inquiry into 'any links and/or coordination between the Russian government and individuals associated with the campaign of President Donald Trump' and related matters,[1] Mueller's investigation, and the documentation it produced, also became a staging post for bipartisan clashes and recriminations, a battleground for differing interpretations of the US Constitution and law and a testing ground for the authority of the US presidency and the sway presidents have over those who serve them. These battles, recriminations and differing interpretations continued even after the bulk of a report Mueller had submitted at the termination of his investigation to the Department of Justice (DOJ) was publicly released in April 2019. Indeed, when Mueller provided testimony to two congressional committees in July 2019, these divisions were as pronounced as ever, with Democrats and Republicans drawing on different parts of the report (or its – real or perceived – flaws) to lay claim to the moral, legal and political high ground and align themselves with the rule of law.[2]

Among other elements of the Official Record, this chapter draws heavily on the two volumes of the Mueller report, formally titled the *Report on the Investigation into Russian Interference in the 2016 Presidential Election*, with extracts of the executive summaries of Volumes I and II provided, respectively, as **Document 1** and **Document 2** in the Document Appendix and in-text. Extracts from a 2000 DOJ Office of Legal Counsel (OLC) Legal Opinion titled *A Sitting President's Amenability to Indictment and Criminal Prosecution*, which informs discussions of the dichotomous relationship between the Official Record and the rule of law, is found as, and hereafter referred to as, **Document 3**. As with other chapters, the extracts for documents 1–3 are chosen to reflect broader points or themes. While some of the references to these documents in this chapter refer to material in the Document Appendix, some refer to material elsewhere in these documents. Readers are encouraged to seek out the full documents.

The main body of this chapter evolves in four sections. To begin, the roots of Mueller's investigation, which were laid by prior investigations by the Federal Bureau of Investigation (FBI), are documented. This is followed by a consideration of the legal context and frameworks that led to Mueller's appointment. Two similar investigations, into the administrations of presidents Richard Nixon and Bill Clinton, are touched upon. Next, the actions of Trump relating to Mueller's investigation are explored. As we shall see, Mueller was subject to public attacks from Trump, efforts by the President to manipulate the shape that the Public Record of the Mueller investigation took and presidential attempts to remove Mueller from his position. This section also summarises the Mueller report's main findings. Finally, this chapter reflects on some key aspects of the relationship between the Official Record and the rule of law that arise from the consideration of the Mueller investigation, as well as the conjecture that can emerge from differing interpretations.

Roots of the Mueller investigation

The Mueller report and investigation had their roots in a July 2016 Australian tip-off to the FBI about a 'May 2016 encounter with Trump Campaign foreign policy advisor George Papadopoulos' and Alexander Downer, an Australian diplomat.[3] During this encounter Papadopoulos 'suggested [...] the Trump Campaign had received indications from the Russian government that it could assist the Campaign through the anonymous release of information damaging to Democratic presidential candidate Hillary Clinton'. This 'prompted the FBI on July 31, 2016, to open an investigation into whether individuals associated with the Trump Campaign were coordinating with the Russian government in its interference activities'.[4] As **Document 1** highlights, between the opening of this investigation and the US presidential election in early November 2016 'two [US] federal agencies jointly announced that the Russian government "directed recent compromises of e-mails from US persons and institutions, including US political organizations," and, "[t]hese thefts and disclosures are intended to interfere with the US election process"'.[5] Investigations into Russian interference continued during the transition period between Trump's election on 8 November 2016 and his inauguration as US President on 20 January 2017. On 6 January 2017 Trump was briefed by, among others, the National Security Agency (NSA) Director Mike Rodgers and FBI Director James Comey that a joint Central Intelligence Agency (CIA), FBI and NSA assessment had 'high confidence that Russia had intervened in the election through a variety of means to assist Trump's candidacy and harm Clinton's'.[6] Comey also briefed Trump individually about the existence of the so-called Steele Dossier, so named because it was written by the former UK intelligence officer Christopher Steele, which claimed that the Russian state had compromising material on Trump relating to a 2013 visit to Moscow.[7]

On 2 March 2017 the US Attorney General Jeff Sessions recused himself (stood back) from responsibility for the Russia investigation because he had been involved in the Trump campaign, which itself was a focus of scrutiny. Both directly and via the White House Counsel Donald McGahn, Trump attempted to stop Sessions recusing himself and, once Sessions did so, tried to get him to 'unrecuse' himself.[8] Meanwhile, in public congressional testimony the same month, Comey confirmed that the FBI was 'investigating "the Russian government's efforts to interfere in the 2016 presidential election," including any links or coordination between the Russian government and the Trump Campaign'.[9] Following this, Trump 'reached out' to the Director of National Intelligence and the heads of the CIA and NSA 'to ask them what they could do to publicly dispel the suggestion that the President had any connection to the Russian election-interference effort' and, 'notwithstanding guidance from McGahn to avoid direct contacts with the Department of Justice' (of which the FBI is a part), Trump 'directly' called Comey, who 'had previously assured the President that the FBI was not investigating him personally', and asked him to '"lift the cloud" of the Russia investigation' by stating so 'publicly'.[10] On 3 May 'Comey testified in a congressional hearing, but declined to answer questions about whether the President was personally under investigation'. This caused Trump to decide to 'terminate Comey' as FBI Director. Initially the White House stated that the 'termination resulted from independent recommendations from the Attorney General and Deputy Attorney General that Comey should be discharged for mis-handling' a prior investigation into the emails of Hillary Clinton, Trump's presidential election Democratic opponent. However, 'after firing Comey, the President told Russian officials that he had "faced great pressure because of Russia,"' and 'acknowledged in a television interview that he was going to fire Comey regardless of the Department of Justice's recommendation and [...] he "decided to just do it"' because "'this thing with Trump and Russia is a made-up story"'.[11] Comey was fired on 9 May 2017.[12]

The Mueller investigation and the law

On 17 May the Acting Attorney General Rod Rosenstein appointed Robert Mueller as Special Counsel 'to conduct the investigation confirmed' by Comey in March 2017. Rosenstein tasked Mueller with investigating 'any links and/or coordination between the Russian government and individuals associated with the campaign of President Donald Trump', 'any matters that arose or may arise directly from the investigation' and matters 'within the scope' of laws governing special counsels. Mueller was also given the power to 'prosecute federal crimes arising from the investigation of these matters'.[13] Mueller's investigation ran until 22 March 2019, when he submitted a 'confidential report explaining' prosecution and declination decisions to William Barr, who became Attorney General on 14 February 2019.[14] During the investigation Mueller 'employed 19 lawyers[,] [...] approximately 40 FBI agents, intelligence analysts, forensic accountants, and other professional staff'. His investigation 'issued more than 2,800 subpoenas [witness summonses], executed nearly 500 search warrants, obtained more than 230 orders for communication records, issued almost 50 orders authorizing use of pen registers [used to collect telephone metadata], made 13 requests to foreign governments for evidence, and interviewed approximately 500 witnesses'.[15] During his investigation Mueller 'obtained criminal indictments against' more than thirty 'people and entities',[16] with key Trump campaign and administration officials found guilty of, or pleading guilty to, among other things, 'making false statements to FBI agents' and Mueller's office, 'witness tampering' and 'conspiracy to commit money laundering, tax fraud, failing to file Foreign Bank Account Reports and Violating the Foreign Agents Registration Act, and lying and misrepresenting to the Department of Justice'.[17]

The term Special Counsel arises from guidelines within the US federal code. However, it is often used interchangeably, or confused with, the related terms Independent Counsel and Special Prosecutor. In short all three terms have been used to describe those in charge of federal-level investigations arising from the 'potential conflicts of interest' related to 'the fact' that '[c]riminal investigations and prosecutions [...] are generally regarded as core executive functions assigned to the executive branch'. This, on occasion, leads to calls for 'criminal investigations by prosecutors with independence from the executive branch'.[18] Famous prior examples of such investigations include the Watergate inquiry into the Nixon Administration led by Special Prosecutor Archibald Cox and the similarly named White Water investigation into the Clinton Administration overseen by Independent Counsel Kenneth Starr.[19] Cox was appointed by Attorney General Elliot Richardson, who, during confirmation hearings with the Senate Judiciary Committee, 'agreed to name an independent special prosecutor' to investigate 'the break-in and burglary of the Democratic National Committee Headquarters at the Watergate Hotel in 1972 [that] led to widespread allegations of wrongdoing by senior officials in the executive branch'.[20] Nixon resigned on 8 August 1974 when, 'because of the Watergate matter', he did not 'have a strong enough political base in the Congress to justify continuing'.[21] Starr, meanwhile, was tasked with investigating 'potential violations of federal criminal or civil law related to President Clinton or First Lady Hillary Rodham Clinton's relationship with Madison Guaranty Savings and Loan Association, White-water Development Corporation, or Capital Management Services, as well as any allegations arising out of that investigation'.[22] Starr's investigation eventually led to Clinton's impeachment in the House of Representatives, and acquittal in the Senate, for 'perjury before a grand jury and [...] obstruction of justice' that related to an 'effort to conceal a sexual affair'.[23]

Rosenstein appointed Mueller under the authority of DOJ guidelines resulting from Title 28 (Part 600) of the United States Code, which, inter alia, provides for the grounds for appointing a Special Counsel and the jurisdiction, power and authority of a Special Counsel.[24] These guidelines came into force in 1999 when post-Watergate era guidelines providing for the appointment of independent counsels expired following bipartisan 'concerns over whether the independent counsel possessed too much power'.[25] As a Congressional Research Service report explains, Title 28 (Part 600) authorises 'the Attorney General (or, if the Attorney General is recused from a matter, the Acting Attorney General) to appoint a "special counsel" from outside the federal government to conduct specific investigations or prosecutions that may be deemed to present a conflict of interest if pursued under the normal procedures of the agency'. As the report notes, a special counsel has 'relatively broad authority',[26] with Title 28 (Part 600) stating that 'the Special Counsel shall exercise, within the scope of his or her jurisdiction, the full power and independent authority to exercise all investigative and prosecutorial functions of any United States Attorney'.[27]

Trump and the Mueller investigation

Mueller's appointment was treated as a grave threat by Trump. Upon hearing about it, Trump stated, 'Oh my God. This is terrible. This is the end of my

Presidency. I'm fucked.'[28] Whilst Special Counsel, Mueller was, among other things, subject to public attacks from Trump, to efforts by the President to manipulate the shape the Public Record of the Mueller investigation took and to presidential attempts to remove Mueller from his position.[29] In a typical jibe Trump tweeted that 'Bob Mueller (who is a much different man than people think) and his out of control band of Angry Democrats, don't want the truth, they only want lies. The truth is very bad for their mission!'[30] Meanwhile, in summer 2017, after learning that 'media outlets were asking questions about' a 9 June 2016 'meeting at Trump Tower between senior campaign officials, including Donald Trump Jr., and a Russian lawyer who was said to be offering damaging information about Hillary Clinton as "part of Russia and its government's support for Mr. Trump"', Trump 'directed aides not to publicly disclose the emails setting up the [...] meeting'. After the emails became part of the Public Record, Trump 'edited a press statement for Trump Jr. by deleting a line that acknowledged that the meeting was with "an individual who [Trump Jr] was told might have information helpful to the campaign" and instead said only that the meeting was about adoptions of Russian children'. Despite this 'the President's personal lawyer repeatedly publicly denied the President had played any role' in editing the statement.[31] On 17 June 2017, after 'the media reported that the Special Counsel's Office was investigating whether the President had obstructed justice', Trump called the White House Counsel Don McGahn and 'directed him to call the Acting Attorney General and say that the Special Counsel had conflicts of interest and must be removed'. However, 'McGahn did not carry out the direction' after 'deciding' to 'resign rather than trigger [...] a potential Saturday Night Massacre'.[32] Once Trump's direction to McGahn became public in 2018, Trump then directed 'White House officials to tell McGahn to dispute the story and create a record stating that he had not been ordered to have the Special Counsel removed'. McGahn informed 'those officials that the media reports were accurate in stating that the President had directed' him to remove Mueller. Trump then 'met with McGahn in the Oval Office and again pressured him to deny the reports' and 'asked McGahn why he had told the Special Counsel about the President's effort to remove the Special Counsel and why McGahn took notes of his conversations with the President'.[33]

The report, formally titled *Report on the Investigation into Russian Interference in the 2016 Presidential Election*, which Mueller delivered to Barr in March 2019 consisted of two volumes labelled **Document 1** and **Document 2** in this chapter. **Document 1** deals with 'Russia's interference in the 2016 presidential election and its interactions with the Trump Campaign'.[34] The report documents how 'Russia interfered in the 2016 presidential election' via two methods. Firstly, 'a Russian entity', named the Internet

Research Agency, 'carried out a social media campaign that favored presidential candidate Donald J. Trump and disparaged presidential candidate Hillary Clinton'. This campaign is known as the 'Russian Social Media Campaign'. Secondly, Russian intelligence 'conducted computer-intrusion operations against entities, employees, and volunteers working on the Clinton Campaign and then released stolen documents'. These operations are collectively known as the 'Russian Hacking Operations'. **Document 1** also evidences 'numerous links between the Russian government and the Trump Campaign'. Though Mueller found that 'the Russian government perceived it would benefit from a Trump presidency and worked to secure that outcome, and that the Campaign expected it would benefit electorally from information stolen and released through Russian efforts', he did not 'establish that members of the Trump Campaign conspired or coordinated with the Russian government in its election interference activities'.[35] **Document 2**, meanwhile, documented Trump's 'actions towards the FBI's investigation into Russia's interference in the 2016 presidential election and related matters, and his actions towards the Special Counsel's investigation'.[36] It did so with relation to the possibility that Trump obstructed justice via the consideration of behaviour such as that highlighted in the previous paragraph. Relying on **Document 3**, which argues that the 'indictment or criminal prosecution of a sitting President would unconstitutionally undermine the capacity of the executive branch to perform its constitutionally assigned functions',[37] **Document 2** does not make 'a traditional prosecution or declination decision' and thus 'did not draw ultimate conclusions about the President's conduct'.[38] Instead, though the 'evidence [...] obtained about the President's actions and intent presents difficult issues that would need to be resolved if' Mueller had made 'a traditional prosecutorial judgment', they did not do so. However, **Document 2** also states that had Mueller's office 'had confidence [...] the President clearly did not commit obstruction of justice', the report would 'so state'. Therefore, though the 'report does not conclude' that Trump 'committed a crime, it also does not exonerate him'.[39] Extracts from the OLC legal opinion can be found as **Document 3** in the Appendix.

Conjecture, the law and the Official Record

The content and findings of Mueller's report, along with the broader investigation, have been the subject of conjecture. Trump and his allies have used it to claim that he was exonerated of any wrongdoing and that stories of collusion between his campaign and the Russian state were false, whilst his adversaries argued that the report provides ample evidence of co-ordination between the Trump campaign and the Russian government as well as sustained obstruction of justice by the President. Both sides claimed to have the rule of law on their side.[40] In a typical tweet Trump said that '[n]ow that the long awaited Mueller Report conclusions have been released, most Democrats and others have gone back to the pre-Witch Hunt phase of their lives before Collusion Delusion took over. Others are pretending that their former hero, Bob Mueller, no longer exists!'[41] However, when asked by the Democratic chair of the House Judiciary Committee during congressional testimony whether Trump's claims that the report 'found there was no obstruction and that it completely and totally exonerated him' were correct, Mueller replied by stating '[t]hat is not what the report said'.[42]

There were also similar disputes between Mueller and Barr, who, as Attorney General, oversaw the submission, initial summation of the report for congress, redaction and public release of the report. Barr summarised the report's findings as follows in a 24 March 2019 public letter to Congress: on co-ordination between Russia and the Trump campaign, Barr stated that Mueller 'did not find that the Trump campaign, or anyone associated with it, conspired or coordinated with the Russian government in these efforts, despite multiple offers from Russian-affiliated individuals to assist the Trump campaign', whilst on the question of obstruction of justice, Barr highlighted that Mueller 'determined not to make a traditional prosecutorial judgment', meaning that he 'did not draw a conclusion – one way or the other – as to whether the examined conduct constituted obstruction'. Barr further stated it was his responsibility to 'determine whether the conduct described in the report constitutes a crime'. In this vein Barr said that after 'reviewing' the report, 'consulting with Department officials, including the Office of Legal Counsel; and applying the principles of federal prosecution that guide our charging decisions', he, along with Deputy Attorney General Rosenstein, 'concluded that the evidence developed during the Special Counsel's investigation is not sufficient to establish that the President committed an obstruction-of-justice offense'. Interestingly, Barr stated that this decision did not relate to 'the constitutional considerations that surround the indictment and criminal prosecution of a sitting president' discussed in **Document 3**, the 2000 OLC legal opinion that Mueller relied upon.[43] However, three days later Mueller sent Barr a letter, which was leaked to the *Washington Post*, to coincide with testimony by Barr to the Senate Judiciary Committee,[44] stating that his summation of the report and its findings did 'not fully capture the context, nature, and substance of this Office's work and conclusions', something that, to Mueller's mind, created 'public confusion about critical aspects of the results of our investigation' that threatened 'to undermine a central purpose for which the Department appointed the Special Counsel': namely 'to assure full public confidence in the outcome of the investigations'. To 'alleviate the misunderstandings that have arisen', Mueller urged the immediate release of the introductions and executive summaries of the report's two volumes. This would 'answer congressional and public questions about the nature and outcome of' the investigation. Mueller noted that he had previously 'communicated' his 'concern' on 25 March.[45]

Unsurprisingly, the leaking of Mueller's letter to Barr was the subject of partisan wrangling, with the Democratic Chair of the House Judiciary Committee, Jerry Nadler, stating that the issues Mueller raised in the letter 'reflect' Democratic concerns that Barr had 'taken it upon himself to describe the Special Counsel's findings in a light more favorable to the President'.[46] However, Chris Stewart, Republican member of the House Intelligence Committee, argued that the leaked letter was 'designed to weaken or embarrass the president' and had been 'disruptive to the American people'.[47] Rather than resolve disputes or decrease tensions, differing interpretations of the Official Record can therefore amplify rather than resolve disputes or provide conclusive answers (or at least answers accepted by all) to divisive questions. This is especially true when that record pertains to issues, such as Russian interference in the 2016 election and the actions of Trump and his campaign, that have come to be viewed through a hyper-partisan lens in an era defined by 'vitriol and division'.[48]

A particularly interesting aspect of the relationship between the Official Record and the rule of law with regard to the Mueller investigation can be found in **Document 3**. As we have seen, this opinion argues that the 'indictment or criminal prosecution of a sitting President would unconstitutionally undermine the capacity of the executive branch to perform its constitutionally assigned functions'.[49] It further states that, where 'a sitting President' is concerned, 'only the House of Representatives has the authority to bring charges of criminal misconduct through the constitutionally sanctioned process of impeachment'.[50] Explaining its adherence to the memo, the Mueller report stated that, as an attorney of the Department of Justice and the 'framework of the Special Counsel regulations', Mueller 'accepted OLC's legal conclusion for the purpose of exercising prosecutorial jurisdiction'.[51] So Mueller's decision not to make a decision about whether Trump engaged in the obstruction of Justice with relation to his investigation was based on a legal finding from the OLC that had formed part of the Official Record for nearly two decades and was written in the shadow of a previous presidential scandal, namely the scandal (or more accurately scandals)[52] that engulfed the presidency of Bill Clinton and ultimately led to his impeachment in February 1999.[53] However, **Document 3** essentially restated the position of a September 1973 OLC legal opinion written in the midst of the Watergate scandal that ended Richard Nixon's administration.[54] Yet, rather than develop its position that a sitting president should not be indicted by focusing on the specifics of the Nixon Administration, the 1973 memo (along with an accompanying June 1973 memo considering judicial subpoenas and the presidency)[55] considered judicial cases and commentator opinions dating back to the early years of the US republic in the late eighteenth century. Indeed the memo draws from historic figures such as Alexander Hamilton and James Madison.[56] This memo ultimately concluded that, as a result of the particular pressures of the US presidency and the fact the US Constitution explicitly lays out impeachment as a mechanism for dealing with 'Treason, Bribery, or other high Crimes and Misdemeanors' committed by presidents (as well as 'Vice President and all civil Officers of the United States'),[57] impeachment 'is the only appropriate way to deal with' potential criminal or political offences of a sitting president.[58] Therefore the decision by Mueller to decline to take a position on whether Trump should have been indicted for obstruction of Justice was based on a memo that was almost two decades old written in the shadow of Clinton era scandals, which itself was a restatement of a position developed during the Watergate era relying on commentary and legal cases stretching back almost two hundred years. In short, rather than solely relating to contemporary events, the intellectual and legal arc of the official, public and historical records that influenced Mueller's decision to decline to take a prosecutorial decision can be traced back over two centuries.

Conclusion

In one sense, this chapter differs from others in this book: with the issues considered resulting from Russian actions to disrupt the 2016 US Presidential elections rather than those of the US, the UK, or another member of the so-called Western Alliance such as Canada. Indeed, for those wishing to adopt a critical standpoint, what might unite an analysis of some of the other chapters in this volume is that the members of this alliance could be interpreted as 'the villain'. Likewise, most other chapters in this book focus on actions taken by such states beyond their borders rather than within them. However, if the citizens of a democracy cannot have faith in elections over a prolonged period, then surely its democratic status is under existential threat? If the reason for such a lack of faith is a foreign power, then the circle between the realms of national security and democracy is squared. For these reasons the Mueller investigation provides an illuminating case study for the consideration of the intersection of the official and public records. Via the production of dozens of publicly available documents such as indictments, statements of criminal information, a two-volume report running to over four hundred pages, as well as plea agreements documenting key figures admitting to wrongdoing and judicial procedures that have produced both convictions and significant further material, the Mueller investigation placed a wealth of material into the Public Record of use to those interested in the relationship between the Official Record and the rule of law.

The issue of US meddling in the elections of other states often looms over discussions of the 2016 presidential election and the Mueller investigation. Among other places the US has interfered in elections in states as diverse as Russia, Guyana, Italy, Japan, Israel, Laos and Sri Lanka.[59] As a result some who highlight such US meddling string together a pot-kettle-black narrative: with the irony of a state that has disrupted elections in other places having seen similar tactics applied to its own elections. In the most simplistic version of this narrative, concerns about the negative effects of Russian meddling in the 2016 election are dismissed when seen in the light of decades of US interference abroad.[60] Yet, while such critics are clearly correct to highlight US attempts to corrupt democratic processes, those who dismiss the validity of US complaints are doing their own arguments a disservice. Firstly, if one believes in democracy and the right of individuals to contribute to the political life of a state, then it is as much an aberration if a person's vote is corrupted within the US as it is when the US is involved in distorting electoral processes abroad. Secondly, Mueller's investigation, along with the partisan conjecture that has driven the interpretation of his work, provided ample evidence of the deleterious effects of subverting democratic processes that can be pointed to next time US policy-makers are tempted to meddle abroad. Put another way, surely the fact that Mueller forensically documented a campaign to alter the result of a US election, along with the many political reverberations recorded within the broader official and historical records, provides ample evidence to those looking to trumpet the importance of free and fair democratic elections? As one commentator put it in 2017, the US has 'been handed a mirror, and the reflection should disturb them'.[61] The Mueller investigation extended this mirror to a panorama.

As of 2023 only four US presidents have been subject to proceedings that, realistically, might have led to their removal from office via impeachment. The first of these occurred in 1868 when the Democratic President Andrew Johnson was impeached in the House of Representatives after clashing with Congress over his veto of 'legislation that Congress passed to protect the rights of those who had been freed from slavery'. He was acquitted by the Senate in May 1869.[62] However, since the early 1970s, three more presidents (two Republican, one Democrat) have been subject to similar proceedings. Trump, as noted at the start of this chapter, was the first president to be impeached twice, and he followed in the footsteps of Nixon, who resigned when it became clear that he would be removed from office if he did not leave of his own accord, and Clinton, who was, like Johnson and Trump, impeached in the House of Representatives and acquitted in the Senate. Moreover, articles of impeachment, pertaining to the Iran-Contra scandal, were introduced against Republican presidents Ronald Reagan and George H. W. Bush, whilst the 'Democratic speaker of the House, Nancy Pelosi, was pushed to launch an impeachment inquiry into whether [Republican President] George W. Bush [...] intentionally misled' congress over the Iraq War.[63] Given the partisan fissures that appear likely to continue to define US politics, at least in the near term, it is probable that the use of special counsel investigations, and the impeachment inquiries that can follow them, will continue to be used with ever-increasing frequency in the coming decades. Moreover, if, as Mueller did, special counsels continue to accept the validity of **Document 3** (and centuries-old legal reasoning) that sitting presidents should not be indicted, then the likelihood of impeachment proceedings is, one presumes, likely to increase with legal avenues for recourse for wrongdoing (whether real or perceived) shut off, but the political choice of impeachment open and encouraged by a circular logic present in the Official Record.

Document appendix

1) Extract from: *Mueller Report: Executive Summary of Vol. I* (2019)
2) Extract from: *Mueller Report: Executive Summary of Vol. 2* (2019)
3) Extracts from: US Department of Justice Legal Opinion: *A Sitting President's Amenability to Indictment and Criminal Prosecution* (2000)

1) Extract from: *Mueller Report: Executive Summary of Vol. I* (2019)

The Internet Research Agency (IRA) carried out the earliest Russian interference operations identified by the investigation – a social media campaign designed to provoke and amplify political and social discord in the United States. The IRA was based in St. Petersburg, Russia, and received funding from Russian oligarch Yevgeniy Prigozhin and companies he controlled. Prigozhin is widely reported to have ties to Russian President Vladimir Putin, [Redacted: Harm to Ongoing Matter]
[...]
At the same time that the IRA operation began to focus on supporting candidate Trump in early 2016, the Russian government employed a second form of interference: cyber intrusions (hacking) and releases of hacked materials damaging to the Clinton Campaign. The Russian intelligence service known as the Main Intelligence Directorate of the General Staff of the Russian Army (GRU) carried out these operations.

[...]

The social media campaign and the GRU hacking operations coincided with a series of contacts between Trump Campaign officials and individuals with ties to the Russian government. The Office investigated whether those contacts reflected or resulted in the Campaign conspiring or coordinating with Russia in its election-interference activities. Although the investigation established that the Russian government perceived it would benefit from a Trump presidency and worked to secure that outcome, and that the Campaign expected it would benefit electorally from information stolen and released through Russian efforts, the investigation did not establish that members of the Trump Campaign conspired or coordinated with the Russian government in its election interference activities.

[...]

Between mid-January 2017 and early February 2017, three congressional committees – the House Permanent Select Committee on Intelligence (HPSCI), the Senate Select Committee on Intelligence (SSCI), and the Senate Judiciary Committee (SJC) – announced that they would conduct inquiries, or had already been conducting inquiries, into Russian interference in the election. Then-FBI Director James Comey later confirmed to Congress the existence of the FBI's investigation into Russian interference that had begun before the election.

[...]

The investigation continued under then-Director Comey for the next seven weeks until May 9, 2017, when President Trump fired Comey as FBI Director – an action which is analyzed in Volume II of the report.

[...]

On May 17, 2017, Acting Attorney General Rod Rosenstein appointed the Special Counsel and authorized him to conduct the investigation that Comey had confirmed in his congressional testimony, as well as matters arising directly from the investigation, and any other matters within the scope of 28 C.F.R. § 600.4(a), which generally covers efforts to interfere with or obstruct the investigation.

President Trump reacted negatively to the Special Counsel's appointment.

2) Extract from: *Mueller Report: Executive Summary of Vol. 2* (2019)

Our obstruction-of-justice inquiry focused on a series of actions by the President that related to the Russian-interference investigations, including the President's conduct towards the law enforcement officials overseeing the investigations and the witnesses to relevant events.

[...]

The Campaign's response to reports about Russian support for Trump

During the 2016 presidential campaign, questions arose about the Russian government's apparent support for candidate Trump. After WikiLeaks released politically damaging Democratic Party emails that were reported to have been hacked by Russia, Trump publicly expressed skepticism that Russia was responsible for the hacks at the same time that he and other Campaign officials privately sought information [Redacted: Harm to Ongoing Matter] about any further planned WikiLeaks releases. Trump also denied having any business in or connections to Russia, even though as late as June 2016 the Trump Organization had been pursuing a licensing deal for a skyscraper to be built in Russia called Trump Tower Moscow. After the election, the President expressed concerns to advisors that reports of Russia's election interference might lead the public to question the legitimacy of his election.
[...]

The President's reaction to the continuing Russia investigation

In February 2017, Attorney General Jeff Sessions began to assess whether he had to recuse himself from campaign-related investigations because of his role in the Trump Campaign. In early March, the President told White House Counsel Donald McGahn to stop Sessions from recusing.
[...]

The President's termination of Comey

On May 3, 2017, Comey testified in a congressional hearing, but declined to answer questions about whether the President was personally under investigation. Within days, the President decided to terminate Comey.
[...]

The appointment of a Special Counsel and efforts to remove him

On May 17, 2017, the Acting Attorney General for the Russia investigation appointed a Special Counsel to conduct the investigation and related matters. The President reacted to news that a Special Counsel had been appointed by telling advisors that it was 'the end of his presidency' and demanding that Sessions resign. Sessions submitted his resignation, but the President ultimately did not accept it. The President told aides that the Special Counsel had conflicts of interest and suggested that the Special Counsel therefore could not serve. The President's advisors told him the asserted conflicts were meritless and had already been considered by the Department of Justice.
[...]

Because we determined not to make a traditional prosecutorial judgment, we did not draw ultimate conclusions about the President's conduct. The evidence we obtained about the President's actions and intent presents difficult issues that would need to be resolved if we were making a traditional prosecutorial judgment. At the same time, if we had confidence after a thorough investigation of the facts that the President clearly did not commit obstruction of justice, we would so state. Based on the facts and the applicable legal standards, we are unable to reach that judgment. Accordingly, while this report does not conclude that the President committed a crime, it also does not exonerate him.

3) **Extracts from:** *US Department of Justice Legal Opinion: A Sitting President's Amenability to Indictment and Criminal Prosecution* (2000)

The indictment or criminal prosecution of a sitting President would unconstitutionally undermine the capacity of the executive branch to perform its constitutionally assigned functions.

Memorandum opinion for the Attorney General

In 1973, the Department concluded that the indictment or criminal prosecution of a sitting President would impermissibly undermine the capacity of the executive branch to perform its constitutionally assigned functions. [...] We believe that the conclusion reached by the Department in 1973 still represents the best interpretation of the Constitution.
[...]
In this memorandum, we conclude that the determinations made by the Department in 1973, both in the OLC memorandum and in the Solicitor General's brief, remain sound and that subsequent developments in the law validate both the analytical framework applied and the conclusions reached at that time.
[...]
Given the unique powers granted to and obligations imposed upon the President, we think it is clear that a sitting President may not constitutionally be imprisoned. The physical confinement of the chief executive following a valid conviction would indisputably preclude the executive branch from performing its constitutionally assigned functions.
[...]
To be sure, the Twenty-fifth Amendment provides that either the President himself, or the Vice-President along with a majority of the executive branch's principal officers or some other congressionally determined body, may declare that the President is 'unable to discharge the powers and duties of his office,'

with the result that the Vice President assumes the status and powers of Acting President. [...] But it is doubtful in the extreme that this Amendment was intended to eliminate or otherwise affect any constitutional immunities the President enjoyed prior to its enactment.

Notes

1 R. Rosenstein, *Order Number 3915–2017: Appointment of Special Counsel to Investigate Russian Interference with 2016 Presidential Election and Related Matters* (2017). Available at: https://www.justice.gov/archives/opa/press-release/file/967231/download (Accessed 29 October 2023).

2 House Intelligence Committee, *Mueller Testimony and Questioning, 24 July* (2019); House Judiciary Committee, *Mueller Testimony and Questioning, 24 July* (2019). Both available at: https://www.nbcnews.com/politics/congress/full-transcript-robert-mueller-house-committee-testimony-n1033216 (Accessed 29 October 2023).

3 D. Chaitin, 'Australian Diplomat Whose Tip Prompted Trump-Russia Inquiry: FBI Doesn't Spy' (2019), *Washington Examiner*. Available at: https://www.washingtonexaminer.com/news/australian-diplomat-whose-tip-prompted-trump-russia-inquiry-fbi-doesnt-spy (Accessed 4 September 2019); G. Hutchens, 'Alexander Downer's Secret Meeting with FBI Led to Trump-Russia Inquiry' (2018), *Guardian*. Available at: https://www.theguardian.com/us-news/2018/may/17/alexander-downers-secret-meeting-with-fbi-led-to-trump-russia-inquiry-report (Accessed 4 September 2019); House Judiciary Committee, *Mueller Testimony*; R. Mueller, *Report on the Investigation into Russian Interference in the 2016 Presidential Election*, Vol. I (2019), 1. Available at: https://www.justice.gov/archives/sco/file/1373816/download (Accessed 29 October 2023).

4 Mueller, *Mueller Report*, Vol. I, 1.

5 Mueller, *Mueller Report*, Vol. I, 1.

6 James Comey, *A Higher Loyalty*, Kindle Edition (London: Macmillan, 2018), 218–24; Mueller, *Mueller Report*, Vol. I, 8.

7 Comey, *A Higher Loyalty*, 222–5.

8 Mueller, *Report on the Investigation into Russian Interference in the 2016 Presidential Election* (2019), Vol. II, 3–4.

9 Mueller, *Mueller Report*, Vol. II, 3–4.

10 Mueller, *Mueller Report*, Vol. II, 4.

11 Mueller, *Mueller Report*, Vol. II, 4.

12 Mueller, *Mueller Report*, Vol. II, 68–9.

13 Rosenstein, *Order Number 3915–2017*.

14 W. Barr, *Letter to Congress Outlining the Main Findings of the Mueller Report* (2019), 1; US Department of Justice, *Meet the Attorney General* (2019). Available at: https://www.justice.gov/ag/staff-profile/meet-attorney-general (Accessed 28 August 2019).

15 Barr, *Letter to Congress*, 1.

16 Jerry Nadler in House Judiciary Committee, *Mueller Testimony*.

17 US Department of Justice, *Special Counsel's Office* (2019). Available at: https://www.justice.gov/archives/sco-mueller (Accessed 17 February 2023).

18 J. Cole and C. Brown, *Congressional Research Service Report R44857: Special Counsel Investigations: History, Authority, Appointment and Removal* (2019). Summary. Available at: https://sgp.fas.org/crs/misc/R44857.pdf (Accessed 8 November 2023).

19 Cole and Brown, *Special Counsel Investigations*, 3–4.

20 Cole and Brown, *Special Counsel Investigations*, 3.

21 R. Nixon, *August 8th Resignation Speech* (1974). Available at: https://www.pbs.org/newshour/spc/character/links/nixon_speech.html (Accessed 29 October 2023). R. Nixon, *August 8th Resignation Letter* (1974). Available at: https://www.nixonlibrary.gov/sites/default/files/virtuallibrary/documents/jul11/gergen07.pdf (Accessed 29 October 2023).

22 Cole and Brown, *Special Counsel Investigations*, 4.

23 Richard A. Posner, *An Affair of State* (London: Harvard University Press, 2000).

24 Rosenstein, *Order Number 3915–2017*; US Government *28 CFR Part 600: General Powers of Special Counsel* (1999).

25 Cole and Brown, *Special Counsel Investigations*, 8, 25 (see Chapter 0, note 000).

26 Cole and Brown, *Special Counsel Investigations*, 12.

27 US Government, *28 CFR Part 600.6: Powers and Authority* (1999). Available at: https://www.ecfr.gov/current/title-28/chapter-VI/part-600/section-600.6 (Accessed 29 October 2023).

28 Mueller, *Mueller Report*, Vol. II, 78.

29 Mueller, *Mueller Report*, Vol. II, 4–6.

30 D. Trump, *Dec 3rd Tweet* (2018). Available at: https://twitter.com/realdonaldtrump/status/1069621305245409281?lang=en (Accessed 22 February 2023).

31 Mueller, *Mueller Report*, Vol. II, 5.

32 Mueller, *Mueller Report*, Vol. II, 4. The term 'Saturday Night Massacre' refers to the events of 20 October 1973, when President Richard Nixon ordered his Attorney General, Elliot Richardson, to fire the Watergate Special Prosecutor Archibald Cox. Richardson refused and resigned. Deputy Attorney General William Ruckelshaus then also resigned when Nixon asked the same of him. Robert Bork, by then Attorney General, finally fired Cox.

33 Mueller, *Mueller Report*, Vol. II, 5–6.

34 Mueller, *Mueller Report*, Vol. I, 2.

35 Mueller, *Mueller Report*, Vol. I, 1–4.

36 Mueller, *Mueller Report*, Vol. I, 3.

37 R. Moss, *A Sitting President's Amenability to Indictment and Criminal Prosecution*. Legal Opinion of Assistant Attorney General Office of Legal Counsel for the Attorney General (2000), 222. Available at: https://www.justice.gov/d9/olc/opinions/2000/10/31/op-olc-v024-p0222_0.pdf (Accessed 29 October 2023).

38 Mueller, *Mueller Report*, Vol. II, 1, 8.

39 Mueller, *Mueller Report*, Vol. II, 8.

40 See, for instance: John Ratcliffe (Rep), Cedric Richmond (Dem) in House Judiciary Committee, *Mueller Testimony*.

41 D. Trump, *April 1st Tweet* (2019). Available at: https://twitter.com/realdonaldtrump/status/1112687993528217602?lang=en (Accessed 22 February 2023). See also: Doug Collins in House Judiciary Committee, *Mueller Testimony*.

42 House Judiciary Committee, *Mueller Testimony*.

43 Barr, *Letter to Congress*, 2–3.

44 E. Beech and K. Freifeld, 'Mueller Complained to Barr about His Summary of Russia Probe – Washington Post' (2019), Reuters. Available at: https://uk.reuters.com/article/uk-usa-trump-mueller/mueller-complained-to-barr-about-his-summary-of-russia-probe-washington-post-idUKKCN1S72X1 (Accessed 22 February 2023).

45 R. Mueller, *Letter to Attorney General William Barr RE: Report of the Special Counsel on the Investigation into Russian Interference in the 2016 Presidential Election and Obstruction of Justice, March 27th*, March 2019. Available at: https://apps.npr.org/documents/document.html?id=5984399-Mueller-Letter-to-Barr (Accessed 29 October 2023).

46 J. Nadler, *Chairman Nadler's Statement on Mueller's Letter to the Attorney General* (2019). Available at: https://medium.com/@HouseJudDems/chairman-nadlers-statement-on-mueller-s-letter-to-the-attorney-general-79cecd7ab125 (Accessed 4 September 2019).

47 Chris Stewart (Rep) in House Intelligence Committee, *Mueller Testimony*.

48 A. Abramson and L. Villa (2019), 'What Elijah Cummings Left Unfinished', *Time Magazine* (4 November 2019), 15.

49 Moss, *A Sitting President's Amenability*, 222.

50 Moss, *A Sitting President's Amenability*, 259–60.

51 Mueller, *Mueller Report*, Vol. II, 1.

52 Cole and Brown, *Special Counsel Investigations*, 25 (see Chapter 0, note 000).

53 Moss, *A Sitting President's Amenability*; Posner, *An Affair*.

54 R. Dixon, *Amenability of the President, Vice President and Other Civil Officers to Federal Criminal Prosecution while in Office* (1973), Memorandum Opinion of Assistant Attorney General Office of Legal Counsel for the Attorney General. Available at: https://irp.fas.org/agency/doj/olc/092473.pdf (Accessed 29 October 2023).

55 R. Dixon, *President's Amenability to Judicial Subpoenas* (1973). Memorandum Opinion of Assistant Attorney General Office of Legal Counsel for the Attorney General. Available at: https://www.justice.gov/media/964346/dl?inline (Accessed 29 October 2023).

56 Dixon, *Amenability of the President*, 10–11.

57 US Constitutional Convention, *US Constitution* (1787). Art. II, Sec. 4.

58 Dixon, *Amenability of the President*, 32.

59 P. Beinhardt, 'The U.S. Needs to Face Up to Its Long History of Election Meddling' (2018), *The Atlantic*. Available at: https://www.theatlantic.com/ideas/archive/2018/07/the-us-has-a-long-history-of-election-meddling/565538/ (Accessed 18 February 2023); D. Levin, 'Partisan Electoral Interventions by

the Great Powers: Introducing the PEIG Dataset', *Conflict Management and Peace Science* 36:1 (2016), 88–106, 96.

60 J. Mueller, 'Hypocrisy on Election Interference' (2017), CATO Institute. Available at: https://www.cato.org/blog/hypocrisy-election-interference (Accessed 12 November 2019).

61 O. Jones, 'Americans Can Spot Election Meddling Because They've Been Doing it for Years' (2017), *Guardian*. Available at: https://www.theguardian.com/ commentisfree/2017/jan/05/americans-spot-election-meddling-doing-years-vladimir-putin-donald-trump (Accessed 12 November 2022).

62 US Senate, *The Impeachment of Andrew Johnson (1868) President of the United States* (2019). Available at: https://www.senate.gov/about/powers-procedures/ impeachment/impeachment-johnson.htm (Accessed 12 November 2022).

63 D. Huckabee and S. Stathis, *Congressional Resolutions on Presidential Impeachment: A Historical Overview* (1998). Available at: https://www.everycrsreport.com/ files/19980916_98–763_9d27a8aa0761f1bf0148170a80258d47a16e2dc7.pdf (Accessed 22 February 2023); J. Lawrence, 'Why Calls for Impeachment Have Become Commonplace' (2019), *The Hill*. Available at: https://thehill.com/opinion/ white-house/465534-why-calls-for-impeachment-have-become-commonplace (Accessed 12 November 2022).

Afterword

Peter Finn and Robert Ledger

Finalised in spring 2023, the draft of this book has been more than four years in the making. The aim of exploring the Official Record in the context of the national security operations of democratic states saw the formation of a panel at the 2019 annual conference of the British International Studies Association in London, which was also where one of us had our initial meeting with Manchester University Press. In the interim, a book proposal was submitted, two rounds of (very useful) external peer-review of the proposal, a series of online workshops, multiple rounds of internal peer-review, various false dawns and line-up changes have all transpired. There has also been a global pandemic, and the constant industrial strife and restructures that are, once again, increasingly a fact of life in academia and beyond. This Afterword draws together strands of thought explored in the volume and looks forward to how we and others may wish to engage with the intersection of the official, public and historical records, national security, oversight and democracy in the future. It begins by highlighting some key insights drawn from volume chapters, as well as some potential blind spots. It closes the volume by looking forward to some of the many avenues available for those wishing to explore document-related territory.

Insights and blind spots

In this volume we have, along with chapter authors, attempted to address a lacuna in the literature around the Official Record, with the aim of providing both the basis for theoretical discussions and empirical material that can be used as springboards for others to judge the validity of our collective works and, as importantly, where the literature should go next.

In the Preface we provided definitions for the Official Record, Public Record and Historical Record. Crucially, rather than treat these terms as stand-alone definitions, we have attempted to introduce definitions that highlight the interconnected relationship between them, as well as the ability for documents and material to move between these categories, and to be part of more than one category at a time. In the Introduction we fleshed out our discussions of the Official Record, Public Record and Historical Record with relation to oversight, national security and democracy, and touched on the construction, control and preservation of the Official Record, drawing from related literature in the process. The Introduction also surveyed the relationship of individuals to the Official Record, Public Record and the Historical Record, illustrating how people are able to generate material that can be located across all three depending on the capacity they are operating in at any one particular time.

Across seven chapters, material broadly (though not exclusively) from the post-Second World War era has been drawn on to gain insights into case studies. To begin, Luca Trenta explored the place of assassination in the Official Record, language and foreign policy of the US. In so doing Trenta highlighted an aversion to outright admissions of assassination, but not necessarily to the practice itself. Next Robert Ledger engaged with public inquiries and UK parliamentary oversight in the context of UK foreign and aid policy scandals. Drawing from official reports and Hansard, the Official Record of Westminster, this chapter demonstrated how events that, for those involved, may initially appear peripheral, can store up problems for those tasked with crafting national security policies and operations. In Chapter 3 Rubrick Biegon teased out differences between US policy as stated officially and as shown by the WikiLeaks cables archive during the presidency of Hugo Chávez of Venezuela. Looking forward, those seeking ways to illustrate more fine-grained understandings of US foreign policy could do worse than taking note of the methodology adopted by Biegon in this chapter.

In the volume's fourth chapter Peter Finn examined the actions of the Canadian government with relation to the Canadian citizen Maher Arar. Drawing from a Canadian public inquiry, this chapter illustrated issues that can arise from the sharing of the Official Record between states, and the very real consequences this can have for individuals if erroneous information is shared. Next, drawing from both contemporary documentation and the US Constitution, Christine Sixta Rinehart discussed targeted killing of US citizens during the War on Terror. In so doing, the chapter documents tensions between the process as enacted and Article V of the Bill of Rights of the US Constitution. In the penultimate chapter Louise Kettle uses material related to the Chilcot inquiry into the UK's involvement in the invasion and occupation of Iraq. Kettle highlights various aspects of the political-legal dynamics of the conflict and the inquiry revealed by such material. In the final chapter Peter Finn documents one of the most contested US legal processes of recent times, the Mueller investigation. Utilising the report of the investigation, among other documents, this chapter illustrates that the legal logic underpinning findings of the Mueller investigation can be traced back hundreds of years within the US Official Record.

Yet any volume that covers territory as expansive conceptually and empirically as the official records of the national security operations of three democratic states would leave out key case studies, creating gaps that would be seen by others as mistaken. In this regard (and though we have done our best), this volume is no different. These gaps, some of which we expand on and encourage others to explore in the second section of this Afterword, are partly a mirror image of what we, and the authors featured in this volume, are interested in and able to traverse thanks to our own prior expertise and knowledge. They are also a reflection of what the author line-up of this volume is not. We have aimed for a diverse makeup of contributors and case studies, and on some counts we have succeeded, though on others less so.

On the positive side of the ledger, there are contributions from authors based in three countries (the US, the UK and Germany), and the volume draws from a broad range of primary material, in some cases stretching back hundreds of years. Yet there are imbalances in terms of gender and ethnicity of volume contributors. While all volume chapters are, we believe, important contributions to the literature, additional contributions from a greater diversity of authors moving forward will bring important insights and perspectives to bear on the discussion of the Official Record, national security, oversight and democracy. Another obvious lacuna relates to an imbalance in the focus of chapters, with four focused on the US, two on the UK, and just a single chapter on Canada.

In all cases the imbalances and lacuna noted above, as well as others that will clearly exist, represent not any predisposition on our part that the authors who have contributed tell the only stories of relevance to these topics, though we would certainly argue that each chapter adds valid insights to the literature. However, we would like this volume to act as a starting point for greater discussions of the Official Record, Public Record and Historical Record, and the dichotomous and evolving relations between the three. Likewise, rather than the final word on the subject, we hope the conceptual material introduced in the Preface and the Introduction is the start of an intellectual conversation. In this vein we look forward to hearing the strengths and weaknesses others find in our work.

Future avenues

The potential for future exploration of the intersection between the Official Record, national security, oversight and democracy is almost unlimited.

Each week, often multiple times, documents are released, or events occur, that could form case studies, and influence the development of related concepts and theories. Even as we worked on the final draft of this volume, material for potential related work on topics included the 6 January attack on the US Capitol,[1] the discovery of classified material at the home of US President Joe Biden,[2] amendments to a UK national security bill,[3] the publication of a Public Inquiry report into the Manchester Arena bombing of May 2017 and a statement from the President of the Treasury Board of Canada Secretariat announcing a ban on TikTok being downloaded on 'government mobile devices' because the 'Chief Information Officer of Canada determined that it presents an unacceptable level of risk to privacy and security'.[4]

One area where research could occur, for instance, is in the mistaken placing of documents into the public realm or, as in the Biden case, kept, deliberately or otherwise, in a manner that did not meet prescribed guidelines (to be fair to Biden, the balance of evidence in this case strongly suggests the documents discovered at his property were being mistakenly held). As noted in the Introduction, classified material from the British state was left at a bus stop in Kent. On face value this appears relatively amusing as an anecdote (unless, of course, one is serving on the HMS *Defender*, which some of the documents concerned), but events elsewhere suggest it is not a one-off. The involvement of MI5 in research at Imperial College, London, related to a 'covert bug and drone research project' came to light when '[p]aperwork produced by Imperial [College] initially cited the apparently obscure Government Communications Planning Directorate (GCPD) as a backer – a moniker used in Whitehall as a codename for MI5'was brought to the attention of the *Guardian* newspaper.[5] Most structurally, though not related to national security, a Japanese man working 'for a company tasked with providing benefits to tax-exempt households' in the city of Amagasaki, Japan, lost a USB stick containing 'personal details of nearly half a million people' after 'several hours drinking in a local restaurant before eventually passing out on the street'. According to the BBC, 'city officials said the data contained on the drive is encrypted and locked with a password' and it appears that no one tried to use the information.[6] However, what these incidents collectively illustrate is that the accidental misplacement and loss of aspects of the Official Record should likely be the focus of future research.

Another area where research may lead to interesting conceptual and empirical insights is the manner in which material and documents move between the official records of different states. As highlighted in the Introduction, states do not exist in a vacuum. Indeed there are untold numbers of instances every day where thousands of documents and pieces of information move between states. In some instances these transfers of documents and material are very much part and parcel of the day-to-day operation of states working together, while in others they may reflect agreements to share sensitive information about matters such as nuclear weapons systems.[7] However, as seen in Chapter 4 of this volume, information passed between states is not always correct, and the impact of falsehoods within the Official Record of a state can be disastrous.

Finally, moving forward, the wealth of material drawn on in this volume helps illustrate the scope and scale of material that can be defined as being part of the Official Record. If we just restrict ourselves to material contained in each chapter appendix, this volume has drawn from: a report of the Senate Select Committee to Study Governmental Operations with Respect to Intelligence Activities: the Family Jewels Directive of James R. Schlesinger; a report of the Rockefeller Commission: minutes of a US National Security Council meeting; executive orders from US presidents; a US National Security Decision Directive; the Hays Park Memorandum; a report on the Pergau Dam scandal by the UK Foreign Affairs Committee; House of Commons Hansard; US congressional testimony of General James T. Hill, Commander, United States Southern Command; US diplomatic cables, reports by, and commission for, the Canadian Commission of Inquiry into the Actions of Canadian Officials in Relation to Maher Arar; a US Department of Justice white paper; the US Bill of Rights; evidence considered by the Chilcot inquiry; the Mueller report; and a US Department of Justice Legal Opinion. Reflecting the complexity and diversity of modern states (democratic or otherwise), this material should act as a reminder for the those of us (academic or otherwise) who feel compelled to 'speak truth to power' of the need to embrace the Official Record (accepting, and highlighting where needed, the deficiencies we find) as an important oversight tool.

Notes

1 House Select Committee to Investigate the January 6th Attack on the United States Capitol, *January 6th Committee Final Report* (2023). Available at: https://www.govinfo.gov/app/details/GPO-J6-REPORT/ (Accessed 26 October 2023).
2 A. Mallin, L. Barr, M. Nagle, B. Gittleson and K. Faulders. 'Key Events in the Biden Classified Documents Probe: Updated Timeline' (2023), ABC News. Available at: https://abcnews.go.com/Politics/key-events-biden-classified-documents-probe-updated-timeline/story?id=96396261 (Accessed 3 April 2023).
3 UK Home Office, *Amendments Laid to Strengthen National Security Bill* (2023). Available at: https://www.gov.uk/government/news/amendments-laid-to-strengthen-national-security-bill (Accessed 3 April 2023).
4 M. Fortier, *Statement by Minister Fortier Announcing a Ban on the Use of TikTok on Government Mobile Devices* (2023). Available at: https://www.canada.ca/en/treasury-board-secretariat/news/2023/02/statement-by-minister-fortier-announcing-a-ban-on-the-use-of-tiktok-on-government-mobile-devices.html (Accessed 3 April 2023).

5 D. Sabbagh, 'MI5 Involvement in Drone Project Revealed in Paperwork Slip-up' (2021), *Guardian*. Available at: https://www.theguardian.com/uk-news/2021/mar/06/mi5-involvement-in-drone-project-revealed-in-paperwork-slip-up (Accessed 3 April 2023).

6 M. Murphy, 'Japanese Man Loses USB Stick with Entire City's Personal Details' (2022), BBC. Available at: https://www.bbc.co.uk/news/world-asia-61921222.amp (Accessed 3 April 2023).

7 US State Department, *New START Treaty* (2023). Available at: https://www.state.gov/new-start/ (Accessed 4 April 2023).

Sources for appendices

Chapter 1

1) Extract from: Senate Select Committee to Study Governmental Operations with Respect to Intelligence Activities, *Alleged Assassination Plots Involving Foreign leaders*, Interim Report (1975), 6-7. Reproduced from the Central Intelligence Agency's Freedom of Information Act Electronic Reading Room, www.cia.gov/readingroom/docs/CIA-RDP83-01042R000200090002-0.pdf (date accessed: 20 July 2023)
2) James R. Schlesinger, *Family Jewels Directive* (9 May 1973). Reproduced with the permission of the National Security Archive, https://nsarchive2.gwu.edu/NSAEBB/NSAEBB222/schlesinger_jewels.pdf (date accessed: 20 July 2023)
3) Extract from: Rockefeller Commission, *Final Report*, (1975), xi. Reproduced from Gerald R. Ford Presidential Library & Museum, www.fordlibrarymuseum.gov/library/document/0005/1561495.pdf (date accessed: 20 July 2023)
4) NSC Meeting, minutes, Henry Kissinger's view of assassination (15 May 1975). Reproduced from Gerald R. Ford Presidential Library & Museum, www.fordlibrarymuseum.gov/library/document/0312/750515.pdf (date accessed: 20 July 2023)
5) The US ban on assassination as featured in:
   A: *Executive Order 11905* (Ford Administration). Reproduced from the Federation of American Scientists, https://irp.fas.org/offdocs/eo11905.htm (date accessed: 20 July 2023)
   B: *Executive Order 12036* (Carter Administration) (https://irp.fas.org/offdocs/eo/eo-12036.htm (date accessed: 20 July 2023)
   C: *Executive Order 12333* (Reagan Administration) (www.reaganlibrary.gov/archives/speech/executive-order-12333-united-states-intelligence-activities (date accessed: 20 July 2023)
6) Extract from: *National Security Decision Directive 138* (1984). Reproduced from the Ronald Reagan Presidential Library & Museum,

www.reaganlibrary.gov/public/archives/reference/scanned-nsdds/nsdd138.
pdf (date accessed: 20 July 2023)

7) Extract from: *Hays Parks Memorandum* (1989). Reproduced from
Lawfire, https://sites.duke.edu/lawfire/files/2019/01/ParksMemo1989.pdf
(date accessed: 20 July 2023)

Chapter 2

1) Extract from: Foreign Affairs Committee, *Public Expenditure: The Pergau
Hydro-electric Project, Malaysia, the Aid and Trade Provision and Related
Matters*. Vol. I, Report together with the Proceedings of the Committee.
(House of Commons, 1994). Reproduced from https://parlipapers.
proquest.com/parlipapers in accordance with the Open Government
Licence of the British National Archives. Available at: https://parlipapers.
proquest.com/parlipapers/docview/t70.d75.1993-093322?accountid=
14557 (date accessed: 17 July 22023)

2) Extract from: Robin Cook, House of Commons Hansard, Deb 26 Feb
1996, Vol. 272, col. 589-694. Reproduced from https://hansard.parliament.
uk/ in accordance with the Open Parliament Licence. Available at: https://
api.parliament.uk/historic-hansard/commons/1996/feb/26/scott-report
(date accessed: 17 July 2023)

Chapter 3

1) Extracts from: United States Congress, Testimony of General James T.
Hill, Commander, United States Southern Command, Hearing of the
House Armed Services Committee: 'Fiscal Year 2005 National Defense
Authorization Budget Request', March 24 (2004). Reproduced from
https://adamisacson.com. Available at https://adamisacson.com/files/
old_cip_colombia/040324hill.htm (date accessed: 10 July 23)

2) Extracts from: WikiLeaks Cable. *Is Chavez Losing It?*, 3 May. Reference
ID: 06CARACAS1169. (2006), https://wikileaks.org/plusd/cables/
06CARACAS1169_a.html (date accessed: 10 July 2023)

3) Extracts from: WikiLeaks Cable. *Iran-Russia-Venezuela Triangle Threatens
Regional Stability*, 13 November. Reference ID: 07BRASILIA2132 (2007),
https://wikileaks.org/plusd/cables/07BRASILIA2132_a.html (date accessed:
10 July 2023)

4) Extracts from: WikiLeaks Cable. *President Jose Manuel Zelaya Rosales:
Personal*, 15 May. Reference ID: 08TEGUCIGALPA459 (2008), https://
wikileaks.org/plusd/cables/08TEGUCIGALPA459_a.html (date accessed:
10 July 2023)

Chapter 4

1) Extract from: Commission of Inquiry into the Actions of Canadian Officials in Relation to Maher Arar, *Report of the Events Relating to Maher Arar: Analysis and Recommendations* (2006). Reproduced with the permission of the Government of Canada following the granting of Crown Copyright File No. 2023/2024-02125, https://epe.lac-bac.gc.ca/100/206/301/pco-bcp/commissions/maher_arar/07-09-13/www.ararcommission.ca/eng/AR_English.pdf (date accessed: 17 July 2023)
2) Extract from: S. J. Toope, *Report of Professor Stephen J. Toope, Fact Finder, October 14, 2005* (2005), Appendix 7 in Commission of Inquiry into the Actions of Canadian Officials in Relation to Maher Arar, *Report of the Events Relating to Maher Arar: Factual Background*, Vol. II (2006), 789–819. Reproduced with the permission of the Government of Canada following the granting of Crown Copyright File No. 2023/2024-02125, https://epe.lac-bac.gc.ca/100/206/301/pco-bcp/commissions/maher_arar/07-09-13/www.ararcommission.ca/eng/Vol_II_English.pdf (date accessed: 17 July 2023

Chapter 5

1) Extract from: Department of Justice, *White Paper 020413* (2011). Reproduced from www.documentcloud.org/documents/566483-020413-doj-white-paper (date accessed: 10 July 2023)
2) Extract from: US Government, *Bill of Rights* (Ratified 1791). Reproduced from www.archives.gov/founding-docs/bill-of-rights-transcript (date accessed: 10 July 2023)

Chapter 6

1) Note from Foreign Secretary Jack Straw to Michael Wood (FCO Legal Adviser), *Iraq: Legal Basis for Use of Force*, 29 January (2003). Reproduced from https://warningsfromthearchive.exeter.ac.uk/ in accordance with the Open Government Licence of the British National Archives. Available at https://humanities-research.exeter.ac.uk/warningsfromthearchive/items/show/94 (date accessed: 10 July 2023)
2) Note from Attorney General Lord Goldsmith to Foreign Secretary Jack Straw, minute, no title, 3 February 2003. Reproduced from https://webarchive.nationalarchives.gov.uk/ in accordance with the Open Government Licence of the British National Archives. Available at: https://webarchive.nationalarchives.gov.uk/ukgwa/20100919030826/http:/www.iraqinquiry.org.uk/transcripts/declassified-documents.aspx (date accessed: 10 July 2023)

Chapter 7

1) Extract from: *Mueller Report: Executive Summary of Vol. I* (2019).
   Reproduced from www.justice.gov/archives/sco/file/1373816/download
   (date accessed: 10 July 2023)
2) Extract from: *Mueller Report: Executive Summary of Vol. 2* (2019).
   Reproduced from www.justice.gov/archives/sco/file/1373816/download
   (date accessed: 10 July 2023)
3) Extracts from: US Department of Justice Legal Opinion: *A Sitting
   President's Amenability to Indictment and Criminal Prosecution* (2000).
   Reproduced from www.justice.gov/olc/opinion/sitting-president%E2%80
   %99s-amenability-indictment-and-criminal-prosecution (date accessed
   10 July 2023)

Index